BUSINESS CASES
IN ETHICAL FOCUS

BUSINESS

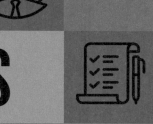

CASES

IN ETHICAL

edited by

Fritz Allhoff & *Alexander Sager*

FOCUS

b

broadview press

BROADVIEW PRESS – www.broadviewpress.com
Peterborough, Ontario, Canada

Founded in 1985, Broadview Press remains a wholly independent publishing house. Broadview's focus is on academic publishing; our titles are accessible to university and college students as well as scholars and general readers. With over 600 titles in print, Broadview has become a leading international publisher in the humanities, with worldwide distribution. Broadview is committed to environmentally responsible publishing and fair business practices.

Library and Archives Canada Cataloguing in Publication

Title: Business cases in ethical focus / edited by Fritz Allhoff and Alexander Sager.
Names: Allhoff, Fritz, editor. | Sager, Alex, editor.
Description: Includes bibliographical references.
Identifiers: Canadiana (print) 20190192046 | Canadiana (ebook) 20190192089 | ISBN 9781554813742 (softcover) | ISBN 9781770487291 (PDF) | ISBN 9781460406854 (HTML)
Subjects: LCSH: Business ethics—Case studies. | LCGFT: Case studies.
Classification: LCC HF5387 .B864 2019 | DDC 174/.4—dc23

Broadview Press handles its own distribution in North America:
PO Box 1243, Peterborough, Ontario K9J 7H5, Canada
555 Riverwalk Parkway, Tonawanda, NY 14150, USA
Tel: (705) 743-8990; Fax: (705) 743-8353
email: customerservice@broadviewpress.com

Distribution is handled by Eurospan Group in the UK, Europe, Central Asia, Middle East, Africa, India, Southeast Asia, Central America, South America, and the Caribbean. Distribution is handled by Footprint Books in Australia and New Zealand.

Canada

Broadview Press acknowledges the financial support of the Government of Canada for our publishing activities.

Copy Edited by Michel Pharand
Book design by Michel Vrana

PRINTED IN CANADA

CONTENTS

PART 4: BUSINESS PRACTICES

UNIT 4.1: BUYING AND SELLING

UNIT 4.2: DOING BUSINESS AT HOME AND ABROAD

ACKNOWLEDGMENTS

The editors thank Anand Vaidya for his work on *Business in Ethical Focus*, from which this casebook is inspired. Furthermore, they thank T.J. Broy and Alex Hoffmann, who served as research assistants and helped with manuscript preparation. They also thank Don LePan and Helena Snopek for editorial work, and Michel Pharand for copyediting the entire manuscript. Finally they thank Stephen Latta, the commissioning editor, for his support of this project.

A NOTE TO READERS

BUSINESS CASES IN ETHICAL FOCUS BRINGS TOGETHER 36 DETAILED case studies covering most of the major areas of business ethics from around the world. The study of business ethics prepares students to reflect on the ethical implications of their own actions in the workplace. It also encourages students to think more broadly about the role of business in society and across borders. One way to accomplish this is through careful analysis of cases to build critical thinking skills and ethical awareness.

Business Cases in Ethical Focus builds on the model of *Business in Ethical Focus, Second Edition*, while adding 24 newly commissioned cases. Authors give students the necessary background to thoroughly understand the topic, followed by an analysis that provides tools and insights from business ethics. Every case ends with discussion questions and resources that can be brought into the classroom or assigned for further exploration.

Business Cases in Ethical Focus is ideal for instructors who structure their business ethics course around cases studies, as well as for those who want to supplement their course materials.

PART 1:
INTRODUCTION

A BRIEF GUIDE TO BUSINESS ETHICS AND CASE STUDY ANALYSIS

ALEX SAGER

GRAVITY PAYMENTS, A CREDIT CARD PROCESSING COMPANY THAT serves small businesses, received national media coverage when founder and CEO Dan Price announced his plan to raise the salary of all employees to $70,000. Price said that his inspiration came from an article by Daniel Kahneman and Angus Deaton that reported emotional well-being does not increase over $75,000.[1] Price paid for the increase in wages for the company's 70 employees by cutting his own salary from $1.1 million to $70,000 and by diverting most of the company's anticipated profit to wages.[2] In an interview on the *Today Show*, Price said:

> I see everything I do as a responsibility and seeing growing
> inequality and how it's harder to just make ends meet and live the
> normal American dream. You know, things are getting more and
> more expensive, especially in a city like Seattle and the wages aren't
> keeping up. And so for me, we're here to serve our clients primarily
> and that's how we're going to be successful. It's not about making
> money. It's about making a difference.

3

Price's decision drew widespread praise, but also controversy. Some employees quit, outraged by colleagues in less skilled and demanding positions receiving large pay raises. Several customers ended their business with the firm, objecting to what they perceived as a political statement or fearing fee hikes despite reassurances that this would not occur.[3] As a result of legal fees and the use of profits and executive salary to fund the salary increase, Price had to rent out his house to make ends meet.[4]

GRAVITY PAYMENT'S STORY PROVIDES A HELPFUL CASE FOR thinking about how to do business ethics. Business ethics courses ask students to analyze cases from an ethical perspective. Many students wonder what this involves. Though ethical reasoning and decision-making plays a major role in our everyday lives, most of us have not been taught to make our ethical thinking explicit. Most of us make decisions about what to do, how to interact with others, and what values to endorse without reflecting on how this involves ethical reasoning. We take norms for granted, without devoting significant effort to asking if they are justified, how they fit with other norms, or how they should be applied. As a result, students taking an ethics class often wonder what it means to think philosophically about ethical issues and how to analyze cases philosophically.

Thinking ethically involves what Aristotle called *phronesis*, or practical wisdom, something we acquire over time by experiencing and by working through ethical issues. It is hard to substitute for life experience, but moral cognition and imagination necessary for business can be developed by reading novels, non-fiction (including biographies), and watching movies and television programs that explore moral issues involving work.[5] We can also prepare ourselves to confront ethical issues in the workplace by studying case studies that raise ethical issues.

Business Cases in Ethical Focus provides the opportunity to expand one's critical and imaginative understanding of ethics in a business context through a series of complex, real-world case studies. Each case includes a description of facts necessary to understanding what occurred and to begin to grapple with the ethical issues. It also includes analyses of some of the major ethical issues, raises central questions, and provides insights from business ethicists. The analyses are not meant to tell students what to think about the cases, but rather to provide tools for deepening their thinking about the ethical issues. Lastly, authors have included references to works that students can explore.

Cases cover the major areas of business ethics. These include questions about the responsibilities of corporations to the community and the environment and the rights and obligations of employers and employees, with particular attention to issues of diversity and of sexual harassment. The case book also examines the ethics of doing business, including questions about bluffing, employee incentives, big data, and advertising. Lastly, they situate business ethics in the larger context of distributive justice and address some of the dilemmas that arise when doing business across borders.

HOW, THEN, SHOULD STUDENTS APPROACH THESE CASES? CASE study analysis can be divided into a number of components that sometimes overlap. A rough division can be made between facts and values, what we know about the case and how we evaluate the actions of the people and organizations involved. Many ethical disputes turn on matters of fact rather than on values or moral principles. People often reach moral conclusions based on false, inaccurate, or one-sided beliefs. For example, to effectively analyze Gravity Payments, it is important to understand that it is a private business. This is crucial for understanding Price's obligations to shareholders. If Gravity Payments were a publicly traded company, Price would have faced legal constraints and quite possibly moral obligations to honor expectations and contracts.[6] Another fact to keep in mind is that Gravity Payments is a small company, so a redistribution of executive compensation and profits made it possible to substantially raise wages. In firms that employ thousands or more workers, redistributing executive compensation and profits would not substantially raise their salaries.[7] These facts alert us to the possibility that if our concern is equality, it might be better to look at other redistributive practices such as taxation, rather than salaries.

It is also necessary to know a great deal about business, economics, law, psychology, and other fields. People (including philosophers) who attempt to practice business ethics with little practical and theoretical knowledge of business often advance naïve views. For example, the popular view that corporate leaders invariably seek to maximize profits or shareholder value regardless of the harm caused to stakeholders does not survive scrutiny of companies' business practices. Some business leaders are ruthless and unscrupulous, but there are plenty of cases in which businesses and their leaders strive to meet moral ideals. Indeed, the possibility of business ethics rests on evidence that businesses sometimes meet ethical standards and that, if they were to increasingly do so, it would increase their value to society.

Ethical disputes may also depend on what empirical theories tell us about the world. People may generally agree on morally desirable outcomes, but dispute which institutions or social arrangements are most likely to produce these outcomes. Many of the most fundamental controversies in business ethics concern how markets function—or do not function—in different contexts. For example, people who argue that businesses' primary obligation is to maximize the value of their organization's stock do not believe that shareholders are all that matter morally. Rather, their conviction is that when business is structured around benefiting shareholders, society benefits: competition between firms aiming to increase shareholder value increases efficiency, leading to lower prices and more innovation.

To assess these debates, business ethicists need to understand markets, where they succeed, and, perhaps even more importantly, under which circumstances they fail.[8] They need to understand firms and should acquire a working knowledge of areas such as institutional economics and theories such as agency theory.[9] Business does not exist in a vacuum. Government regulation is also important. This brings in the study of law and policy and also of human psychology, which is often relevant for business ethics. Learning these subjects can occupy a lifetime, but a basic knowledge of them helps identify, understand, and assess authors' theoretical convictions. Perhaps even more importantly, learning a little bit about these topics should teach us modesty about the complexity of the world and the limits of our understanding.

For example, when evaluating Price's decision to pay employees the same at Gravity Payments, we can ask what would occur if all or even many businesses followed his lead. Ignoring the issue that part of the reason that Price *could* (legally) take this measure is that Gravity Payments is a small, privately owned company,[10] we can wonder how generalizing this policy would affect recruitment, motivation, investment, and much else. It may be that Price's ability to pay each worker significantly over the median wage is parasitical on a larger economic system where wages are largely set by supply and demand. If this is true, Gravity Payments cannot serve as a general model for corporate social responsibility even if we find it morally attractive.

Students approaching a case study for the first time should pay close attention to the facts of the case. What do we explicitly know about the case? What information is implicit? How well-supported (e.g., by what we know in the social sciences) are the claims? Students should also make a note of areas for further research. What questions occurred to you while reading? What would you like to know more about?

Knowing the details of the case and the relevant social science for understanding it is necessary, but not sufficient for an ethical analysis. A case study analysis also requires identifying the central values necessary to morally assess actions, organizations, and rules.

The first challenge that students face in business ethics is identifying *when* an ethical issue exists. Ethics is bound up with all aspects of social life. In our everyday interactions, ethics is embedded in our norms, customs, and habits. People are able to work together, to purchase what they need to live, or, for that matter, to walk safely down a busy street because they share ethical assumptions about promises, responsibility, fairness, rights, and much else. The challenge is that these are often not identified as *ethical* assumptions. In real life, ethical considerations are often implicit, bound up with other types of considerations such as efficiency, and embedded in largely unexamined rules, regulations, and habits.

For example, in the infamous Ford Pinto case, Ford failed to recall cars that were prone to fires from low-level rear-end collisions. Though many people are outraged by what they perceive as Ford's pursuit of profit regardless of the cost of human lives, it did not occur to the recall coordinator Dennis Gioia that an *ethical* issue was at stake.[11] The danger posed by the Pinto did not register in the mental script that Gioia used to identify when a recall was warranted. Similarly, until recently, employers considered sexual harassment a personal issue, not a matter of ethics that needed to be addressed by workplace policies.[12] Some ethical wrongdoing occurred because the wrongdoers did not realize ethics was at stake.

How, then, do we identify when an ethical issue is present? Unfortunately, there is no straightforward answer or test. We come to identify ethical issues through exposure to them and through reflection. Though there is no formula for identifying ethical issues, we can use clues to help determine if an ethical issue is at stake. Applied ethics often deals with the impact of individual conduct and institutions on well-being and freedom. Does business as a social institution contribute to well-being and human flourishing? Does it have an *obligation* to do so? This is related to the topic of distribution: what role should business and the market have in determining the distribution of goods? For example, debates surrounding corporate social responsibility concern businesses' obligations—if any—to different stakeholders. Questions about freedom often address government regulations. When are governments morally justified in restricting what businesses can do? How much power ought democratic decision-making have over the private sector? Many other questions concern employees' rights. What rights do employees have and what do these imply for employers' obligations?

A reaction some people may have to Gravity Payments' wage raise is that it is an *amoral* action, i.e., an action that is neither right nor wrong. On this view, Price's action is simply his choice and not one that can be criticized morally (though we might criticize its wisdom or view it as an action that we do not personally endorse). Though many of us would agree that Price had a *right* to raise his employees' salaries and that nobody should have had the power to stop him from doing so, the *ethics* of his decision is more complicated. That an agent has a right to do or not to do something does not necessarily settle whether it is a moral (or the morally best) action, only that the agent should be allowed to perform it.

We can think about the Gravity Payments case on a number of levels. First, we can ask about the moral issues at stake in the workplace, especially those that concern managers and employees. Many issues in business ethics concern how corporations treat the people who work for them (and in some cases non-employees affected by their actions). Do businesses have a right to monitor their employees' social media activity? Can they demand certain forms of behavior of their employees outside of working hours? What safety standards must they meet? How much do they have to compensate workers? What control, if any, should employees have over company decisions?

In the case of Gravity Payments, many of the major ethical issues concern distributive justice—*who gets what for what reasons*? We can ask whether it was just for Price to have paid himself a $1.1 million salary in the first place. Though Price has suggested that his salary was set by the market rate, it appears that he received significantly more than other CEOs working at companies similar in size and profitability to Gravity Payments. Moreover, we can question if salaries should be set simply by what employees or CEOs can command on the market, as opposed to merit, need, equality, or other criteria. The view that Price received excessive compensation may also be at the heart of a lawsuit filed by his brother and major shareholder.[13] What counts as *excessive* is ultimately a value-related question.

Price's shift to radically egalitarian compensation where everyone makes $70,000 also raises issues of fairness and merit. Is it just for employees who contribute more with their education, skills, experience, and hours worked to receive the same compensation as employees who offer less? Even worker cooperatives such as Spain's Mondragon Corporation allow for some inequality in wages. Morality may demand that workers be paid *differently*.

Beyond issues of compensation within the company, there are larger questions about the purpose of business and the nature of corporate social responsibility. Karen Weise from *Bloomberg Business* reports Price asking, "Is [the purpose of business] to maximize shareholder returns? Or is it to best serve the customers and provide for employees?"[14] Price represents himself as advocating a new vision of business, where one set of stakeholders—in this case employees—benefits more than is typically the case. This is a controversial view.

How we view distributive justice within Gravity Payments will also be influenced by our macro-level views about how goods ought to be distributed. If we think that distributive justice mostly involves allowing the free market to allocate resources through supply and demand, then we will likely be attracted to a view of corporate social responsibility where businesses should focus on competing in the market. If our view of distributive justice instead emphasizes government redistribution to correct inequities caused by unbridled capitalism, then we may think corporations have broader obligations to diverse stakeholders.

SO FAR I HAVE TRIED TO SHOW THAT THE CASE OF GRAVITY Payments raises many fundamental issues in business ethics related to distribution and also to our vision of businesses' role in a just economy. Once we've identified ethical issues, the next step is analyzing them. How does one defend an ethical position? What role, in particular, can ethical theory play?

Ethical theories seek to provide a systematic account of ethical concepts and principles.[15] They advance some sort of test to guide actions, such as asking whether a proposed action or principle would maximize happiness or whether it would be assented to by an impartial observer. A fully developed ethical theory would provide guidance on how we should live and act, and help alert us to morally salient information. For example, consequentialist theories based on maximizing happiness lead us to ask if policies and institutions promote the overall good. Theories based on the work of Immanuel Kant remind us of the importance of autonomy and of treating people as ends in themselves and not as mere means. Feminist theories alert us to the possibility of gender-based discrimination and oppression. The diversity of ethical theories can help us recognize moral considerations that our preconceptions or prejudices may have led us to overlook.

Many people new to applied ethics imagine that applied ethics involves merely taking an ethical theory and applying it to the matter at hand. In fact, many early textbooks in applied ethics, including business ethics, took this approach. Though this approach is initially appealing in its simplicity, the proper role of ethical theory is considerably more complex. *There is no formula for determining how to use ethical theory in applied ethics.*

Though applied ethicists sometimes work within an ethical theory when thinking through moral issues, this is rarely done through a straightforward top-down application of their preferred theory to an issue. Even if we accept that moral issues should ideally be addressed within an ethical theory, judgment is needed to determine what the ethical theory tells us. For example, a consequentialist may believe that we should strive to maximize happiness. But even if we can reach agreement on what happiness is (a topic of considerable disagreement among philosophers and psychologists), we still need to ask how to maximize happiness, when intervention is warranted, and who is responsible for acting. In the case we have been considering, it is far from clear whether Dan Price's actions would be recommended by a consequentialist ethical theory. Does Price's decision in fact improve the happiness of his employees and other stakeholders associated with Gravity Payments? Is it likely to do so in the long run?

A deeper concern with employing an ethical theory as the basis for ethical analysis is that philosophers have not reached an agreement about which ethical theory to endorse. Even if we believe that Price's decision maximizes his employees' happiness, we may argue that happiness is not all that matters. In paying all employees the same regardless of differences in their skills, education, or position, is Price treating his employees with proper respect? Sometimes equitable treatment demands that we recognize differences. Fundamental issues such as whether actions can be right or wrong independently of their consequences have not been resolved, at least to the satisfaction of advocates of competing theories. This creates a problem: if we see applied ethics as the application of ethical theory, then it would seem that we need to resolve longstanding controversies about ethical theory first. This would be a bleak conclusion for anyone hoping that philosophical ethics can provide guidance for how we should live and act.

Fortunately, we can normally consider the ethics of a given situation without relying on a developed ethical theory by drawing on widespread (though not universal) points of agreement. Often, moral issues can be analyzed based on factors that most people accept regardless of their preferred ethical theory. We do not need an ethical theory to tell us that wanton cruelty is wrong or that causing undue harm is impermissible. And so, if a proposed action is cruel, or if it causes harm to customers, employees, or other stakeholders, we can pass judgments on whether that action is ethical without attempting to address broader philosophical questions about which ethical theory is best.

ETHICS IS PART OF LIFE, AND THE ABILITY TO IDENTIFY AND ANALYZE ethical issues is acquired through practice. There is no formula available on how to do this. Nonetheless, this is not the same thing as saying ethics is simply a matter of personal opinion. There are better and worse answers to ethical questions, and reasons that we can give to justify our views. By studying the actions of other people and organizations, and by thinking through the ethical quandaries they have faced, we may improve our own ability to make ethically sound judgments. Ultimately, we need to be able to defend our positions to people they affect and our defense will include ethical reasons. Thinking hard about case studies provides valuable training for navigating many of the ethical issues we confront as workers, managers, and citizens.

NOTES

1   Daniel Kahneman and Angus Deaton, "High Income Improves Evaluation of Life but Not Emotional Well-Being," *Proceedings of the National Academy of Sciences* 107.38 (2010): 16489–493. doi:10.1073/pnas.1011492107.

2   Patricia Cohen, "One Company's New Minimum Wage: $70,000 a Year," *New York Times* (2015).

3   Patricia Cohen, "A Company Copes with Backlash against the Raise That Roared," *New York Times* (2015).

4   Kellan Howell, "Dan Price, Seattle CEO Who Set Company Minimum Wage at $70K, Struggles to Make Ends Meet," *Washington Times* (2015).

5   Ellen J. Kennedy and Leigh Lawton, "Business Ethics in Fiction," *Journal of Business Ethics* 11.3 (1992): 187–95.

6   Chris MacDonald, "Why Gravity Payments' $70,000 Minimum Salary, Sadly, Won't Catch On," *The Business Ethics Blog* (April 16, 2015). businessethicsblog.com.

7   Matthew Yglesias, "What We Can Learn from the CEO Who Took a 93% Pay Cut to Give His Team a Raise," *Vox* (2015).

8   Two useful overviews of economics for the general reader are Charles Wheelan, *Naked Economics: Undressing the Dismal Science*, fully rev. and updated (New York: W.W. Norton, 2010), and Ha-Joon Chang, *Economics: The User's Guide* (New York: Bloomsbury Press, 2014).

9   Joseph Heath, "The Uses and Abuses of Agency Theory," *Business Ethics Quarterly* 19.4 (2009): 497–528.

10   MacDonald (2015).

11   Linda Klebe Treviño and Michael E. Brown, "Managing to Be Ethical: Debunking Five Business Ethics Myths," *Academy of Management Executive* 18.2 (2004): 69–81.

12   For an overview of the issue of sexual harassment in business ethics, see Keith Dromm, *Sexual Harassment: An Introduction to the Conceptual and Ethical Issues* (Peterborough, ON: Broadview Press, 2012).

13   Karen Weise, "The CEO Paying Everyone $70,000 Salaries Has Something to Hide," *Bloomberg Business* (2015).

14   Weise (2015)

15   For a systematic overview of ethical theory, see Dan DeNicola's *Moral Philosophy: An Introduction* (Peterborough, ON: Broadview Press, 2018).

PART 2:
THE
RESPONSIBILITIES
OF BUSINESS

1.

CORPORATE LOBBYING ON GMO LABELING LEGISLATION: OREGON BALLOT MEASURE 92

BRAD BERMAN

BACKGROUND

SIXTY-FOUR COUNTRIES CURRENTLY REQUIRE GENETICALLY ENGI-neered (GE) foods to be labeled as such. The United States is not among them. As of 2019, newly proposed requirements from the United States Department of Agriculture (USDA) may change this situation. But on the whole, legislative efforts to label GE foods have met with little success in the United States.

In 2014, Oregon voters rejected one such effort, a state ballot initiative (Measure 92) that would have required the labeling of broad classes of GE foods. Supporters grounded their core arguments for the measure in a presumed right of consumers to know how their food is produced. Mandatory labeling, they claimed, would enable consumers to make informed purchasing decisions, ones that reflect not only their values, ethical and otherwise, but also their own estimations of the relevant consequences of producing and consuming GE foods.

Grassroots support for Measure 92 was relatively strong. Thousands of individuals, mostly in-state, made small donations to PACs and campaigned on its behalf. Nonetheless, the measure's principal backers primarily consisted of consumer advocacy groups, environmental organizations, and corporations—Dr. Bronner's Magic Soaps and Mercola.com Health Resources foremost among them—which collectively contributed millions in cash and in-kind support.

The results were the closest in state history, with little more than one-twentieth of a percentage point separating the two sides. Initial polling, however, had shown overwhelming support for a mandatory labeling scheme. Just four months before the vote, for example, Oregon Public Broadcasting found that 77 per cent of residents favored the labeling of GE foods.[1] Related ballot initiatives in the region, such as California's Proposition 37 (2012) and Washington State's Initiative 522 (2013), were likewise voted down by narrow margins after early support eroded.

In each case, corporate lobbying played an outsized role in turning the tide of public opinion. In Oregon, in a campaign that shattered prior state spending records, the PAC opposing Measure 92 outspent its rivals by a nearly 2-to-1 margin. Well over 99 per cent of its war chest was financed by national and multinational corporations.[2] Monsanto and DuPont Pioneer alone donated almost $11 million, effectively offsetting the entire fundraising effort in support of the measure. PepsiCo, Coca-Cola, and Dow AgroSciences also made seven-figure contributions to defeat the initiative, and another dozen companies, food and agrochemical conglomerates for the most part, donated sums in the hundreds of thousands.

A key stratagem that those donations financed focused on depicting Measure 92 as a poorly written piece of legislation. On the one hand, detractors argued that the measure went too far. They claimed, for example, that it would require some foods to bear a GE label despite neither containing nor being produced from GE ingredients.[3] On the other hand, and perhaps more surprisingly, detractors argued that the measure did not go far enough, citing exemptions for food prepared in restaurants, alcoholic beverages, and foods whose production indirectly involved genetic engineering, such as beef from cows fattened on GE feed.

That tactic might encourage the suggestion that Measure 92's corporate adversaries took issue more with the measure itself than with GE labeling generally. This construal of their target cannot be sustained. Those who donated to defeat Measure 92 in Oregon, with few exceptions, lobbied the US House of Representatives just a year later to pass H.R. 1599. In addition to prohibiting the FDA from requiring GE foods to be labeled as such, this federal bill, the so-called "Safe and Accurate Food Labeling Act of 2015," would preclude *any* further state-level GE labeling initiatives and invalidate those already passed.

ANALYSIS

THE SHEER VOLUME OF CORPORATE DONATIONS AND THEIR DIS-proportionate role in the campaigns for and against Measure 92 bred complaints that corporations had an undue influence on both the debate over the measure and its eventual fate. The extent to which corporate political activity can sway public opinion raises concerns about its appropriate place, if any, in a liberal democracy. Discussions of corporate lobbying thus often assume the burden of justifying such activity.

In the US, corporations have legal rights to various forms of polit-ical activity that, since *First National Bank of Boston v. Bellotti* (1978), have explicitly included a First Amendment right to contribute to ballot initiative campaigns. Insofar as corporations can direct their political activity to shaping public policy in ways that promote their competitive advantage, they often have strong financial incentives to exercise those legal rights. But whether it is ethically permissible for corporations to engage in political activity is another matter.

A principle of free expression commonly plays a crucial role in dis-cussions to that end. The classic defense of free expression, John Stuart Mill's *On Liberty* (1859), hinges upon three points: that holding well-reasoned and true opinions is valuable, that we are fallible, and that the best, if not only, way to reliably improve our opinions is to subject them to unrestricted critical assessment. Free expression, in Mill's view, is both indispensable for personal autonomy, since it uniquely enables our development as reasonable persons, and conducive to the public good, since better decisions will be reached as more opinions—whatever their progeny or perceived merit—enter into the public debate and challenge one another.

Still, one might wonder whether even a Millian advocate of free expression would sanction all the various forms of corporate speech engaged in over Measure 92.[4] The issuing of public statements express-ing political opinions or reasons for them would seem to be most clearly protected, and all the more so if it is an extension of a corporation's public relations or branding platform since that would, in effect, associate those political views with the very identity of the corporation. Chipotle Mexican Grill's endorsement of Measure 92 is a good example on this front. As part of their "food with integrity" campaign, in 2013 the company began disclosing which of their menu offerings contained GE ingredients and, after developing suppliers, switched to solely serving non-GE foods in 2015.

Corporate campaign donations are a more complicated category of political activity to analyze. In the US, *Buckley v. Valeo* enshrined a line of legal interpretation taking political donations to constitute speech. In its decision, the Court argued that "because virtually every means of communicating ideas in today's mass society requires the expenditure of money," prohibiting or restricting the financing of political campaigns "necessarily reduces the quantity of expression by restricting the number of issues discussed, the depth of their exploration, and the size of the audience reached."[5]

On this point, it is perhaps useful to consider what the fight over Measure 92 might have looked like had corporate financing been removed from the process. The result would presumably have differed, but so, too, would the debate over GE labeling. Absent corporate funding, the No on 92 Coalition would have had roughly $1,000 to spend, leaving a non-negligible minority with few resources to publicly advance their case. A notable issue in their media campaign concerned the healthfulness of GE foods. Many supporting the measure appealed to "potential" but as-yet unknown health risks of consuming GE foods. Yet, for the most part, such fears are unfounded, or at least highly exaggerated in the public perception. The overwhelming scientific consensus is that consuming GE foods is no riskier than consuming their non-GE counterparts. Whether or not one concurs with that assessment, the debate over the measure was better for grappling with it.[6]

Nonetheless, the *Buckley* decision, which focused on money as a *means* of effective political speech, remains controversial. One question that the fight over Measure 92 reiterates concerns the *content* of the speech that money might be said to constitute. Once money has been donated to a political action committee, the matter of how it is to be spent is often out of the donor's hands. It cannot be assumed, therefore, that DuPont Pioneer, for example, endorsed the views presented in ads commissioned and paid for by the No on 92 Coalition. At best, it supports the conclusion that Pioneer had an interest, self-appraised at no lower than \$4.5 million, in seeing Measure 92 fail. If so, Pioneer's donations were plausibly a form of speech about a political issue, but not speech that, in itself, made a particularly valuable contribution to the debate over that issue. Indeed, the speech in question might not even properly count as political speech, despite concerning a political topic, since the interest expressed could have had little to do with an estimation of the public good.

Should such corporate political speech be constrained, then? If so, who should regulate it, in which circumstances, and how? Answers depend in large part upon the competing values one recognizes. In the present case, two are especially pressing. The first is a principle of equal political representation. As matters stand, those who have more money to spend have more power to impact the shape of the political debate. Corporate donations accounted for over 80 per cent of the total spending on Measure 92, with 4 out of every 5 corporate dollars going to defeat it. The overwhelming majority of corporate donors, to compound the issue, were headquartered out of state. Influence is of course harder to quantify than spending, but the conclusion that corporate donations cost citizens of Oregon control over at least some aspects of their election is hard to avoid.

A second challenge to free expression engages the nature of the measure, in contrast to the debate over it, more directly. Producers of GE foods contended that, in forcing them to label their products, Measure 92 would have compelled them to speak against their will. Supporters of the measure countered that mandatory labeling was needed to promote their personal autonomy. Without knowing how one's food is produced, supporters claimed, one's ability to make purchases in line with one's normative beliefs is undermined. The operative assumption here, typically unstated, is that one does not just buy a product, one buys into it, sharing in responsibility for the act of its production.

Hansen has argued that concerns for personal autonomy are not sufficient to justify the mandatory labeling of GE foods. She notes, first, that systematically enabling the choice between GE and non-GE foods would be achieved equally well by labeling the latter as by labeling the former. Second, she argues, the mandatory labeling of either category of food is excessive, at least for those who might wish to avoid GE foods, since those who want to do so already can. They need only assume that foods that are not reliably flagged as being GE-free—by, for example, bearing a USDA Organic label—may contain GE ingredients. As Rubel and Streiffer caution, though, most consumers, in fact, do not make that assumption.[7]

On the other hand, the distinction between GE and non-GE foods is perhaps not the appropriate place to focus with respect to labeling and autonomy, as few of the ethical issues raised by GE foods pertain to them as a class. Soybeans, Rainbow papayas, and Golden rice all routinely appear in discussions of the ethics of genetic engineering, although they typically do so to rather different ends. For this reason, the first state-wide labeling initiative in the US, 2002's failed Measure 27 in Oregon, proposed requiring far more specific information on GE food labels, including both the sources and purposes of genes transferred by genetic engineering techniques: for example, "this squash contains viral genetic information designed to make it resistant to viral infection."[8] While this information is often publicly available to consumers willing to do the research, the likelihood of its being required on US food labels any time soon is slim. For now, legal deference to free expression, corporate expression included, is simply too strong.

NOTES

1   Devan Schwartz, "Most Northwest Residents Say They Want Labeling for Genetically Modified Food," *OPB* (July 7, 2014).

2   The No on 92 Coalition received no more than a few dozen, relatively small contributions from local industry associations and private individuals.

3   This claim is misleading, as nothing in the measure would have legally required such foods to bear a GE label. Yet, it is not unreasonable to think that, had the measure passed, GE labels would have been more liberally applied. Under the legislation's enforcement conditions, lack of a GE label would have potentially opened a food's producer to lawsuits, and so some producers, particularly small ones, might have opted to give their non-GE foods a GE label in an attempt to forestall costly, even if baseless, legal battles.

4   Others types of corporate political activities, while not properly speech, no doubt merit attention as well. For example, Ben & Jerry's served up free scoops of ice cream (an "in-kind" campaign contribution) at one of its Portland locations while the eponymous Jerry gave a talk promoting the labeling of GE foods. The company regularly gives away its ice cream, but

the context is important here since small gifts are a fairly effective means of influencing voter behavior. Such gifts are a far cry from the outright buying of votes, but they raise an analogous worry to the extent that they promote political decisions to be made independently of the actual issues in play.

5   *Buckley v. Valeo*, 424 U.S. 1 (1976).

6   On the other hand, many philosophically interesting arguments were given little attention despite the massive media campaigns. A local chapter of the NAACP argued, for example, that increased food costs associated with labeling would disproportionately burden the poor since food purchases consume a larger share of their budget. The NAACP submitted the argument for inclusion in the voters' pamphlet, but it was not picked up for wider dissemination by the PAC challenging the measure and went largely unanswered.

7   On the prevalence of GE foods in the US and public misperception of it, see Maarten J. Chrispeels, "Yes Indeed, Most Americans Do Eat GMOs Every Day!," *Journal of Integrative Plant Biology* 56.1 (2014): 4–6.

8   "Measure 27," in *Oregon Voters' Pamphlet: November 5th General Election* (Salem: Oregon Secretary of State, Elections Division, 2002), 116–37.

DISCUSSION QUESTIONS

(1)   Just whose speech is corporate speech? Whose opinions and interests should it represent and to what ends?

(2)   Political debates are notoriously suffused with trickery. Is it fair to demand, then, that corporations meet higher standards when they enter those debates?

(3)   Does free expression live up to Mill's construal of its public good? In particular, does the debate over Measure 92 support his view, famously expressed by the Supreme Court, that truth will ultimately prevail in the marketplace of ideas?

(4)   To what extent, if any, are consumers ethically responsible for the actions that companies take to produce and market the goods they buy?

(5)   What kinds of information are companies ethically obliged to disclose to the public? What grounds those obligations?

FURTHER READINGS

Jeffrey Birnbaum, *The Lobbyists: How Influence Peddlers Get Their Way in Washington* (New York: Times Books, 1992).

Mark Friesen, "2014 Oregon GMO Measure Fundraising," *OregonLive.com* (2014).

Brooke J. Hamilton III and David Hoch, "Ethical Standards for Business Lobbying," *Business Ethics Quarterly* 7.3 (1997): 117–29.

Shane Leong, James Hazelton, and Cynthia Townley, "Managing the Risks of Corporate Political Donations: A Utilitarian Perspective," *Journal of Business Ethics* 118.2 (2013): 429–45.

"Measure 92," in *Oregon Voters' Pamphlet: November 4th General Election (2014)* (Salem: Oregon Secretary of State, Elections Division), 137–53.

Alan E. Singer, "Corporate Political Activity, Social Responsibility, and Competitive Strategy: An Integrative Model," *Business Ethics: A European Review* 22.3 (2013): 308–24.

Andrew Stark, "Business in Politics: Lobbying and Corporate Campaign Contributions," in *The Oxford Handbook of Business Ethics*, ed. George G. Brenkert and Tom L. Beauchamp (Oxford: Oxford University Press, 2010).

Paul Weirich, ed., *Labeling Genetically Modified Food: The Philosophical and Legal Debate* (New York: Oxford University Press, 2007).

2.

THE ETHICS OF THE PORNOGRAPHY INDUSTRY

VANESSA CORREIA

BACKGROUND

PORNOGRAPHY IS A BIG BUSINESS. THOUGH EXACT FIGURES ARE unavailable, it's estimated that the pornography industry generates at least $6 billion in annual revenue in the US, and possibly closer to $15 billion.[1] Technological innovation, particularly the Internet, has produced both opportunities and challenges for the pornography industry as a whole, but ultimately the opportunities appear to have prevailed; while pornography has suffered significantly from online piracy and the wide availability of free amateur content, the industry continues to grow due to other developments, including mobile applications and faster Internet speeds. The pornography industry is, however, fraught with ethical concerns. There are at least two forms of harm that the industry has been alleged to cause. First are the harms done to performers during the creation of pornography. These harms may include an increased risk of sexually transmitted diseases and the potential of being coerced into performing or enduring humiliating, painful, or otherwise objectionable acts.[2] Second is the harm created through the consumption of pornography—a type of harm that may directly affect those who consume pornography, but which may also affect society more broadly.[3] Both of these harms are often discussed within the context of violent pornography, which portrays rape, torture, battery, and other forms of physical and sexual violence.

Many ethical analyses of pornography have started by considering the personal histories of performers and their reasons for entering the industry. Reliable statistics on this are, however, notoriously difficult to come by. Many people believe that pornographic actors are compelled into the industry by factors such as poverty, addiction, or a history of sexual abuse, and thus condemn the industry as deeply exploitative. However, while it is probable that *some* pornographic actors come from such backgrounds, others from within the industry have challenged this as an unfounded stereotype. For example, one actor comments that she has a college education, a supportive circle of family and friends, and led an otherwise "normal" life. Additionally, a performer in the industry may well have a positive sense of self-worth and feel happy with his or her job choice, regardless of its purported moral implications.[4]

But even if we cannot establish a solid basis for condemning pornography based on the experience of performers, the consumer side of the equation remains to be considered. Numerous studies have sought to demonstrate that those who watch violent pornography may have an increased willingness to aggress against females. This may have in large part to do with the common pornographic trope of women being aroused by physical and sexual aggression.[5] This fact is particularly concerning when we consider the amount of physical and verbal aggression depicted in popular pornographic materials. Estimates of the extent of this aggression are varied: on the low end, some studies have concluded that as little as 1.9 per cent of scenes in bestselling pornographic materials display aggression,[6] but on the high end, another study shows that almost 90 per cent of popular pornographic videos involve physical or verbal aggression, and that approximately 95 per cent of this aggression is not met with an attempt to avoid the harm.[7] Other studies focus on pornography's tendency to be degrading to women, especially in scenes depicting dominance and penis worship, and in its frequently objectifying portrayal of women.[8] Correlations have been found between the consumption of degrading pornography and men expressing a willingness to commit rape in a variety of hypothetical circumstances.[9]

Even watching non-violent pornography has been associated with harms. For example, men exposed to non-violent pornography were found to be more tolerant of violent forms of pornography, less supportive of statements regarding sexual and gender equality, and more likely to endorse more lenient punishments for rapists.[10]

If the consuming pornography increases the willingness to aggress against women or decreases support for gender or sexual equality, then the ethics of the industry that profits in perpetuating them appears questionable. Is pornography fundamentally unethical in its commodification of female sexuality? Should all pornography be considered unethical, or only content that is particularly violent or degrading? What rights may be infringed upon by restricting viewers' access to pornography? Philosophers, social activists, and legal scholars disagree on how these questions should be addressed.

ANALYSIS

SOME HAVE ARGUED THAT THE HARMS OF PORNOGRAPHY ARE SO great that the industry should not be permitted to operate at all. The 1970s and 1980s were periods of high activity for anti-porn feminists, with Catharine MacKinnon and Andrea Dworkin among the most outspoken of these critics. MacKinnon and Dworkin were notably involved in a series of attempts to pass anti-pornography civil rights ordinances in the 1980s, intended to censor pornography on the basis of harm to women and to allow those harmed by pornography to legally pursue compensation. Though the ordinances were eventually struck down, the movement brought anti-pornography arguments to the forefront of mainstream feminist activism. These discussions include the argument, voiced particularly by MacKinnon, that pornography actually works to deprive women of their speech rights, especially when it comes to speech against sexual assault: within a context where men are aroused by images of the rape, battery, and torture of women, a woman's recounting of a horrific sexual assault actually becomes pornography.[11] The view that pornography silences women is shared by some more recent feminists. Rae Langton argues that pornography silences women by contributing to a culture in which women's speech—especially speech related to sexual consent—is frequently misinterpreted and ignored. This is exemplified by the common pornographic scenario in which a woman's "no," her voiced refusal to participate in a sexual activity, is portrayed as an implicit "yes" and as part of the sex itself. By making this scenario appear normal, pornography inverts the meaning of women's words and diminishes women's ability to refuse sex. Langton further argues that the same kind of silencing happens in courtrooms with victims of sexual assault. This silencing makes it impossible for women to protest, obtain justice in court, or celebrate their own sexuality.[12]

MacKinnon and Dworkin's ordinances defined pornography as "the graphic sexually explicit subordination of women, whether in pictures or in words," with at least one of six features, including the depiction of women as sexual objects who enjoy pain or humiliation, the depiction of women finding sexual pleasure in being raped, and the depiction of women in scenarios of degradation, injury, or torture.[13] US courts involved in the matter admitted that, defined as such, pornography indeed depicted subordination, leading "to affront and lower pay at work, insult and injury at home, battery and rape on the streets."[14] Ultimately, however, they ruled that pornography does not infringe upon freedom of speech,[15] and that it warrants protection under the First Amendment in the same way that racist speech, anti-Semitism, and violence on television do. Therefore, formally, the pornography industry has not been censored.

Most civil libertarians would agree with the court's decision. Civil libertarian views generally hold that individuals should be free to pursue whatever activities and obtain whatever social goods they see fit, so long as they do not infringe on the rights of others to pursue their preferred activities and obtain their share of social goods. Some political philosophers see this as part of the right to moral independence; this is defined as a citizen's equal right to pursue his or her particular interests and obtain certain goods, even if society as a whole finds those interests and goods morally questionable, distasteful, or reprehensible.[16] The right to moral independence thus protects individuals with minority views and interests from having their social opportunities limited based on the opinions or judgments of the majority. The benefits of acknowledging this right are perhaps most obvious when applied to questions of cultural and religious freedom: most of us would likely agree, for instance, that members of a minority religion should be free to pursue goods and opportunities related to their religious views, even if those religious views conflict with those of the demographic majority.

Some believe that this same reasoning applies to pornography. The argument here is that, even if the majority of individuals find pornography to be distasteful or wrong, the minority of individuals who enjoy pornography should nonetheless be permitted to obtain it. The simple dislike of pornography by the majority of society is not reason enough to censor pornography from those who wish to consume it. Even if it can be positively proven that pornography constitutes an indirect harm to society, a civil libertarian might argue, the violation of the right to moral independence in this context would likely constitute a greater harm. Even according to this view, it might be acceptable to place restrictions on the distribution of pornography, so that pornographic images, for instance, would not be tolerated in public places. But, according to civil libertarians, businesses should not be prevented from producing pornography, and consumers should be at their liberty to obtain pornographic material.

Some feminist critics would agree that censorship is not the answer, but nevertheless maintain that pornography is unethical and something should be done about it. According to this view, the regulation of pornography should not be addressed by legal or political bodies but rather by reforms within society itself. The focus here is on tackling the underlying structures and institutions that perpetuate violence and sexism. Various strategies have been proposed, including protesting sexist events and performances, better integrating positive sex education into school curriculums, and encouraging government subsidization of non-commercial media producers that promote diversity in their work.[17] The bottom line, however, is that while this approach opposes pornography—or at least pornography that can be considered violent or misogynistic—it does not encourage censorship.

None of the approaches yet discussed adopt a positive stance toward pornography. Dworkin and MacKinnon are critical of pornography's existence, as are those feminists who maintain that pornography is harmful but shouldn't be censored; and the civil libertarian view is neutral with regard to whether porn causes harm. But quite another approach has emerged in recent decades from yet another group, a group sometimes labeled "pro-porn feminists." Such feminists see pornography not only as permissible, but actually as a potential stage for furthering feminist aims. Rather than working to censor the pornography industry, or to oppose pornography through social activism, producers of what has been termed "feminist porn" work to reform the industry from the inside. Feminist pornography has become its own genre, one that views sex as "an expression of identity, a power exchange, a cultural commodity, and even a new politics."[18] In its early years, feminist porn was understood as a gentler form of pornography that focused on storylines and female pleasure; over time it broadened in focus to depict underrepresented minorities, a variety of sexualities, and a wide range of sexual fantasies, including but not limited to the fantasy of relinquishing control in sexual situations. As such, feminist porn has been seen by many as a site of sexual liberation.

Feminist pornography has grown from a small niche to become an industry of its own within the category of adult entertainment, and it enjoys a growing market. Quite apart from the *kind* of product the feminist pornography industry creates, the industry also focuses heavily on an ethical *production* process. It boasts fair, safe, and consensual work environments, has a higher proportion of female producers and other production leaders, and tends to cast a more diverse range of performers. Feminist Porn Awards, given out in the United States and in Europe, focus on pornography that celebrates the female viewer with a focus on active desire, consent, real orgasms, power, and agency.[19]

Nevertheless, pornography continues to face opposition as an industry. In 2011, psychologist Melissa Farley described pornography as a form of prostitution. This comparison relies in part on the understanding that pornography inherently, or at least very frequently, exploits its female performers, who are alleged—much like many women in prostitution—to come from backgrounds of poverty and abuse. The comparison also draws attention to the frequent sexual exploitation and abuse of children in both industries (a topic rarely addressed in feminist critiques of pornography[20]), and further asserts that women in both industries are routinely hurt, raped, and pressured to perform extreme sexual acts.[21] If such analyses are true, pornography raises a new set of ethical and legal considerations.

If pornography is a kind of prostitution, then pornographers are pimps, the global pornography industry is a form of human trafficking, and pornography consumers are analogous to "johns" or buyers. Some might even say that women in pornography are worse off than women in prostitution: they receive compensation only once, by a producer, after which their performances are distributed online and made accessible forever. Abigail Bray argues that the pornography prostitute is in virtual slavery because her ongoing labor is unpaid.[22] But is this a problem with pornography itself, or rather a problem created by the lack of a fair, established payment system for performers? Unlike performers of pornography, women in prostitution must repeatedly perform sexual acts directly for the end consumer, and thus put themselves at continual risk of harm. To equate pornography with prostitution may be to ignore this significant difference in risk of harm (and potentially to underrate the uniquely unsafe circumstances faced by many sex workers). Ultimately, trying to draw direct analogies between the two industries may be likely to create more questions than it solves.

NOTES

1   Ross Benes, "Porn Could Have a Bigger Economic Influence on the US Than Netflix," *Quartz* (June 20, 2018).

2   Catharine A. MacKinnon, *Only Words* (Cambridge, MA: Harvard University Press, 1996), 20–21.

3   For a discussion of some of the complexities regarding the social harms of pornography, see Alisa L. Carse, "Pornography: An Uncivil Liberty?" *Hypatia* 10.1 (1995): 155–82.

4   Dylan Ryder and Dave Monroe, "The Jizz Biz and Quality of Life," in *Porn—Philosophy for Everyone: How to Think with Kink*, ed. Fritz Allhoff (New York: Wiley-Blackwell, 2010), 11–21.

5   Edward Donnerstein, Daniel Linz, and Steven Penrod, "The Impact of Violent Pornography," in *The Question of Pornography: Research Findings and Policy Implications*, ed. Donnerstein et al. (New York: The Free Press, 1987), 86–107.

6   Alan McKee, "The Objectification of Women in Mainstream Pornography Videos in Australia," *The Journal of Sex Research* 42.4 (2005): 277–90.

7   Ana J. Bridges, Robert Wosnitzer, Erica Scharrer, Chyng Sun, and Rachael Liberman, "Aggression and Sexual Behavior in Best-selling Pornography Videos: A Content Analysis Update," *Violence against Women* 16.10 (2010): 1065–85.

8   Gloria Cowan and Kerri F. Dunn, "What Themes in Pornography Lead to Perceptions of the Degradation of Women?," *The Journal of Sex Research* 31.1 (1994): 11–21.

9   Edward Donnerstein, Daniel Linz, and Steven Penrod, "Changes in Viewers' Attitude and Beliefs," in *The Question of Pornography: Research Findings and Policy Implications*, ed. Donnerstein et al. (New York: The Free Press, 1987), 74–85.

10 Ibid.

11 Catharine A. MacKinnon, *Only Words*, 67.

12 Rae Langton. "Speech Acts and Unspeakable Acts," in *Sexual Solipsism* (New York: Oxford University Press, 2009), 25–64.

13   MacKinnon, *Only Words*, 67.

14   Ibid.

15   *American Booksellers, Inc. v. Hudnut*, 771F. 2d 329 (7th Cir. 1985).

16   Ronald Dworkin, "Is There a Right to Pornography?," *Oxford Journal of Legal Studies* (1981): 177–212.

17   Varda Burstyn, "Beyond Despair: Positive Strategies," in *Women Against Censorship*, ed. Varda Burstyn (Vancouver: Douglas & McIntyre, 1985), 152–80.

18   Constance Penley, Celine Parrenas Shimizu, Mireille Miller-Young, and Tristan Taormino, "Introduction: The Politics of Producing Pleasure," in *The Feminist Porn Book: The Politics of Producing Pleasure*, ed. Taormino et al. (New York: The Feminist Press, 2013), 9–22.

19   Ibid.

20   Abigail Bray, "Merciless Doctrines: Child Pornography, Censorship, and Late Capitalism," *Signs* 37.1 (2011): 133.

21   Melissa Farley, "Pornography Is Infinite Prostitution," in *Big Porn Inc: Exposing the Harms of the Global Pornography Industry*, ed. Melinda Tankard Reist and Abigail Bray (North Melbourne: Spinifex Press, 2011), 150–59.

22   Abigail Bray, "Capitalism and Pornography: The Internet as a Global Prostitution Factory," in *Big Porn Inc: Exposing the Harms of the Global Pornography Industry*, ed. Melinda Tankard Reist and Abigail Bray (North Melbourne: Spinifex Press, 2011), 160–66.

DISCUSSION QUESTIONS

(1) Suppose we accept that pornography, in all or most of its forms, is morally objectionable. Who is more at fault for the industry's success—the consumers who continue to watch pornography, or the producers who continue to make and distribute it?

(2) More generally, how much freedom should businesses have to produce morally questionable products when there is evidently a strong consumer base wanting those products? Try to think of another industry that relies on consumer demand for a product that is arguably unethical: does moral responsibility lie with the industry or with the consumers of the product?

(3) Suppose we accept that some forms of pornography, such as feminist pornography, are morally acceptable, while other forms, such as violent pornography, are morally wrong. What implications would this have for the regulation of the industry as a whole?

(4) Despite the vocal protests of many feminists against pornography, especially violent and misogynistic pornography, the industry has continued to grow over recent decades. Why do you think that is? What does this say about pornography as an industry?

(5) What implications does the ethical debate on pornography have for the ethical debate on prostitution?

FURTHER READINGS

Carolyn Bronstein, *Battling Pornography: The American Feminist Anti-Pornography Movement, 1976–1986* (Cambridge: Cambridge University Press, 2011).

The Feminist Porn Book: The Politics of Producing Pleasure, ed. Tristan Taormino et al. (New York: The Feminist Press, 2013).

Gert Martin Hald, Neil M. Malamuth, and Carlin Yuen, "Pornography and Attitudes Supporting Violence against Women: Revisiting the Relationship in Nonexperimental Studies," *Aggressive Behavior* 36.1 (2010): 14–20.

Mireille Miller-Young, "Hip-Hop Honeys and Da Hustlaz: Black Sexualities in the New Hip-Hop Pornography," *Meridians: Feminism, Race, Transnationalism* 8.1 (2007): 261–92.

Paul J. Wright, Robert S. Tokunaga, and Ashley Kraus, "A Meta-Analysis of Pornography Consumption and Actual Acts of Sexual Aggression in General Population Studies," *Journal of Communication* 66.1 (2016): 183–205.

THE BUSINESS ETHICS OF RECREATIONAL MARIJUANA

M. BLAKE WILSON

BACKGROUND

ON JANUARY 1, 2018, THE STATE OF CALIFORNIA BEGAN ISSUING licenses for the cultivation and commercial sale of marijuana, or cannabis, to adults for their recreational use. The licenses are the direct result of Proposition 64, better known as the Adult Use of Cannabis Act (AUMA). The AUMA was approved by the people of California on November 8, 2016, by a vote of 57 per cent to 43 per cent. These voters agreed that cannabis—a substance which has been illegal in the state since 1913 and remains illegal under Federal law—shall be legal for individuals to possess, use, and cultivate in small amounts (as consumers) and legal for their suppliers (as producers) to cultivate and sell in much larger amounts. Although permitted to grow up to six plants at home, most consumers will choose to act as cannabis consumers of the flowers of the plant (for smoking) as well as processed derivatives for oral consumption (or "edibles"). In 2017, *Fortune Magazine* predicted that Californians would purchase $7 billion of cannabis products in 2018, generating $1 billion in tax revenue for the state.[1] In fact, the numbers were substantially smaller: 2018 saw $2.51 billion in sales[2] and just over $345 million in tax revenues.[3] Still, California has emerged as the world's largest market for cannabis, which stands to surpass almonds, grapes, strawberries, and tomatoes as California's biggest cash crop. The prospects for investment, entrepreneurship, income, and wealth for producers are enormous.

For the past 20 years, California attorney Omar Figueroa has specialized in defending individuals accused of running afoul of the state's medical cannabis regulations. The author of *Cannabis Codes of California*, the first reference guide to the new and old regulations, Figueroa has also represented hundreds of individuals accused of violating state and federal criminal cannabis laws, and is currently advising many more who are attempting to comply with California's new cannabis licensing codes and regulations. The majority of these regulations have arisen from the AUMA's provision that regulation can be augmented by "legislative amendments" enacted by the elected members of California's legislature.

Figueroa is on the cutting edge of the regulation surge, although he is careful to stress that he and his fellow attorneys cannot legally represent the architects of the new cannabis industry as business attorneys; rather, they are practicing a kind of regulatory compliance law for their clients. "Even with Proposition 64," he says, "there are still lots of black and gray markets for cannabis." With that in mind, many of Figueroa's former criminal clients are seeking permits and licenses in order to avoid the threat of criminal prosecution and incarceration, but, as Figueroa emphasizes to his clients, cannabis remains illegal at the Federal level, and even the new California rules and regulations continue to subject cannabis users and products to a wide range of possible criminal sanctions. Although the new statutes designate many of the former felony cannabis offenses as misdemeanors, each misdemeanor can result in up to one year in jail. The new regulations also impose substantial punishments for environmental and workplace offenses, not to mention substantial civil fines that can become liens on property as a result of operating unpermitted grow sites.[4]

According to Figueroa, "Proposition 64 did not truly legalize cannabis. Cannabis would be legal if there were no penalties for possession, like coffee." In this sense, his services are not markedly different from his previous services to clients as a criminal defense attorney. When he was acting in that role, cannabis cultivation and production were fully criminalized through massive efforts to eradicate the plant, and the combined law enforcement/prosecution effort resulted in cannabis-based convictions of over one million people in California alone, where 6,000 people are currently serving felony prison sentences for trafficking in the substance. During that era, producers and users spent time in jails and prisons but also huge sums of money on penalties, fines, and attorney's fees. Now, says Figueroa, they are employing marketing consultants and finding demographic niches. Figueroa's own experiences as well as those of his clientele set the stage for the story of this sea change not only in law and regulation, but also in the ethical challenges to both producers and consumers as cannabis moves from crime to commerce.

ANALYSIS

THE LEGALIZATION OF CANNABIS AND OTHER SUBSTANCES FOR recreational use raises a number of interesting issues for business ethics, including the role of property rights, the permissibility of governmental regulation of so-called "vice" (commonly known as paternalism), and the moral obligations of producers of intoxicants. There is no doubt that cannabis producers are meeting a tsunami of consumer demand for their product. But "meeting demand with supply" is no substitution for ethics. If a market in cannabis opens the floodgates for more dangerous drugs, or if the cannabis market itself does more harm than good, then ethicists have good reason to challenge the wisdom of making cannabis available in the produce department—right next to the carrots and cucumbers—at the neighborhood grocery store.

In the cannabis business story (*cannabusiness* for short), there are two categories of moral agents. The first category comprises *producers* of cannabis products and includes growers, wholesalers, and retailers, or anyone who is involved in cannabis in order to make a profit. Producers create and distribute cannabis products designed to be used by the second category: *consumers*. This second category also includes anyone who is not directly involved in the production of the product for commercial use and therefore includes the legislators who regulate the product as well as the end-use consumers. So, the first category consists of producers, and the second category includes everyone else. After all, it's "the public"—acting as a democratic majority—who made this happen through the ballot initiative process.

Moral agents have moral obligations, and there is a variety of moral obligations that govern all trade. Producers of cannabis products—or any other commodity, such as carrots—are obligated to sell products that conform with a general warranty of merchantability, to avoid false or misleading advertising, and to be liable to their consumers for damages if they sell an inherently defective product. Although cannabis is now legal in small amounts for recreational use in California as well as ten other states (plus the District of Columbia),[5] over two dozen more states permit it to be legally possessed with a doctor's recommendation. In these states, cannabis is permitted to be used as medicine, which clearly indicates a meaningful distinction between cannabis and carrots. As a producer of a pharmaceutical product, cannabis producers certainly have more ethical obligations to consumers (or, in this case, patients) than producers of carrots. They must, for example, ensure that dosage amounts are correctly indicated on the label of the product, and that the proper strain or variety of cannabis is being provided pursuant to the directive of the prescription. But this case study is not about medical cannabis: it's about cannabis as a recreational product, where it is presumably more like wine or coffee than antibiotics or opioids. So, from an ethical standpoint, is trade in recreational cannabis meaningfully different than trade in carrots?

One way to approach an answer to this question is to determine what kinds of *rights* are involved in commercial transactions generally, and then to inquire about cannabusiness rights in particular. According to legal philosopher H.L.A. Hart, "[r]ights are typically conceived of as possessed or owned or belonging to individuals, and these expressions reflect the conception of moral rules as not only prescribing conduct but as forming a kind of moral property of individuals to which they are as individuals entitled."[6] If people have a right to engage in a particular kind of behavior, then it is usually wrong to interfere with them when they choose to exercise that right. After all, rights are important, and rights should only be violated when there are substantial justifications for doing so.

One group of rights that is indispensable for most, if not all, commercial transactions is *property rights*, and property rights play a major role in business ethics. If producers have a property right to produce and sell carrots, and consumers have a similar right to buy and consume carrots, then respect for the property rights of carrot farmers and carrot consumers might be analogous to respecting the property rights of producers and consumers of other agricultural products such as recreational cannabis.

It is often said that property is protected by a bundle of rights. According to this theory, property consists of the group of rights or incidents "inhering in the citizen's relation to the physical thing, as the right to possess, use, and dispose of it."[7] Property is therefore the "set of government backed rights one has in the physical thing,"[8] and these rights are often termed "sticks" in the bundle.[9] A person becomes the full owner of a property when he or she possesses certain rights, or "standard incidents of ownership," in a mature, liberal legal system.[10]

In terms of property rights and business ethics, the actions and behaviors involved in trade can be evaluated from at least two ethical standpoints: consequentialist ethics and deontological ethics. The buying and selling of cannabis products can be evaluated from these two perspectives as well.

The consequentialist argument claims that cannabis ought to be protected by property rights and bought and sold like any other commodity, provided that those commodities produce good consequences. If the cannabis trade does not produce good consequences, then it—like any other commodity that produces more bad outcomes than good ones—can be heavily regulated or even outlawed because it is *harmful*. Strong property rights in both producers (the right to sell) and consumers (the right to buy) turn upon this empirical fact. Under this approach, the property right is granted (or not) based upon the observable and quantifiable outcomes in regards to the amount of welfare produced by it.

The deontological argument, on the other hand, justifies property rights independently of the outcomes. From this perspective, cannabis ought to be bought and sold like any other commodity because people have a right to engage in this kind of behavior. By ignoring the consequences of commodification, this approach focuses upon the individual rights of producers and consumers. If persons have such rights, then it is wrong to violate them through extensive regulation or criminalization. If persons lack such rights, then it is not wrong to regulate or criminalize this kind of behavior.

Let's look at the consequentialist argument in more detail. According to Bernard Williams, consequentialism "is the doctrine that the moral value of any action always lies in its consequences and that it is by reference to their consequences that actions, and indeed such things as institutions, laws, and practices, are to be justified if they can be justified at all."[11] The consequences aimed for by utilitarianism—the most well-known form of consequentialism—include "people's desires or preferences and their getting what they want or prefer."[12] The general rules governing these acts also form the basis for the operation of the institutions that govern commerce and industry.

John Stuart Mill famously wrote that utilitarianism—the most popular form of consequentialism—seeks to provide "the greatest good for the greatest number of people," and actions that succeed in providing such goods promote human welfare. From a moral point of view, consequentialists tell us that we ought to engage in those kinds of actions. Do property rights, in carrots or cannabis, help satisfy this moral *ought*? For consequentialists, society grants property rights to producers and to consumers only insofar as the general welfare is promoted. If the general welfare is not promoted, the consequentialist is obligated to *deny* these rights through extensive regulation or even criminalization because the actions and behaviors associated with legalization cause more harm than good. Of course, criminalization and regulation can themselves also create new harms, and consequentialists need to weigh the costs of those as well.

Unlike alcohol and cigarettes, which are subject to a variety of *paternalistic* controls (including restrictions based on age and areas of use), there are very few regulatory or paternalistic constraints on the marketing or the consumption of carrots. Consequentialists can claim this to be the case because carrots do not have the same potential for harm or abuse as alcohol, cigarettes, or cannabis. These items, along with knives, guns, and chainsaws, are certainly harmful under certain circumstances, and consequentialists can consistently regulate or outlaw them because of their potential for harm. In terms of cannabis, millions of people wish to buy and use cannabis recreationally, and many others wish to provide it to them. If negative social consequences (which would include concerns about harm as well as cannabis's possible status as a 'gateway' drug) are the result of the commercialization and use of cannabis, but those consequences are outweighed by positive consequences in terms of general welfare, then the consequentialist will lean towards property rights in cannabis. If the negative consequences are not outweighed by the positive, then society should not respect those rights.

From the deontological perspective, cannabis production and use are not tied into questions about the general welfare. Unlike consequentialism, where rights are determined only after considerations of welfare are made (here, it is said that the good precedes the right), deontologists *begin* their moral evaluation with rights, which are meant to be foundational to any further considerations of welfare (here, the right precedes the good). Morality, for the deontologist, is not the result of welfare-promoting actions, but their basis. In terms of business ethics, the great deontological ethicist Immanuel Kant illustrated this principle with his story of the ethical shopkeeper.[13] Writing in the late eighteenth century, Kant tells us that an ethical shopkeeper does not overcharge an inexperienced customer, and sells his goods at an honest price, because it is the right thing to do, and not because he wants a good reputation or because he is required by law to do so. For Kant, the foundation of morality consists in treating others with respect because that is how we want to be treated in return, and we show respect for others by treating them as persons who possess certain rights simply by virtue of being persons and not as mere means to each other's ends. One of those rights, for Kant, is the right to hold and own property. This right is not the product, or consequence, of considerations about welfare or efficiency, and societies cannot take away this and other rights if their exercise fails to enlarge the aggregation of social welfare. If persons have a deontological right to truck and barter their possessions, then consequentialist considerations are irrelevant.

Whether derived from consequentialist or deontological justifications, the property right as it pertains to commerce can be thought of as an exercise in *economic liberty*, which can be defined as "the right to acquire, use, and possess private property and the right to enter into private contracts of one's choosing."[14] Like the other fundamental rights, particularly those involving bodily integrity, private property permits us to create what Paul Fairfield calls *moral spaces*, which are "demarcations in the social sphere" and "less metaphorical than many other rights."[15] Although all rights create a sphere or domain of noninterference, what is interesting about the private property right is the fact that it does so "in a more direct and literal way, establishing relatively unambiguous territorial distinctions between physical, intellectual, or personal domains and the realm of public affairs."[16] In other words, because private property rights are grounded in spaces, they are more directly observable and therefore more capable of expressing the moral agency of both the owner, who makes choices about their acquisition, use, and alienation of their property, as well as the agency of others.

The classic restriction on property rights involves the ownership of a knife: knife owners do not have the right to use their knife by sticking it in someone's back.[17] But in this case, *ownership* of the knife is irrelevant:

non-owners of knives are under the same duty not to harm others as owners. Owners, of course, have a strong exclusionary right to keep non-owners from their knife, but non-owners have an even stronger duty of noninterference (i.e., they must refrain from stealing it) as long as the owner/user is not violating their duty not to unjustly harm others with it. This illustrates the moral and legal maxim *sic utere tue ut alienum non laedas*, or "use your own property in such a manner as to not harm that of another."[18] Interestingly, both consequentialists and deontologists might agree with this maxim.

Let's return to carrots and paternalism for a moment. Carrots are perfectly legal: there are no restrictions on their possession or, for the most part, on their use. However, were someone to harm another by using a very large carrot as a club, or to harm themselves by intravenously injecting carrot juice, then the state can legitimately intervene in the first example, but probably not in the second. A law that prohibits the use of carrot juice in this manner is considered paternalistic, and paternalism is the practice of restricting a person's actions on the grounds that it is harmful to themselves, but not others—or, at least not *directly* harmful to others. Parents might tell their child "it's for your own good" when they deny that child a second bowl of ice cream, and the state similarly acts like a parent by purporting to know what is in their citizens' best interests. Seat belt laws, motorcycle helmet laws, and laws against drug use are all paternalistic. Can they be justified?

Interestingly, few of these laws punish violators for *actually* harming themselves: rather, they sanction behavior that has the *potential* for harm. For example, the state can mandate that motorcyclists wear helmets to protect themselves from being harmed by their own negligence, but also by the negligence of others. Street drugs such as heroin or crack are also potentially dangerous—even to an experienced user—for the same reason: the manufacturer or supplier might negligently provide a product that seriously harms the user in much the same way that a reckless driver can seriously harm a helmetless motorcyclist. But, by coercing the motorcyclist to wear a helmet—and coercing the drug user not to use—both actual and potential harms are reduced. Clearly, it's good for motorcyclists to wear helmets, and it's good for drug addicts to avoid dangerous street drugs. Paternalism, in this sense, protects persons from *both* themselves and others.

So, what's wrong with paternalism? Opponents argue that these laws violate the legal principle *volenti non fit injuria*—"to a willing person, injury is not done." It stands for the idea that no one can claim that a harm was unjust when they have willingly consented to it. In civil law, *volenti non fit injuria* means that a spectator at a baseball game cannot sue the batter or the ball park owners after being hit in the head by a foul ball. In criminal law, it means that a person should not be held answerable to the state when they harm only themselves. It is also the basis for several other legal principles such as assumption of risk and informed consent. In the context of drug use—including the use of recreational cannabis—it means that persons are not unjustly injured when they voluntarily consent to engage in risky behavior. They may suffer harm, but the harm is not wrongful, and the agent causing the harm cannot be held liable for giving the user the opportunity to harm themselves. Purveyors of street drugs, legalized cannabis, chainsaws, and baseball contests might defend their actions on similar grounds.

The legitimacy of paternalism is closely tied to criminalization. What, exactly, is a crime, and when can states punish those who commit them? At first blush, it appears that crimes cause harms, but torts and broken contracts are also harmful—yet they are not categorized as crimes. Unlike torts, crimes entail punishment, and criminalization punishes behaviors that *are* categorized as crimes. In accord with the principle of *volenti non fit injuria*, legal philosopher Douglas Husak makes the claim that states may only punish behavior that *unjustly* harms others, and such behavior must be *malum in se*, or bad in itself. Harm to others is the product of behavior that is *malum in se*, and it constitutes one—and perhaps the only—justification for the imposition of punishment. The classic examples of conduct that is *malum in se* are murder, rape, and theft. Paternalistic laws typically do not punish conduct that is *malum in se*, but rather conduct that is *malum prohibitum*: conduct that is bad by virtue of it being against the law.

Husak argues that these kinds of laws (which would include motorcycle helmet laws as well as most drug laws) violate what he calls the *right against punishment.* For Husak, the right against punishment is derived from a general right not to be subjected to "intentional deprivation and censure through state action."[19] State punishments necessarily include the deliberate infliction of both hard treatment and the imposition of stigma, both of which conflict with a general right not to have these harms inflicted upon rightsholders. Such a right, Husak argues, is a fundamental one and on par with the rights of speech, religion, and privacy. Legally, these rights are protected by what the Supreme Court has labeled the *strict scrutiny* test: if legislation implicates fundamental rights such as speech, religion, or privacy, courts ought to strike down the legislation unless it is "necessary to achieve a compelling governmental objective."[20]

In regards to behavior that does not implicate these fundamental rights, states enjoy very broad powers to outlaw or regulate just about anything (including cannabis production and use) by adhering to the far less demanding *rational basis* test, which permits the state to implement a wide variety of legislation—even legislation that punishes, incarcerates, or even executes offenders—so long as the legislation is "rationally related to a conceivable public purpose."[21] If the right not to be punished was determined to be constitutionally fundamental (such a determination could be made by either the courts or the legislature), then the state would be required to satisfy strict scrutiny in order to maintain *any* legislation that punishes. A fundamental right not to be punished would therefore place the burden of proof squarely upon the state to justify laws that subject those within its jurisdiction to any punishment whatsoever.

It is well known that laws that are strict in theory are fatal in fact, and "precious few laws survive strict scrutiny."[22] For Husak, only certain kinds of acts are punishable, and the state's compelling interest in preventing violence or other harms satisfies strict scrutiny and justifies responsive punishments. *Malum in se* crimes would therefore survive strict scrutiny, but most (if not all) *malum prohibitum* conduct would not. Drug offenses, prostitution, and other so-called victimless crimes would clearly not satisfy strict scrutiny, and the right against punishment would probably vitiate most paternalistic laws as well—including, of course, laws that criminalize the production and use of cannabis.

Lastly, no discussion of cannabis legalization can escape the inevitable charge that it will lead to the legalization of drugs *tout court*. Can we legalize pot but consistently and reasonably continue to outlaw far more dangerous drugs? After all, what's to prevent further citizen-led initiatives, like Proposition 64, permitting the recreational use of crack, heroin, and LSD? Don't the same arguments for a market in pot support a market in PCP? Philosophers call this a *slippery slope* argument, and it is fallacious when it creates bogus causal links between unrelated things and events. It also plays upon a fear of the final link in the chain, which might be completely rational on its own, by fallaciously linking it backwards to an irrational fear of the first link. So, is there a slippery slope from the cannabis market to the methamphetamine market, or is this a legitimate objection to the commercialization of cannabis in the first place?

Attorney Figueroa thinks the link is imaginary. Cannabis, according to Figueroa, is *sui generis*: as its own category—situated somewhere between mild intoxicant and euphoriant—cannabis is fundamentally different than alcohol and harder drugs such as methamphetamine and PCP. As a naturally occurring substance that is used by millions of people every day without harm to themselves or others, cannabis products are more like coffee, chamomile, and carrots than crack or cocaine. Whereas the long-term use of harder drugs can be fatal, there is no evidence that cannabis products promise similar fates for users. In terms of efforts at legalization, Figueroa reports that "we can draw the line at cannabis, and we don't need to open the floodgates to every other substance."

Perhaps not coincidentally, California also leads the nation in microbreweries, and Figueroa foresees a cannabis industry that echoes the microbrew phenomenon, where producers sell artisanal products directly to consumers without the middleman or distributional network that seems to lend itself to gray and black markets. And although there is widespread abuse of alcohol, most users learn to self-regulate their intake in the same way coffee users learn self-regulation. Time will tell whether California cannabis users will follow suit, and whether the state will pave the way towards further legalization of cannabis nationwide, or be the proving grounds for claims that the costs of legalization do not outweigh the benefits due to the decline in social welfare. The eyes of the nation's cannabis users, producers, and regulators are on you, California.[23]

NOTES

1   Grace Donnelly, "The Marijuana Tax Problem: Why Prices Could Increase 70% in 2018," *Fortune* (2017). It is estimated that the national market will grow to $30 billion by 2021. Debra Borchardt, "The Marijuana Industry Is Getting Supersized," *Forbes* (2017).

2   "The 2018 California Cannabis Marketplace in Review," https://bdsanalytics.com/the-2018-california-cannabis-marketplace-in-review/ (accessed July 18, 2019)

3   "California's Marijuana Tax Revenue Badly Misses the Mark," https://www.fool.com/investing/2019/02/24/californias-marijuana-tax-revenue-badly-misses-the.aspx (accessed July 18, 2019)

4   One such county, Humboldt, is proposing a $10,000 fine per day for unpermitted cannabis operations.

5   Those states are Alaska, Colorado, Illinois, Massachusetts, Maine, Michigan, Nevada, Oregon, Vermont, and Washington.

6   H.L.A. Hart, "Are There Any Natural Rights?" in *Theories of Rights*, ed. Jeremy Waldron (Oxford: Oxford University Press, 1984), 83.

7   *Ruckelshaus v. Monsanto Co.*, 467 U.S. 986, 1003 (1984) (quoting *U.S. v. General Motors*, 323 U.S. 373, 377–78 (1945)). See also Stephen R. Munzer, *A Theory of Property* (Cambridge: Cambridge University Press, 1990), 16.

8   Robert Meltz, Dwight H. Merriam, and Richard M. Frank, *The Takings Issue: Constitutional Limits on Land Use Control and Environmental Regulation* (Washington, DC: Island Press, 1999), 27.

9   Munzer, *A Theory of Property*, 16.

10 On one analysis, there are eleven such incidents: (1) the right to possess; (2) the right to use; (3) the right to manage; (4) the right to the income of the thing; (5) the right to the capital; (6) the right to security; (7) the incident of transmissibility; (8) the incident of absence of term; (9) the duty to prevent harm; (10) liability to execution; and (11) the incident of residuarity. See Tony Honoré, "Ownership," in *Making Law Bind* (Oxford: Clarendon Press, 1987).

11 Bernard Williams and J.C.C. Smart, *Utilitarianism: For and Against* (Cambridge: Cambridge University Press, 1973), 79.

12 Ibid.

13 Immanuel Kant, *Groundwork of the Metaphysics of Morals* (Cambridge: Cambridge University Press, 1996), 53.

14 Randy Barnett, "Does the Constitution Protect Economic Liberty?" *Harvard Journal of Law & Public Policy* 35.1 (2012): 5.

15 Paul Fairfield, *Public/Private* (Lanham: Rowman & Littlefield, 2005), 124.

16 Ibid.

17 The example is from Robert Nozick.

18 1 *Blackstone's Commentaries* 306.

19 Douglas Husak, *Overcriminalization: The Limits of the Criminal Law* (Oxford: Oxford University Press, 2008), 57.

20 See *Moore v. City of East Cleveland*, 431 U.S. 494 (1977).

21 *Hawaii Housing Authority v. Midkiff*, 467 U.S. 229, 241 (1984).

22 Husak (2008), 127.

23 Many thanks to Omar Figueroa for agreeing to be interviewed for this case study.

DISCUSSION QUESTIONS

(1) Do people have a right to use mind-altering drugs? If so, can others claim a right to supply those drugs to users? Are property rights important in either case?

(2) What kinds of issues should democratic majorities take into consideration when they criminalize or decriminalize drugs such as cannabis?

(3) Do illegal cannabis producers have a different set of moral obligations than legal ones?

(4) What amount of regulation of substances like cannabis or alcohol is acceptable in a free market?

(5) What kinds of facts would prove whether cannabis or other drugs are beneficial or harmful to society, and should those facts influence our understanding of their ethical production and use?

FURTHER READINGS

Jason Brenna and Peter Jaworski, *Markets without Limits* (New York: Routledge, 2016).

Omar Figueroa, *Cannabis Codes of California* (Sebastopol, CA: Lux Law Publishing, 2017).

Douglas Husak, *Overcriminalization: The Limits of the Criminal Law* (Oxford: Oxford University Press, 2008).

Douglas Husak, *Legalize This! The Case for Decriminalizing Drugs* (New York: Verso, 2002).

John Stuart Mill, *On Liberty, Utilitarianism, and Other Essays* (Oxford: Oxford University Press, 2015).

Robert Nozick, *Anarchy, State, and Utopia* (New York: Basic Books, 1974).

Michael Sandel, *What Money Can't Buy* (New York: Farrar, Straus, and Giroux, 2012).

4

OF PRICES AND PILLS: ETHICAL ISSUES IN PHARMACEUTICAL PRICING

BRYAN CWIK

BACKGROUND

CHRONIC MYELOID LEUKEMIA (CML) IS A TYPE OF CANCER THAT affects myeloid cells (the cells that form red blood cells, platelets, and some white blood cells) in the bone marrow.[1] CML primarily affects older adults (age 65 and older); in the United States, there are around 9,000 new cases a year, and approximately 1 in 555 adults are diagnosed with CML. Prior to 2001, the standard treatment for CML was with interferon therapy (synthetic versions of proteins made by the human immune system). CML is very debilitating and deadly; survival rates for CML were approximately three to five years.[2]

In 2001, a drug, imatinib, marketed under the trade name Gleevec, was introduced to treat CML. Dr. Brian Druker, a cancer researcher at the Oregon Health and Science University (OHSU) in Portland, Oregon, pioneered the use of imatinib for the treatment of CML. Imatinib was developed by scientists at a company that eventually became part of

45

Novartis, one of the largest pharmaceutical companies in the world. The idea behind imatinib was to develop a targeted chemotherapy compound that would block an enzyme that is causally responsible for CML.[3] This work built on decades of research in cancer biology, and most proximally by work done by a team at the Hebrew University of Jerusalem. Some of this research was publicly financed, and some was funded by private money.

Research on the clinical use of imatinib to treat CML began in the 1990s, and the compound was patented by Novartis in the late 1990s. A pharmaceutical patent gives its holder exclusive rights to make, market, and distribute a drug for a period of 20 years, though patent exclusivity can be extended through various legal mechanisms (a process known as "evergreening"). Holding a patent on a drug like imatinib can be extremely valuable for a company, as it allows the company to set the price as high as the market will bear, instead of setting a price that is competitive with other manufacturers. When Gleevec was initially introduced to the market in 2001, it was priced in reference to interferon, its main competitor. A yearly course of Gleevec in 2001 was $30,000. However, Gleevec turned out to be a genuine "miracle cure" for CML. With Gleevec, over 80 per cent of CML patients live longer than five years past their initial diagnosis, and it is speculated that treatment with imatinib may enable CML patients to live out a normal lifespan.[4]

As the popularity and the success of the drug took off, Novartis began increasing the price of Gleevec. In 2013, the price of Gleevec was $80,000–90,000 a year, and by 2016 the (wholesale) price had increased to $120,000 a year. That year, a group of oncologists and cancer biologists (including Dr. Druker) wrote an essay in the journal *Blood* condemning the high price of Gleevec, arguing that it greatly restricts access to the drug and adversely affects the health of patients with CML. At the time the essay was written, Gleevec was the most expensive drug in history. Since then, other "miracle cure" pharmaceutical products have entered the market at even higher costs than Gleevec. Sofosbuvir (marketed as Sovaldi or Harvoni and patented by Gilead Pharmaceuticals), which is used to treat Hepatitis C, cost $84,000 per 12-week course when it was first released in 2014, a price of $1,000 a day.[5] In the summer of 2017, Novartis introduced a gene therapy treatment for acute lymphoblastic leukemia (ALL), marketed as Kymriah. The initial price for Kymriah was set at $475,000 for a one-time intravenous injection.[6]

ANALYSIS

THERE ARE SEVERAL ETHICAL ISSUES RAISED BY PHARMACEUTI-
cal pricing in multiple and different areas of practical and applied ethics.
There are profound questions about the way in which drug development
is financed, the role of private companies in provision of health care, and
about balancing rights to property (assuming there is a justification for
property rights in the form of patents on compounds) and other rights
(such as a human right to health). All of these are set against a background of more general ethical issues about health and the provision of
health care, and indeed about the role of medicine in society.

Developed (and an ever-increasing number of developing) countries
have gone through what medical anthropologists call *the epidemiological
transition*.[7] The epidemiological transition is when the majority of deaths
occur not from infectious diseases (such as tuberculosis or malaria) but
from chronic diseases associated with age and lifestyle (such as heart
disease, diabetes, cancer, and dementia). As more societies around the
world "gray" (that is, as the median age of their population gets older),
the burden of chronic disease grows. The great medical advances of the
nineteenth and early twentieth centuries (the germ theory of disease,
antiseptic surgery, antibiotics, and better public health measures) were
huge contributors to the overall increase in life expectancy, health, and
well-being experienced by (many) individuals worldwide. But this process is not without cost; as more people are living longer lives, more people suffer from chronic diseases that are expensive and difficult to treat.

CML is one of these diseases, a chronic disease that is the result
(mostly) of age. As more people live into their 60s, 70s, and 80s, the
number of people with CML and similar diseases goes up, and the more
treatment (and prevention, where possible) for these diseases becomes
a top health priority. Infectious diseases such as cholera or tuberculosis
can be handled fairly cheaply with "low tech" tools (low-cost antibiotics,
vaccination, and improved public health measures), but diseases such
as cancer require intensive (and expensive) medical interventions. In
post-epidemiological transition societies such as the United States, treatments of chronic diseases are primary health care priorities. As a result,
reducing costs and barriers to access associated with the cost of medical
treatment for chronic disease is a major issue. The role of pharmaceutical pricing practices in the overall cost of health care must therefore be

understood against this background of broader social and ethical questions about the burden of chronic disease on developed countries.

New drugs can often be (but are not *always*) significant improvements over existing treatments. The difference between treatment regimens can often be a matter of life or death, or at least of significantly improved health. The difference between treatment with Gleevec (at $120,000/year) and with generic interferon is the difference between three to five more years of life and potentially living much longer and dying of something else. Prices are the result of the aggregation of a great deal of information, but the primary determinant of price is, as every microeconomics student knows, consumer demand. Demand itself is complicated—the level of demand for any product is determined not only by bare desire, but also preference for this particular product over its competitors, other demands on consumers' income and time, marketing and brand recognition, and the simple vagaries of taste and culture. But for some things, demand can sometimes be fairly straightforward. Most people prefer more to fewer years of life and most people would, when faced with the choice between three to five years of life or five plus years, be willing to reorganize their preferences and devote a significant amount of resources to achieving the latter. Pharmaceutical companies that have patents on "blockbuster" drugs like Gleevec are thus in a position to set prices very high, as they control access to a product that, for many consumers, can make the difference between life and death.

There is thus a significant question about whether companies should exploit their position relative to their customers to charge as high a price as they wish. Even very staunch defenders of property rights, such as Robert Nozick, balk at the idea that companies controlling "the only water hole in the desert" can be free to price their products at any level the market will bear.[8] There is a substantial case to be made that setting the price of a lifesaving drug like Gleevec as high as it can go is deeply unethical, as it amounts to something like holding people's lives and health for ransom.

Critics of this line of argument point to three complicating factors. First, in most cases, the prices charged for drugs are not paid directly by consumers but by a third-party payer. In the United States, these are entities such as private insurance companies and government (in the form, for instance, of Medicare drug subsidies); in other countries pharmaceuticals are purchased at wholesale prices by government national health services (as in Canada). In fact, in some countries pharmaceutical markets take the form of a *monopsony*—a market where there is only a single buyer (in this case the government that provides for a national health service), and the single buyer thus has a great deal of power to set the actual price paid for a drug. One explanation for why drug prices in the United States are often so high is that the market is significantly distorted by the existence of third-party payers, which insulates people from the real cost of their medicines. If consumers had to pay directly for access to drugs such as Gleevec, companies like Novartis could not charge $120,000 a year, because the average consumer could not pay that much.

Second, patents do not last forever—they are legally limited to 20 years after their filing date (which can be extended by "evergreening"), and drugs that are under patent and very expensive today will be off-patent and available in generic forms at much cheaper prices in the future. The high cost of new drugs such as Gleevec is necessary for companies to recoup the cost of drug development and—most importantly—to attract new investment to support research and development of new medications. If companies did not charge high prices while drugs were under patent, then they could not pay for new medical innovation, and so the loss of access to a new drug due to high prices today is offset by the benefits to everyone of greater access in the future and of the medical innovation that profit can finance.

Third, critics argue that it is not the responsibility of pharmaceutical companies to boost access to their products; pharmaceutical companies are responsible to their employees and shareholders, and it is government or individuals themselves who are responsible for the health of people with diseases such as CML. All three arguments are further complicated by numerous additional issues (for instance, about whether or not high prices for patented drugs are really necessary to boost medical innovation). Many of these issues turn on complicated empirical questions, about things like the factors affecting wholesale drug prices and the structure of pharmaceutical markets.

The third point is particularly significant in business ethics. To what extent—if any—do companies have responsibilities to their customers over and above providing products and requirements of transparency, product safety, and the like? Debates about corporate social responsibility (CSR) in the pharmaceutical industry are particularly heated and acute, precisely because they involve questions about the role of these companies in promoting the health and well-being of people in their societies. Many pharmaceutical companies play a role in promoting access to medicines to be part of their CSR models, and have access pro-grams to provide medicines to people who have trouble affording them.[9] Many ethicists argue that this does not go far enough. There is heated debate about whether the price of such things as life-saving drugs should be set solely by a market, or whether there are ethical considerations that should also determine how high a price should be. The idea of a "fair price" goes all the way back to medieval European philosophy. In the context of pharmaceuticals, the notion of a fair price would involve building requirements to boost access directly into pricing models, to ensure that companies set prices at levels that provide maximum access while bringing in a "reasonable" or fair profit.

Critics of the fair price idea for pharmaceuticals argue that prices cannot be distorted in this way without having detrimental effects on pharmaceutical markets, and that it would, at any rate, be very difficult to legislate and enforce. Others argue that enforcing obligations to boost access can be done informally, by tracking which companies do well in meeting their obligations and by "naming and shaming" those who don't. Behind all of these are significant and larger questions about the role of private companies in providing medicines, and about the justifiability in the first place of patents and private markets for drugs. Under the current structure of pharmaceutical markets, de facto control over who can and cannot access drugs and who controls the supply of medicines is delegated by law to pharmaceutical companies and health care providers. Cases like those of Gleevec raise serious ethical questions about whether this is the fairest, or even the most efficient, means of governing access to medicines.

NOTES

1   American Cancer Society, "About Chronic Myeloid Leukemia," online.
2   American Cancer Society, "Survival Rates for Chronic Myeloid Leukemia," online.
3   Michael Deininger, Elisabeth Buchdunger, and Brian Druker, "The Development of Imatinib as a Therapeutic Agent for Chronic Myeloid Leukemia," *Blood* 105.7 (2005): 2640–53.
4   Carolyne Y. Johnson, "This Drug Is Defying a Rare Form of Leukemia—and It Keeps Getting Pricier," *Washington Post* (2016).
5   Margo Sanger-Katz, "$1,000 Hepatitis Pill Shows Why Fixing Health Care Costs Is So Hard," *New York Times* (2014).

6 Gina Kolata, "New Gene Therapy Treatments Will Carry Whopping Price Tags," *New York Times* (2017).

7 Abdel R. Omran, "The Epidemiologic Transition," *Milbank Memorial Fund Quarterly* 49.1 (1971): 509–38.

8 Robert Nozick, *Anarchy, State, and Utopia* (New York: Basic Books, 1974), 180.

9 See, for example, Novartis' Access Initiative (online) aimed at developing countries.

DISCUSSION QUESTIONS

(1) Should pharmaceutical companies be able to charge whatever prices they can for medicines?

(2) Should there be a "fair price" for pharmaceuticals, set not just by demand but also by duties to boost access?

(3) Should private entities control the supply of medicines?

(4) What responsibilities do pharmaceutical companies have to their consumers, and for the health and well-being of society?

(5) How do we balance the tradeoff between more and better medical innovation for the future, and access to medicines in the present?

FURTHER READINGS

Access to Medicines Index, https://accesstomedicineindex.org/.

Marcia Angell, *The Truth about the Drug Companies: How They Deceive Us and What to Do about It* (New York: Random House, 2005).

Allen Buchanan, Tony Cole, and Robert O. Keohane, "Justice in the Diffusion of Innovation," *Journal of Political Philosophy* 19 (2011): 306–32.

"Experts in Chronic Myeloid Leukemia. The Price of Drugs for Chronic Myeloid Leukemia (CML) Is a Reflection of the Unsustainable Prices of Cancer Drugs: From the Perspective of a Large Group of CML Experts," *Blood* 121 (2013): 4439–42.

Jessica Flanigan, *Pharmaceutical Freedom: Why Patients Have a Right to Self-Medicate* (Oxford: Oxford University Press, 2017).

Ian Maitland, "Priceless Goods: How Should Life-Saving Drugs Be Priced?" *Business Ethics Quarterly* 12 (2002): 451–80.

Alex Rosenberg, "On the Priority of Intellectual Property Rights, Especially in Biotechnology," *Politics, Philosophy and Economics* 3 (2004): 77–95.

5.

PRIVATE PRISONS IN THE UNITED STATES: A CASE OF PROFIT AT ANY COST?

TOM MCNAMARA, IRENA DESCUBES, AND CYRLENE CLAASEN

BACKGROUND

IMAGINE BEING CONVICTED OF A CRIME AND SENT TO PRISON. While ready to pay your debt to society, you tell prison staff that you are concerned for your safety. Your pleas are ignored. You are then held hostage in your cell for 24 hours and repeatedly raped and physically abused. Other inmates have been stabbed and beaten as well, and the people who work at the facility are fully complicit in the violence. The United Nations asserts that "All prisoners shall be treated with the respect due to their inherent dignity and value as human beings."[1] What kind of government would blatantly disregard such basic human rights and allow these things to happen at one of its prisons?

The above events didn't happen in a gulag in some far-off dictatorship. They took place in a detention facility near Jackson, Mississippi, known as the Walnut Grove Youth Correctional Facility. What's more, the day-to-day operation of the facility was not overseen by the government, but was rather the responsibility of a private company.

Home to just 5 per cent of the planet's population, the US is home to almost 25 per cent of the planet's prisoners—about 2.2 million people (a fourfold increase since the 1970s). Compared to other Western nations, the US detains people at an astounding rate: an estimated 666 per 100,000 citizens. This is anywhere from 5 to 10 times higher than rates seen in similar industrialized democracies, surpassed perhaps by North Korea, which is estimated to punish her already suffering citizens at a rate of up to 800 per 100,000 (reliable statistics are hard to come by).

The associated cost of detaining one out of every four prisoners in the world is about $60 billion a year, a fivefold increase from two decades ago. And with increased government spending comes an increased opportunity for private companies to make a profit by offering to provide the same service at a lower cost. In theory, this should be a win-win proposition for the US taxpayer. Increasingly, however, the private prison industry is receiving bad publicity for questionable practices.

Just how did the US end up being the world's jailer? A lot of it had to do with the launching of President Nixon's "War on Drugs" in 1971. Almost half of the people in Federal prison today are there on drug charges. By any objective measure this war is a failure, having cost the US taxpayer $1 trillion and coming nowhere near to solving America's problems with drugs; in 2016 it was estimated that the number of people who died from drug overdoses was larger than the number of US soldiers killed in the Vietnam War and the Second Iraq War combined. Another reason for the large number of prisoners is the continued efforts by politicians (both Republican and Democrat) to be seen as being "tough on crime." Passing stricter and stricter laws with longer sentences is often seen as an easy way to win votes. The result is a prison system that has been pushed beyond its design limits. Privatizing parts of America's prison system can be seen as a partial cure to its growing ills of overcrowding and poor conditions.

In 1983, the Corrections Corporation of America (CCA) had the novel idea of leasing a motel in Houston, Texas, and then using it to procure a government contract to detain undocumented immigrants (their first "prison" was staffed by relatives of the company's founders). But the use of private prisons didn't really take off until 1997, when the Federal Bureau of Prisons (BOP), the government agency responsible for detaining people convicted of (or facing) federal charges, began giving contracts to privately run facilities (commonly called "contract prisons"). This action was taken in response to intolerable conditions of overcrowding and various directives from Congress. At first their use was on a small scale, but today private prisons can be found at both the federal and state level. An estimated 8 per cent of US prisoners are in facilities run by private corporations, an increase of about 80 per cent between the years 1999 and 2010 (this doesn't even include the hundreds of thousands of undocumented immigrants who get processed every year in private detention facilities as well).

A few companies have decided that their strategic advantage lies in housing, feeding, and reforming prisoners for the government, two of the largest being GEO Group and CoreCivic. Together, these companies saw revenues in 2016 of $4 billion. But increasingly their business model is being threatened. In its 2014 annual report, CCA stated that "the demand for our facilities and services could be adversely affected by the relaxation of enforcement efforts, leniency in conviction or parole standards and sentencing practices or through the decriminalization of certain activities that are currently proscribed by our criminal laws."

The report's prediction proved fateful. In the dying days of the Obama administration, the Department of Justice came to the conclusion that in terms of safety and actually rehabilitating prisoners, the government did a far better job than private companies. It decided that the use of private prisons would be gradually phased out. But Jeff Sessions, the newly appointed head of the Department of Justice, reversed the previous administration's policy. Since the Sessions announcement and the Trump victory, companies specializing in private prisons have seen their stock price increase.

The topic of private prisons raises central questions for business ethics. Is punishment and rehabilitation something that should be in the hands of private companies rather than governments directly accountable to the democratic public? Should we morally evaluate private prisons based on their consequences (e.g., their cost effectiveness and other outcomes) or are there principled reasons for rejecting them? How should business leaders respond when benefits to their shareholders (e.g., profit) are in tension with the public interest (e.g., rehabilitation, less punitive sentencing)?

ANALYSIS

PRIVATE PRISONS ARE A CONTENTIOUS ISSUE IN THE US. Supporters say that their use results in cost savings to the government through greater efficiency, provides better levels of service to inmates, creates jobs and provides tax revenue in areas that are usually somewhat isolated and in need of economic stimulus. Detractors would question the overall cost savings, pointing out that the jobs created are mostly lower paid with poor benefits (and are non-union) as compared to government-run facilities, and that service levels are in fact quite often poor. Also, when you take into account the tax incentives (sometimes costing millions of dollars) that many communities need to provide in order to attract a private prison, their benefit becomes less clear.

The debate over private prisons can be framed in terms of a person's political or economic point of view. People who are against private prisons might take the position that prosecuting and detaining people is essentially a "Public Good," that is, it is a service that is provided for the general well-being of a society without profit. There is also the argument that punishing people is a right that only the government has (state monopoly theory), and that this right can't be delegated to a private company. One can say that there is a moral danger too, in that private prisons could lead to the possible "commoditization" of people, i.e., that the value of a human being comes from their being an entry on a balance sheet and not from some intrinsic value accorded them under the US Constitution or from natural law. Some might go so far as to say that the idea of for-profit prisons is antithetical to a functioning democracy.

Those in favor of private prisons often have a free market perspective, highlighting the usual lower cost and savings associated with market efficiencies and the benefits inherent in providing choice in the face of a government-run monopoly. Furthermore, forcing companies to compete for government contracts (or the renewal of contracts) provides a strong incentive for them to improve services, develop innovative solutions, and reduce costs even further—elements that are sorely lacking in many state-run prisons. Also, by providing additional (clean and new) capacity to alleviate conditions of overcrowding at government-run facilities, private prisons would improve the plight of prisoners and help preserve their dignity, supporting UN principles on human rights.

But the question remains: Are private prisons better or worse than government-run facilities? Some researchers believe that there really is no significant difference in cost between public and private facilities (the primary argument for privatization). In general, when it comes to handling maximum-security detainees, private prisons usually fare better in terms of cost, with government-run facilities having the advantage when it comes to medium- and minimum-security prisoners. Researchers also failed to see any considerable improvements in the level of quality of confinement, something one might not expect from the introduction of free market competition.

Private facilities also reportedly have much higher levels of violence than those run by the BOP, experiencing lockdowns at a rate that is nine times higher than the BOP's.[2] And while private prisons can be up to 10 per cent cheaper than their government-run rivals, this cost advantage is often achieved through reductions in staff, which can lead to poor inmate management and higher levels of violence.

Furthermore, there are some who argue that this cost advantage is a result of "cherry picking." Private prisons can refuse to accept high risk, unhealthy, mentally disturbed, or elderly prisoners, referring them to government-run facilities instead. This means that any cost savings derived from using privately run facilities would most likely be offset by an increase in the cost being borne by the government (and, eventually, the US taxpayer).

Another front on which private prisons are being criticized is in the provision of medical care, something that is considered an Eighth Amendment right for those who are incarcerated. One study found that many healthcare practitioners working for private companies "had their licenses revoked in other states." CoreCivic has been accused of refusing to provide hospital stays to prisoners as well as punishing those who repeatedly request one. More troubling, CCA is being sued by an inmate who lost both of his legs and all of his fingers to gangrene. He says that his complaints about his deteriorating health were systematically ignored.

In defense of contract prisons, it should be noted that prisoners in general tend to be in poorer health than the population at large due to their higher levels of dependence on alcohol and drugs, thus making them more susceptible to complications as a result of any substandard healthcare. Proponents of private prisons also point out that one doesn't need to look very hard to find numerous examples of cruelty, incompetence, and neglect on the part of government-run facilities as well.

Nonetheless, "customer service" levels (i.e., inmate satisfaction) could be considered as being higher in government-run facilities in that prisoners there had fewer grievances as compared to private prisons. Also, public prisons were seen as having an advantage in terms of the amount of training being provided to inmates, a key factor in reducing recidivism rates.

To be fair, many of the problems with the US penal system existed before the rise of private prisons. One of the most disturbing things about the US penal system is that punishment is meted out more severely to people of color, with Blacks and Latinos comprising a higher proportion of the prison population than they do in the population of the country in general. "Well, those are the people who commit the most crimes," is a common remark one often hears. But studies have shown that people of color are more likely to be convicted of a crime than a White person is, even when it's the same type of crime.[3]

What is not clear is how a system of privately run detention centers can (or even should) help alleviate these injustices. In fact, it might very well aggravate it. Studies show that people of color tend to be overrepresented in the percentage of inmates who are sent to private prisons. Therefore, any deficiencies or problems in a privately run facility would affect them in a disproportionate manner.[4]

So far we have considered how well private prisons achieve some of their outcomes—do they more efficiently house, care for, and rehabilitate prisoners? For some legal scholars, however, the concept of due process of the law and maintaining the protections afforded every US citizen under the Bill of Rights would automatically run counter to the primary interests of private prisons. To be profitable these companies need as many inmates as possible and one way to accomplish this is by having high conviction and detention rates (regardless of any extenuating circumstances).

Indeed, on some conceptions of business ethics, private prisons may even have a responsibility to advocate tough sentences and more convictions. Famed economist Milton Friedman argued that the primary responsibility of a company is to deliver profits to shareholders. Any CEO who believes that (or whose bonus depends upon it) would have little incentive to rehabilitate prisoners or address the underlying causes of crime. In fact, their incentive would be the exact opposite. Companies that run private prisons depend on large prison populations as the easiest way to ensure steady profits. This clearly provides incentives for these companies to lobby lawmakers for harsher sentences, whether they are warranted or not. This explains the creation of "model legislation" favorable to the private prison industry, and the promotion of its introduction through lobbying efforts and financial contributions to politicians.

"Good" might be the response from a hard working (and frightened) US taxpayer. "By sending more people to prison we'll lower crime rates!"

Unfortunately, it is not that simple. Crime rates in the US have been falling since the 1980s, but research has shown that there is not much of a connection between higher detention rates and a reduction in crime, with increased incarceration being responsible for at most 10 per cent of the drop off seen in lawlessness in the US.

Compounding concerns over due process is the fact that when a company agrees to run a detention facility for the government, it quite often inserts a clause into the contract guaranteeing a certain occupancy rate (usually 90 per cent). Cynics observe that the CEO of a contract prison provider who is trying to please his shareholders might not have too many qualms about how this 90 per cent objective is achieved. There is also the concern that prescribed detention rates might put undue stress on the courts of a community to continuously send people to prison, even if local crime rates are dropping. This could very well result in the creation of conflicting, or at the very least, questionable, incentives.

There is in fact evidence that these incentives have already played a role. One of the most troubling examples of this was the "Kids for Cash" scandal, in which two Pennsylvania judges were charged with taking $2.6 million in bribes for condemning juveniles to unusually strict sentences for even minor offenses (the convicted minors were then remanded to private detention facilities). Many of the defendants appeared in court without a lawyer, something that would run counter to a 1967 Supreme Court decision, which said that even people under the age of 18 are entitled to legal counsel. It is believed that 50 per cent of the juveniles who waived their right to a lawyer were convicted and sent to a detention center run by a private company. In the name of profit, many young lives were needlessly destroyed.

Disturbingly, there is also evidence that two contract prison providers, CCA and GEO Group, tried to influence the passing of laws regarding the detention of undocumented immigrants in order to create a more favorable business climate for their operations. According to a 2015 law, Immigration and Customs Enforcement (ICE) has a "bed mandate" or quota that requires them to hold 34,000 detainees. Interestingly, almost 75 per cent of immigrants being detained in the US are held in private facilities. For their part, officials with GEO Group, as well as CoreCivic, say that they do not actively promote policies that increase the numbers of prisoners in the US. Nonetheless, any laws that increase punitive actions against criminals or immigrants would most likely improve the bottom line of private prison providers.

NOTES

1   Office of the United Nations High Commissioner for Human Rights, "Basic Principles for the Treatment of Prisoners," adopted and proclaimed by General Assembly resolution 45/111 of 14 December 1990.

2   Office of the Inspector General, US Department of Justice. Review of the Federal Bureau of Prisons' Monitoring of Contract Prisons, Evaluation and Inspections Division 16–06 (August 2016).

3   Marc Mauer and Ryan King, *Uneven Justice: State Rates of Incarceration by Race and Ethnicity* (Washington, DC: Sentencing Project, 2007), 1–23; M. Marit Rehavi and Sonja B. Starr, "Racial Disparity in Federal Criminal Charging and Its Sentencing Consequences" *Journal of Political Economy* 122.6 (2014): 1320–54; Cassia C. Spohn, "Thirty Years of Sentencing Reform: The Quest for a Racially Neutral Sentencing Process," *Criminal Justice* 3 (2000): 427–501; United States Sentencing Commission, "Report on the Continuing Impact of *United States v. Booker* on Federal Sentencing, *Federal Sentencing Reporter* (2013): 327–33; and Bruce Western and Becky Pettit, "Black-White Wage Inequality, Employment Rates, and Incarceration," *American Journal of Sociology* 111.2 (2005): 553–78.

4   Christopher Petrella, "The Color of Corporate Corrections, Part II: Contractual Exemptions and the Overrepresentation of People of Color in Private Prisons," *Radical Criminology* 3 (2014): 81–100; Christopher Petrella and Josh Begley, "The Color of Corporate Corrections: The Overrepresentation of People of Color in the For-Profit Corrections Industry," *Radical Criminology* 2 (2013): 139–48.

DISCUSSION QUESTIONS

(1)   The United States imprisons its citizens at a rate that is 5 to 10 times higher than those seen in comparable Western Democracies. What are some of the reasons behind this apparent anomaly in the US justice system? Do you believe that America's high incarceration rate is justified? Explain.

(2)   What are some of the arguments that one could use to justify the existence, or even expansion, of America's private prison system? Do you agree with them? Explain.

(3)   What ethical and constitutional questions are raised by the privatization of prisons and their use in incarceration in American society?

(4) Canon City in Fremont County, Colorado, is sometimes called the "Corrections Capital of the World" due to its 7,150 inmates who live in 13 federal or state prisons there. The Mayor of Canon City, Ruth M. Carter, has said that the prison industry is "nice, non-polluting, and recession-proof." Do you agree or disagree? Provide a detailed rationale for your answer.

(5) Columbia University and the University of California (UC) divested their holdings of for-profit private prison stocks following student activist campaigns in 2015 and 2016. Do you believe that actions of this nature will help alleviate or aggravate the ethical concerns associated with private prisons? Why?

FURTHER READINGS

American Psychological Association, "Incarceration Nation," *Monitor on Psychology* 45.9 (2014): 56.

Paul Ashton, "Gaming the System: How the Political Strategies of Private Prison Companies Promote Ineffective Incarceration Policies," *Justice Policy Institute* (2011).

Hadar Aviram, "Are Private Prisons to Blame for Mass Incarceration and Its Evils: Prison Conditions, Neoliberalism, and Public Choice," *Fordham Urban Law Journal* 42 (2014): 411.

Michael Cohen, "How For-profit Prisons Have Become the Biggest Lobby No One Is Talking About," *The Washington Post* (April 28, 2015).

Office of the Inspector General, US Department of Justice, "Review of the Federal Bureau of Prisons' Monitoring of Contract Prisons," Evaluation and Inspections Division 16–06 (August 2016).

David Trilling, "Private Prisons: Research, Data and Controversies," Journalist's Resource, Shorenstein Center on Media, Politics and Public Policy, Harvard Kennedy School (July 12, 2017).

6.

PAYDAY LENDING: AMERICA'S UNSECURED LOAN MARKET

ERIC PALMER

BACKGROUND

LOANS OF MONEY ARE CALLED "UNSECURED" IF THEY ARE GRANTED without collateral. Collateral provides a material guarantee against at least some of the loan's value: holding the deed to a house and land in trust, for example, provides a bank with collateral against a home loan. If something can stand in place of collateral, then a similar security for the lender might be ensured. Something of the right sort was found in the United States during the 1990s by owners of check cashing storefront businesses that operated in all cities and many towns.

Check cashing businesses provide a necessary service, charging fees to cash checks and to draft checks and money orders for their clients, many of whom do not have access to personal bank accounts. Check cashing services found that they could expand their business to a new group of customers who did have access to checking accounts by offering "advance check cashing" services. In place of loan collateral, customers could provide the lender evidence, in the form of a recent paystub, of their ability to pay in the future, plus an indication of intent to repay, in the form of a post-dated check or electronic fund transfer agreement for the value of the loan plus interest and fees. The recipient could then purchase the service of "advance check cashing" against a future paycheck, a loan secured by money that would presumably be available in the recipient's checking account on the next payday.

A borrower might take the money and run, as is a concern with any loan. In this case, one might close the bank account or neglect to supply it with sufficient funds, but the penalty incurred would be significant. The value of maintaining a bank account and good credit history is apparent to most borrowers, fees charged to account holders for bounced checks are usually substantial, and, of course, the loan balance remains on the customer's record. Such a balance might also be sold to a debt collection service, which would ask for further fees on top of the balance. With no collateral, lenders have nothing to show in cases of default, but they have found the arrangement to be stable anyway because the penalty of default provides sufficient incentive for repayment. Thus, penalty replaces collateral.

Payday lending storefronts have proliferated across 35 states, increasing from about 500 locations in 1990 to over 24,000 by 2007 and reducing to about 16,500 at present. They serve about 12 million customers in the US, or 5 per cent of the adult census population. The largest company, Advance America, has 2,100 locations in 28 states. It has been owned by Grupo Salinas since 2012.[1] The storefront market has reduced because of rising activity facilitated through the Internet, to which we turn shortly.

Advance check cashing—now more commonly known as payday lending—commonly provides an advance of up to 50 per cent of the value estimated from a paystub plus interest and fees, all due on the date of the next paycheck. The value of a loan is typically about $350. The loans are most frequently advanced for approximately a two-week period, reflecting total charges of roughly 15 per cent of the principal on average. Business owners originally circumvented usury laws, which are upper limits set by states upon interest rates, by introducing the practice under the name of check cashing, rather than lending. Litigation and legislation followed the introduction of the practice, with the result that such loans are now available in most states, with a fee structure that usually reflects a combined fee plus interest rate charge of about 400 per cent per annum.[2]

Unsecured loans are now generally available across the entire nation because transactions may occur across state lines, particularly by loan application on the Internet. An examination of an offering at mypaydayloan.com is illustrative of current Internet arrangements.[3] Online coupon aggregator websites may provide access to a first "Free Loan" opportunity for some customers of the lender. An online application accompanied by photographs of a pay stub and a postmarked envelope with address visible may lead to approval in "less than 5 minutes during normal business hours." If the application arrives early in the business day, funds arrive in the borrower's checking account on the same day. First-time customers are limited to a $600 loan and the ceiling for repeat borrowers is $1,000. Text drawn from the "frequently asked questions" page details the lending arrangements:

> If you have poor credit, it will not affect the approval of your loan. However, if you have filed for bankruptcy within the past year or if you have filed multiple times, we will not be able to extend an advance to you....

> The fee for advancing a payday loan is $30 per every $100 borrowed....

> Online payday loans are intended to be used for quick cash in the case of a financial emergency....

> Payments are normally due every 10 to 14 days, depending on your next payday and regardless of how often you are paid. Even if you are paid once a month, your payments will still be due every two weeks with a payday loan....

> You are allowed to extend your payday loan as many times as necessary; however, keep in mind that a payday loan is a short-term loan that should be paid back quickly....

> The minimum amount [due] is simply the fees associated with your current principal balance.... You have 3 payment options to choose from:

>> 1) Elect to pay the total amount due (fees will be waived if you are a Free Loan customer)

2) Elect to pay the minimum amount and extend the loan with a *new contract

3) Elect to pay more than the minimum amount and extend the loan with a *new contract (payment will initially be applied to the fees and the remainder of the payment will be applied to the principal)

A *new contract means you are entering into a new loan period, which obligates you to pay the finance charge associated with your new principal balance at the end of the next pay period....

If you fail to submit a payment request by the deadline, as a courtesy, we may debit the minimum due only. However, please be aware that this is a courtesy we extend at our discretion. Per the Check Advance Agreement, you are required to submit a payment request prior to each due date to ensure that the payment amount you desire will be debited from your account....

If your payment is returned due to NSF [non-sufficient funds] (or Account Frozen or Account Closed), our collections department will contact you to arrange a second attempt to debit the payment. A return item fee of $25 and a late fee of $50 will also be collected with the next debit.

If you have an issue with a fraudulent lender and require further assistance, please call the OLA Consumer Hotline at ... and they will assist you [in] reporting fraud.

Mypaydayloan.com charges a "fee," rather than interest. Were a two-week loan of this sort to extend over a full year without repayment of principal, fees would total 7.8 times the unpaid principal (780 per cent). In the event that a borrower does not select a payment option by the due date, either the lending fee or a greater sum is automatically debited from the borrower's checking account: in those circumstances, conditions apply that are similar to option 2 or option 3 above. The "OLA Consumer Hotline" mentioned in the final paragraph above rings to the Online Lenders Alliance, which is one of several trade associations that publish best practices and advocate on behalf of member-lending businesses in government.

ANALYSIS

PAYDAY LOANS ARE MARKETED IN THE UNITED STATES AS SHORT-term solutions for debt; that is, they are portrayed as useful tools for individuals facing emergency financial shortfalls.[4] A challenge to that claim, which subsequently drew national attention to payday lending, was introduced a decade ago by the US consumer advocacy group Center for Responsible Lending, which is funded by and affiliated with credit unions that offer alternative models for short-term lending.[5] Center authors argued that payday lending is predatory: both dishonest in its marketing as a solution to debt, and usurious in its fee structure. They held that a study of public records showed that over three-quarters of payday lending was what they called "phantom demand" generated by the requirement of debt service on such loans. The authors argued that, because payday loans require immediate debt cancellation at the date of the next paycheck rather than payment of relatively small installments, such loans do not present the solutions that they advertise. Instead, among the 4/5 of loan recipients who contracted more than one payday loan per year, half took out a new loan at the next opportunity that the law allows, either immediately or within two days, depending upon state legislation. Nearly 9/10 of this group (87 per cent) would initiate a new loan before the next paycheck, and 9/10 of payday lending business went to recipients who contract for at least five payday loans within one year. About a quarter of all borrowers took 21 or more bi-weekly loans per year. A 2012 study by the Pew Charitable Trusts suggests less extreme, but significant levels of debt for a larger group of borrowers: "on average, a borrower takes out eight loans of $375 each per year and spends $520 on interest."[6]

In 2014, Pew also reported on the emerging area of Internet lending, pointing to practices that appear to represent the model found at mypaydayloan.com: "Many online loans are designed to promote renewals and long-term indebtedness. One in 3 online borrowers has taken out a loan that was set up to withdraw only the fee on the customer's next payday, automatically renewing the loan without reducing principal." African American, separated or divorced, and less educated people are disproportionate among borrowers. The most typical borrower is white, female, single, and between 25 and 44 years old. Consequently a high proportion of single heads of households with young children are utilizing these services.[7]

The authors of *Phantom Demand* maintained that, because payday loans are regularly treated as longer-term installment loans by their users, the arguments that were used to relax state regulations in the 1990s should not apply and should be repealed. The authors recommended adherence to US Federal Deposit Insurance Corporation (FDIC) recommendations that include interest rate caps of 36 per cent per annum and minimum lending terms of 90 days. They also suggested that options be made more widely available for installment loans, which require multiple payments over time to reduce and finally cancel lending debt.

Small loans might also be offered by credit unions and private banks. Many national governments, following a trail blazed by India in the 1990s, ensure some forms of lending and savings account access to the poor. India provides funds guarantees, sets regulations and requires private banks to participate in savings and lending for agriculture loans and women's self-help group arrangements. In the US, such schemes would not be favored among some banks—as they are also not among some Indian banks—since the arrangements would very expensive to administer, even with government guarantees.

The National Credit Union Administration (NCUA), an independent US federal agency, has introduced regulations detailing "payday alternative loans" (PAL). Since 2010, PAL has allowed credit unions to lend $200–$1,000 for terms of one to six months. A minimum of at least two substantially equal payments encompass payment of principal as well as charges. Where borrowers cannot close these loans, terms may be extended to six months maximum. Charges are limited to an application fee of up to $20 and an interest rate of up to 28 per cent APR (annual percentage rate). On a $300 loan for a period of two weeks, this would amount to application fee plus $3.23 interest.[8] Credit unions are federally insured institutions, unlike private payday lenders, and their business model, which includes many services at varied scales, does not strictly demand that this particular lending arrangement be profitable.

Another innovative option relies heavily on an empirical finding cited in *Phantom Demand*: "Consumer Federation of America researchers found that households with no savings earning $25,000 or less annually were eight times more likely to use a payday loan than similarly situated households with just $500 in emergency savings." This suggests that incentivizing savings of small amounts might greatly reduce the problem of debt traps. A government scheme that matches savings dollar-for-dollar up to $250 contributed by the individual might greatly reduce the need for payday lending and would perhaps lead people into the habit of saving still more. Another novel possibility is prize-linked incentives for savings account deposits. People generally like lotteries: they see an incentive even in the slim chance that they will win a lottery payment.[9]

Lending law in the US generally proceeds state-by-state, though the Federal Deposit Insurance Corporation (FDIC) presents recommendations for appropriate practices. There are exceptions from the state rules, particularly for US military personnel, for whom there is a national cap of 36 per cent per annum on lending, but state laws apply to most people. Fifteen states have enacted limits at or below 36 per cent, and Arkansas sets interest plus fees at 5 per cent above the Federal Discount Rate. But Internet sales, offshore incorporation, and affiliation of lenders with Native American governance systems erode states' effective control. In states that effectively outlaw payday lending, borrowing rates are about half of what they are in the least restrictive states.[10]

Other states have less restrictive rules, and a dilemma arises for each state, since lenders will set up shop in the most permissive states. States would better serve their people by enacting restrictions; nevertheless, each state would be better served in other respects if they keep lenient arrangements, for tax revenue and business employment accrue to the home states with lower taxation rates and lower regulation. Six states have no cap on fees for payday loans or have no explicit law on fees (Delaware, Idaho, Nevada, Texas, Utah, Wisconsin). Two states have no explicit law concerning maximum loan amount (Utah, Wyoming). Other states indicate either dollar maximums of $1,000 (or less), or a proportion of 35 per cent (or less) of the borrower's salary, if they permit lending at all. The owner of mypaydayloan.com is "Zarvad III S.A.," a Costa Rica corporation registered in Utah in 2009.[11]

The US Bureau of Consumer Financial Protection (CFPB) issued more stringent rules for payday lenders late in 2017, set to take effect in August 2019. The new restrictions explicitly allow NCUA's PAL lending terms, and allow non-credit union lenders to lend under such terms. The new standards for payday lending require lenders to collect detailed information concerning borrowers' credit history and ability to repay before extending loans above $500. These requirements would put a significant burden on payday lenders and would reduce their pool of eligible borrowers. For lower-value loans structured as payday lending, these strictures do not apply, but the new rules restrict sequential loans to three 15-day contract periods, requiring a lending structure that decreases the loan's principal to close out the loan over the three con-tract periods. They also impose a mandatory 30-day "cooling off period" before any lender may offer another such loan. The CFPB anticipated that its rules would increase lenders' expenses and that "payday loan vol-umes will decrease by 62 per cent to 68 per cent, with a corresponding decrease in revenue."

In January 2018 a change in leadership occurred at the CFPB. Sixty days after the CFPB had made these new arrangements official federal policy, on the same day upon which business entities were required to register for compliance with the impending 2019 regulations, the CFPB released a brief statement that included the following: "The Bureau intends to engage in a rulemaking process so that the Bureau may recon-sider the Payday Rule.... Recognizing that this preliminary application deadline might cause some entities to engage in work in preparing an application to become a RIS [Registered Information System], the Bureau will entertain waiver requests from any potential applicant."[12] The Competitive Enterprise Institute released a study on the following day that included this claim: "While the CFPB is statutorily limited from reg-ulating the interest rates of small-dollar loans, it has sought to under-mine the industry through onerous regulations that make these loans unprofitable for lenders."

"Exploitation" refers to a variety of activities that may be deemed appropriate or inappropriate. Exploitation that does not involve the engagement of more than one individual—exploitation of a resource for personal gain, such as the use of the sunshine, or the exploitation of another's writing freely provided on the Internet—are generally accounted as appropriate, and such cases will not be of concern here. Exploitation of another's time or efforts may be judged both ethically appropriate and mutually beneficial: the housepainter may contract with the homeowner; similarly, the caller to a toll-free technical help line might reasonably assume that the worker at the other end has chosen such work and is appropriately compensated. Exploitation of an oppo-nent's weakness in a sport is often judged appropriate, though other val-ues associated with being a *good* sport may reverse the appraisal in a particular case. Exploitation may be ethical, but still be disvalued for other reasons: there may be nothing at all unethical in exploiting the politeness or timidity of others in a group by taking the last cookie, even if doing so shows a disregard for the host's own true intention when the last available one is offered. Even if a violation of politeness results in an unequal final distribution of cookies among guests, the result may be ethical and we need not find that the outcome should have been different: some may just value the cookies more than others, some may have food allergies, and others may prefer to be polite. Social norms like politeness may coincide with ethical norms, but the two may be appropriately distinguished, as the cookie example suggests, and as is shown by common (socially accepted, or normative) practices that ethicists argue should be negatively valued, and that they may intend to address and alter.

Payday lending is exploitation of some kind, then. Should payday lending be disvalued? Should it be disvalued because it is somehow an unethical kind of institutional or structural practice? If so, on what grounds? Is it unethical because it is taking unfair advantage, or generates disproportionate gain for one party? Or does it arise only in cases of harm? Each of these may be a case that some call an "unconscionable contract": debt bondage, dead peasant insurance (i.e., insurance on employees' lives owned by the company), and markets in human organs may display one or several of these aspects. Is payday lending odious for another reason, perhaps because it is taking unfair advantage *and* is coercive, regardless of whether or not it is harmful to either party? An example of this is offering lower pay rates to workers who are evidently more needy and lack other options because of their social status. Philosophers frequently use these terms but they analyze unethical exploitation in very different ways, and those who appear to agree on the terms also may judge the same case differently.

Business ethicists dispute whether the terms of payday lending are justified for both free market and regulated cases. Robert Mayer argues that some payday lending is unethical: it is exploitative in a way that is inequitable (unfair) and coercive. Yet Mayer's analysis may surprise: the defaulting debtor is cast alongside the lender as exploitative of other borrowers in "a sort of conspiracy between the top and the bottom against the middle." So, Mayer finds an interest rate cap justifiable because payday lending addresses an immediate need, and borrowers with such a need have limited opportunity to shop around for better rates: "Unless prices are capped, the more solvent majority of borrowers is compelled to cross-subsidize the least solvent debtors, who have a high rate of default."

Responding to Mayer, Matt Zwolinski argues that payday lending's model displays the marks of a functioning market with usual rates of return on capital. He finds that "payday lending is ... sufficiently constrained by competitive pressures to ensure that no party is in a position to take unfair advantage of the other." Zwolinski also provides a general justification of usury that suggests it may be ethical, even if it is often harmful:

> Even if usury is a form of exploitation, it is usually a form of *mutually beneficial* exploitation. Both parties benefit from the exchange, even if one party benefits less than fairness requires. Suppressing mutually beneficial exploitation prevents unfairness, to be sure, but it also often makes both parties worse off than they otherwise would have been, and this often has a disproportionately harmful effect on the most vulnerable party.

Zwolinski finds no compelling reason for altering open payday lending conditions. Mayer replies that the social role of government demands that limits be placed on the lender for the sake of both the defaulting borrowers, who might then be excluded, and repaying borrowers: "when government caps the price of credit, lenders are prevented from boosting the fee they could charge to the solvent debtors to cover these losses. Their only real option is to lend more cautiously."

So, Zwolinski implies that lenders should price the poorest out of a free market. Mayer instead relies on the judgment of lenders insofar as their rate options have been restricted by regulators, and he suggests a 15 per cent bi-weekly rate is appropriate, as it has been shown to be a viable ceiling rate in the markets of some states. Both authors consider payday lending to be appropriate in one or another form as it is currently pursued in the US.[13]

The arguments of these two authors concern the justice of institutional practices, but their analyses include no discussion of the details of the structure of the payday-lending contract, the frequency of renewals, the unrealized alternative arrangements that have been proposed, and the history of national policy and corporate influence that are detailed above. Those details suggests that, for some theorists who choose to articulate ethics through principles, something other than or more than an analysis of fairness, consent, and government's role may be required for ethical appraisal of payday lending. The details of the case may suggest to other ethicists—virtue and relational (care) ethicists, who focus either upon the case itself or upon the relations of power and vulnerability on display between agents—that unethical exploitation of both non-defaulting and defaulting borrowers generally applies in all current payday lending arrangements.[14]

NOTES

1 Statistics concerning the general characteristics of the industry have been drawn from Consumer Finance Protection Bureau (2017); if not found in that publication, they are drawn from other cited sources dated 2007 to the present.

2 For details of this history, see Katherine Samolyk, "Payday Lending: Evolution, Issues and Evidence," in *Household Credit Usage: Personal Debt and Mortgage*, ed. Sumit Agarwal and Brent W. Ambrose (New York: Palgrave, 2007), 175–201.

3 At MyPaydayLoan.com, https://www.mypaydayloan.com/cash-advance, https://www.mypaydayloan.com/faq. The first of these links was the first link to be displayed on a Google search for "payday loan" using an anonymized browser, accessed January 27, 2018.

4 See, for example, claims at mypaydayloan.com, and see the website of the leading industry advocacy group, Consumer Financial Services Association of America, http://cfsaa.com.

5 The Center for Responsible Lending indicates at its website that Board member Martin Eakes "is CEO and founder of Self-Help, a community development lender that was instrumental in establishing the Center for Responsible Lending."

6 Leslie Parrish and Uriah King, "Phantom Demand: Short-term Due Date Generates Need for Repeat Payday Loans, Accounting for 76 Per Cent of Total Volume," Center for Responsible Lending (2009), 3–6, and see Uriah King and Leslie Parrish, "Springing the Debt Trap," Center for Responsible Lending (2007), 3. Pew Charitable Trusts, "Who Borrows, Where They Borrow, and Why: Executive Summary and Key Findings" (2012).

7 Pew Charitable Trusts, "Fraud and Abuse Online: Harmful Practices in Internet Payday Lending," (October 2014), 1, Appendix A.

8 National Credit Union Administration, "Regulatory Alert: Final Rule— Part 701, Short-term, Small Amount Loans" (October 2010).

9 Shai Akabas and Brian Collins, "Prize-Linked Savings Accounts Are Lotteries with No Losers," Bipartisan Policy Center (May 14, 2014).

10 Pew Charitable Trusts, "Fraud and Abuse Online," 22–23.

11 See proceedings against the corporation by the State of New Hampshire Banking Department in 2013 ("Notice of order to cease and desist" business within the state without a license [Case 10–460]). New Hampshire permits payday lending at an interest rate of 36 per cent per

annum, with no other charges allowed; no such businesses are currently registered in New Hampshire. Zarvad III S.A.'s 2009 registration in Utah lapsed after 10 months.

12 Consumer Finance Protection Bureau, "CFPB Statement on Payday Rule" (2018).

13 See works by Mayer and Zwolinski in Further Readings section.

14 Wertheimer's writing (see Further Readings) is the current standard initial reference for contemporary philosophical analysis of exploitation. Discussion (pp. 8–10) briefly notes the general concerns of case-based and relational approaches. The general terms for a theory of exploitation that might be adapted to a business ethics focus follow, pp. 10ff.

DISCUSSION QUESTIONS

(1) Why do governments enact usury laws? Should these transactions be considered to be loans, or advance check cashing? How are the two distinguished, and what is the importance of the distinction?

(2) If the suggested 36 per cent annual rate caps were to apply to payday lending, then the option may well disappear, since transaction costs and default rates are high for these loans. Does the ethical case for payday loans, in your opinion, outweigh the case against them?

(3) Credit unions in the US now offer payday alternative loans (PAL), as detailed above. Credit unions are not-for-profit, tax-exempt member-owned financial cooperatives: in general terms, credit union account holders own the shop and they don't pay taxes on its activity, which is actually arranged to serve the same account holders, and so is arranged to maximize value for them, and not arranged to maximize profit. Credit unions are federally insured institutions, and their business model, which includes many services at varied scales, does not strictly demand that the PAL arrangement be profitable, since other activity in the business might serve to make up for a loss on PAL loans. None of these claims apply to payday lenders.

Credit unions that offer PAL arrangements target very much the same market as the private businesses that offer payday loans. Is this a just arrangement? What arguments do you see supporting such a claim, what arguments undermine it, and how would you finally accept, qualify, or reject the claim that credit unions should be allowed to offer the PAL alternative?

(4) Mayer and Zwolinski analyze the institution of payday lending in terms of voluntary contractual relations, fairness, coercion, harm, and government's role in promoting good for its people. Each author holds that one or another arrangement that is currently available in payday lending in the US is appropriate. Is one correct in his general analysis? If so, why? If neither is correct, why not?

(5) Are the conditions of payday lending a wrong that should be addressed? Have you an account or analysis of why or why not? How might that wrong be effectively addressed in your society? Or, if the institution is not structurally unjust, but it might be improved anyway, should it be improved? How should it be improved?

FURTHER READINGS

Abhijit Banerjee and Esther Duflo, *Poor Economics* (Public Affairs Press, 2011), especially chapters 6 and 7.

Consumer Finance Protection Bureau, "Executive Summary of the Payday, Vehicle Title, and Certain High-Cost Installment Loans Rule" (October 5, 2017).

Neal Gabler, "The Secret Shame of Middle-Class Americans," *The Atlantic* (May 2016).

David M. Jackson, "Bentham and Payday Lenders," in *Economic Justice: Philosophical and Legal Perspectives*, ed. H.M. Stacy and W.-C. Lee (New York: Springer, 2012), 29–36.

Paul Kiel, "To Dodge Law, High-Cost Lender Offers Cash for Free," *ProPublica* (2013).

Robert Mayer, "When and Why Usury Should Be Prohibited," *Journal of Business Ethics* 116.3 (2013): 513–27.

Robert Mayer, "The Cost of Usury," *Business Ethics Journal Review* 1.7 (2013): 44–49. (A reply to Zwolinski 2013.)

Pew Charitable Trusts, "Fraud and Abuse Online: Harmful Practices in Internet Payday Lending."

Daniel Press, "How the Consumer Financial Protection Bureau's Payday Loan Rule Hurts the Working Poor," Competitive Enterprise Institute (2018).

Alan Wertheimer, *Exploitation* (Princeton, NJ: Princeton University Press, 1999).

Matt Zwolinski, "Are Usurious? Another New Argument for the Prohibition of High Interest Loans?" *Business Ethics Journal Review* 1.4 (2013): 22–27. (A comment on Mayer, 2013.)

7.

CHILDREN AND GAMBLING: THE ETHICAL PROBLEM OF LOOT BOXES

ALEXANDER L. HOFFMANN

BACKGROUND

LOOT BOXES ARE VIRTUAL ITEMS SOLD IN ONLINE STORES ON VARious video game platforms. They are valuable to players because, when opened, a set amount of additional virtual items used in-game are randomly doled out. In April of 2018, The Belgian Gaming Commission deemed loot boxes illegal because they violated gambling legislation.[1] Many liken loot boxes to traditional forms of gambling for two reasons: 1) they are purchased via micro-transactions which demand real money and 2) the variation of prizes, ranging from common to rare, depends on chance.[2]

Electronic Arts, one of the top video game publishers, was one of the main targets in the Belgian investigation due to popular titles like *FIFA Ultimate Team* and *Star Wars Battlefront 2* gaining a notorious reputation for their use of micro-transactions (further purchases within a game, which include virtual items such as loot boxes). The most egregious uses of micro-transactions allowed players to purchase in-game items that improved their gameplay, such as better weapons, players, and gear. Other examples of in-game items available inside loot boxes are cosmetics (different outfits, customizable weapon skins, etc.), experience boosters that make leveling-up faster, and emotes that allow characters to make unique expressions in the forms of dances or player messages. Due to mounting pressure and ridicule from the gaming community, *Star Wars Battlefront* 2 eventually halted its use of micro-transactions completely.[3] Many hailed the concession of EA as a victory for consumers, but others argued that the controversy over loot boxes and micro-transactions had not been resolved. Indeed, EA intends to move forward with loot boxes in the future, with the chief executive, Andrew Wilson, publicly stating that "we don't believe that FIFA Ultimate Team or loot boxes are gambling."[4]

The vice president for the Entertainment Media Software Association, Dan Hewitt, insists there is *not* a strong comparison between gambling and loot crates.[5] When the gamer purchases a loot crate, they are guaranteed something they can use in the game, which Hewitt argues is distinct from traditional gambling. Additionally, other commonly accepted forms of children's entertainment, such as trading cards and arcade machines, operate on a similar model. For example, Pokémon cards are sold in individual booster packs and conform to a predetermined algorithm, which then decides the likelihood of winning a card of high value.

Nonetheless, loot boxes mimic tactics used by gambling industries to keep people coming back. Keith Whyte, the executive director at the National Center for Problematic Gambling, insists that winning rare items in loot boxes and winning money on a lottery ticket are basically the same; what unites the two experiences is "the action and excitement of winning a prize."[6]

Most video game publishers, despite the controversy, are finding it difficult to ignore the benefits of loot crates in their games. Activision Blizzard, creator of the video game *Overwatch*, reported that over $4 billion (more than half their total earnings for the entire fiscal year) came from in-game purchases such as loot crates.[7] With such a strong financial incentive to add loot crates to games, and indecision surrounding the categorization of loot crates as gambling, many publishers are adopting the loot crate model with little hesitation.

Not all consumer feedback has been negative towards micro-transactions. There is a large portion of the video gaming community itself that has embraced the benefits loot boxes give to the players. Creators of content in video games are constantly looking for ways to draw in a crowd and keep people playing their game. Loot boxes have proven themselves to be a successful way to add new content to games over time and keep the fan base interested. Furthermore, after the initial sales of a game dies off, there is no longer a continuous stream of revenue given to the creators to allow additional content to be added. In a way, loot boxes benefit all players, even those who refuse to purchase them, by giving the developers incentives to add more content to old games.

ANALYSIS

A VIDEO GAME PUBLISHER, LIKE ANY OTHER BUSINESS, NEEDS TO make a profit in order to remain sustainable. Loot boxes have proven an incredibly lucrative tool that, when utilized, increases the earnings of a video game substantially. Consumers want the products they buy to retain value over time. Loot boxes give these game publishers the resources necessary to give their products a lasting value that directly benefits the gamers. If both the business and many consumers benefit from loot boxes, then the choice to eliminate them is a weighty decision. This may no longer be a concern in Belgium, where the government has stepped in and established a law banning loot boxes, but the US and other countries have no such restriction. So why not capitalize on loot boxes where they are still legal?

The emphasis on psychological harm has become one of the central ethical issues surrounding loot boxes. State representative Chris Lee from Hawaii argues that loot boxes "are specifically designed to exploit and manipulate the addictive nature of human psychology."[8] If loot boxes do exploit the addictive tendencies of players, then marketing to children becomes an important concern. Many games that offer loot boxes, like Rocket League and FIFA 18, are rated E, which means the game is available for purchase by anyone at any age. It is still unclear whether children are at a point developmentally where the risk/reward model of loot boxes will have lasting harmful effects. For this reason, it could be the case that the addition of loot boxes is sufficient for an M rating, which would force retailers to check the ID of buyers to avoid selling to anyone under 17 years of age in the United States.[9]

On one influential account of business ethics put forward by Milton Friedman,[10] it is not the business's problem to consider social issues, but only to make profit within the appropriate boundaries of the law.

Of course, there are many products offered on the market that can be abused, or are harmful outside of moderation. However, it is often the case that the responsibility to control the abuse of products falls to the consumer. Whether children are mature enough to control how much money they spend on virtual items, like loot boxes, is arguably something parents should decide. Therefore, it could be the case that parents ought to be the ones responsible when loot boxes are abused by their children.

Rohan Miller has argued against this view, claiming that "policies of morality," meaning implicit moral rules, should hold businesses accountable when their actions are legally permissible but morally irresponsible.[11] Thus, even when businesses are acting legally, they ought to be reprimanded for the purely moral wrongs their goods and services cause.

The defense that moderation is the responsibility of the consumer can also be called into question. In some cases, products can be so harmful that the company is held morally responsible for them. An obvious example would be the aggressive marketing tactics employed by cigarette companies in the twentieth century.[12] However, it is not entirely clear whether loot boxes fall under any such policy of morality, especially when opinions on games of chance for children are so divided.

As stated previously, many children's toys have dimensions of chance that are viewed as relatively innocuous. A good example is Chuck E. Cheese, a chain restaurant/play area for children which operates as a kind of casino. Similar to gambling chips, tokens are distributed to children (purchased for real cash) that are used to play games. These games are won either by skill or chance and dispense tickets that are traded for prizes.[13] Despite having a similar design to loot crates and traditional casinos, both the law and the general attitude of the public has accepted this sort of entertainment for several decades now. Either there is a strikingly different quality about loot crates that sets them apart, or these other forms of media, such as trading cards and Chuck E. Cheese, fall under the same category.

Perhaps what is bothersome is the idea that children's media employs similar psychology-exploiting strategies used on adults. Would there still be an uproar if there were no money involved in loot crates, but children had to play for a certain amount of time before opening another one? Now children would have to pay with time in order to try their luck at the next prize. It could be that there is still something unsettling without incorporating micro-transactions into the system. However, if our problem sits solely on psychological manipulation, then a whole swathe of other kinds of media that children consume would also be called into question. Ought we also to rid ourselves of advertisements, product placement in kids' shows, strategic placing of toys in stores, etc.? How could video game designers predict what line they might cross when their goal is to make a product enticing for their desired audience?

NOTES

1 Tom Gerken, "Video Game Loot Boxes Declared Illegal Under Belgium Gambling Laws," *BBC* (April 26, 2018).

2 Ibid.

3 Erik Kain, "EA Removing 'Star Wars Battlefront II' Micro-Transactions Is a Victory, but the War Isn't Over Yet," *Forbes* (November 17, 2017).

4 Andy Chalk, "Electronic Arts Will 'Push Forward' with Loot boxes in Future Games," *PC Gamer* (May 10, 2018).

5 Jason Bailey, "A Video Game 'Loot Box' Offers Coveted Rewards, but Is It Gambling?" *New York Times* (April 24, 2018).

6 Qtd. in Ellen McGrody, "For Many Players, Lootboxes Are a Crisis that's Already Here," *Waypoint* (January 30, 2018).

7 Rob Thubron, "Over Half of Activision Blizzard's $7.16 Billion Yearly Revenue Came from Microtransactions," *Techspot* (February 12, 2018).

8 Bailey (2018).

9 Ibid.

10 Milton Friedman, "The Social Responsibility of Business Is to Increase Its Profits," *New York Times Magazine* (September 13, 1970).

11 Rohan Miller, "Fixing the Game? Legitimacy, Morality Policy and Research in Gambling," *Journal of Business Ethics* 116.3 (2013): 601–14.

12 Richard Pollay, "The Last Straw? Cigarette Advertising and Realized Market Shares among Youths and Adults, 1979–1993," *Journal of Marketing* 60.2 (1996): 1–16.

13 Brad Tuttle, "Chuck E. Cheese: Where a Kid Can Gamble like an Adult," *Time* (May 14, 2013).

DISCUSSION QUESTIONS

(1) Is it the responsibility of the business to judge what is morally right? Or should consumers and public policy shape business practices?

(2) Do corporations have a social responsibility to its consumers and global community? If yes, then how much should social responsibility outweigh the other concerns of the business?

(3) Does it matter whether or not loot crates are categorized as gambling? Or are the psychological effects sufficient to find them morally reprehensible, thus unsuitable to dispense without regulation?

(4) Should businesses worry about what products could be harmful to children outside of moderation? Or is it the duty of the parent to ensure that their children are not exposed to harmful products? If yes to the latter, then are any psychological harms that loot boxes have on children relevant to this discussion?

FURTHER READINGS

Paul Camenisch, "Profit: Some Moral Reflections," *Journal of Business Ethics* 6.3 (1987): 225–31.

Rina Gupta, "The Relationship between Gambling and Video-Game Playing Behavior in Children and Adolescents," *Journal of Gambling Studies* 12.4 (1996): 375–94.

Rohan Miller, "Fixing the Game? Legitimacy, Morality Policy and Research in Gambling," *Journal of Business Ethics* 116.3 (2013): 601–14.

Mirella Yani-de-Soriano, "Can an Industry Be Socially Responsible If Its Products Harm Consumers? The Case of Online Gambling," *Journal of Business Ethics* 110.4 (2012): 481–97.

8.

THE DEEPWATER HORIZON
OIL SPILL

CYRLENE CLAASEN AND TOM MCNAMARA

BACKGROUND

THE PETROLEUM INDUSTRY, ONE OF THE MOST PROFITABLE ON
the planet, is also one that is fraught with risk and danger. This became
apparent on April 20, 2010, when the Deepwater Horizon, an oil rig
operated by a company called Transocean under contract for British
Petroleum (BP), exploded, caught fire, and sank in the Gulf of Mexico.
Eleven workers lost their lives and millions of barrels of oil spilled into
the Gulf of Mexico over the course of 87 days, devastating marine life
and damaging hundreds of miles of sensitive nearby coastline. It would
turn out to be the biggest oil spill in US history.

BP realized immediately that they were the ones who would be ultimately held responsible in any legal judgments. The company set aside
about $42 billion to cover the cost of cleanup, fines and compensation to
victims, with $36 billion of this money already being paid out or assigned
by February of 2013. In the immediate aftermath of the explosion, the US
government forbad BP from bidding on any federal contracts and sought

$21 billion in compensation for the environmental damage (according to the Clean Water Act, for each barrel of oil spilled a polluter can be fined the basic penalty of $1,100, or up to $4,300, depending on the degree of negligence).

Deep-sea drilling for oil, a highly technical and demanding task, has been going on for decades. The companies that engage in this type of activity have millions of hours of experience. So what exactly went wrong one mile below the surface of the ocean? The cause of the accident appears to have been an accumulation of errors and mistakes.

One of the major dangers associated with deep-sea drilling is "kicks," powerful disruptions experienced when a drill comes into contact with a pocket of natural gas. Ominously, Deepwater Horizon was experiencing an unusually large number of these kicks, but BP played down their risk. In order to diminish the threat from explosion, cement is applied to the outside of the bore piping used in the drilling. This is supposed to create a type of seal which prevents flammable gas from working its way back up the drill pipes. A second line of defense is something known as a blowout preventer, basically a giant pair of scissors that sits at the bottom of the ocean and is designed to cut the drilling pipe in the event of an explosion. In the case of Deepwater Horizon, both of these devices apparently failed. It is believed that the explosion was a result of the initial failure of the contracted company Halliburton to properly mix the cement supplied for the seal on the Gulf's floor. This was then compounded by a lack of care and diligence on the part of the rig operators, resulting in the explosion and catastrophic environmental disaster.

BP's actions afterwards also deserve scrutiny. The company claimed that about 1,000 barrels of oil per day were flowing into the Gulf of Mexico. Later, a government scientist estimated the flow at nearly 5,000 barrels, but said he could not vouch for the accuracy of that figure. Complicating matters further, BP's response included using a highly toxic chemical, Corexit, in the cleanup of the Gulf. Corexit contains five chemicals associated with cancer, 10 chemicals that may be harmful to the kidneys, as well as other potentially dangerous chemicals; it is said to be 50 times more toxic than oil itself. Sweden and the United Kingdom (where BP is based) have banned Corexit. 771,000 gallons (2,900,000 L) of this chemical dispersant were injected into the flow of oil near the seafloor to break up oil droplets and cause them to disperse or sink to the seafloor. So, rather than waiting for the oil to rise to the surface and removing it with specialized equipment, BP flooded the Gulf with chemicals which, scientists say, poison coral reefs and other marine life. Not surprisingly, cleanup crews began complaining about health problems during their shifts, ranging from nausea and vomiting to dizziness and chest pains. The Government Accountability Project collected stories from BP cleanup crews, and blood tests confirmed that the majority of these whistleblowers had highly elevated levels of toxins in their blood. It is believed that there is a link between these illnesses, Corexit, and petroleum exposure.

In response to these troubles, workers filed a class-action lawsuit against BP for damages associated with Corexit. Over 12,000 claims were included and to date over 700 people have been compensated. In May 2010, the US Environmental Protection Agency (EPA) directed BP to switch to less-toxic dispersants, but the company said that it could find no suitable alternatives. The EPA has proposed rules that would strengthen standards for dispersants used in oil spill cleanups. This would allow the agency to "delist" certain dispersants that are highly toxic and require companies to find alternatives. The EPA has already received hundreds of comments on the rules, including industry opposition to any restrictions.

Five years after the disaster, wildlife is still struggling to rebound. A new report, released by the NWF, suggests that at least 20 species are still being affected by the spill. "This report, more so than any, shows that science is certain that this is a long-term problem," said Ryan Fikes, a scientist with NWF. "But it's going to take even more time to understand the true magnitude of this." In another scientific study, as part of an unusual mortality event investigation, a team of scientists has discovered that dead bottlenose dolphins stranded in the northern Gulf of Mexico since the start of the Deepwater Horizon oil spill have lung and adrenal lesions consistent with petroleum product exposure. While some phenomena in the Gulf—people getting sick, fishing nets coming back empty—are hard to pin conclusively on BP, experts say the signs of ecological and economic loss that followed the spill are deeply concerning for the future of the Gulf.

In January of 2013, BP pleaded guilty to manslaughter charges over the deaths of the 11 rig workers. It also agreed to a deal in which it would pay $4 billion in fines and penalties (at the time, a record) to the US Justice Department. None of these actions absolved the company of the civil claims it was facing from the federal government.

In September of 2014 a judge arrived at a ruling on the disaster. It was determined that BP would be assigned 67 per cent of the blame, with the rig's owner Transocean getting 30 per cent and Halliburton getting stuck with 3 per cent. In the 153-page court decision, the presiding judge said that BP had shown negligence and was primarily concerned with making "profit-driven decisions" during the exploration activities that immediately preceded the deadly explosion. The ruling meant that BP was now liable for penalties under the Clean Water Act, which theoretically could add up to over $17 billion. In response, BP said that it would appeal the ruling.

In June of 2015 the US Supreme Court rejected BP's bid to have the 2014 ruling against it thrown out. Part of the company's argument was that it should not be held responsible for oil spilled due to equipment failure on a drilling rig that it did not own. For its part, in 2014, Transocean (the rig's owner) agreed to pay the US government $1 billion in fines and penalties for its role in the spill.

Finally, in July of 2015, BP announced that it had reached a settlement. The company said that it had agreed to pay a record $18.7 billion in damages to the US government and the five states directly affected by the spill (Alabama, Florida, Louisiana, Mississippi, and Texas). The terms of the agreement give the company 18 years to pay out any monies related to civil claims and environmental restoration. BP's chief executive Mr. Bob Dudley said, "This is a realistic outcome which provides clarity and certainty for all parties" and that "this agreement will deliver a significant income stream over many years for further restoration of natural resources and for losses related to the spill."[1]

In the aftermath of the Deepwater Horizon oil spill, BP has tried to address its badly dented corporate image by ramping up its effort to convince consumers that life is returning to normal on the Gulf coast. The company has released public relations materials that highlight the Gulf's resilience, as well as a report compiling scientific studies that suggest the area is making a rapid recovery. However, affected communities are not in agreement with the company and its reassurances have done little to quell people's fear. Activists and residents of the area surrounding the Gulf of Mexico say that oil is still being found on beaches, on private land, and in the water. They complain that in addition to having to deal with economic hardships and environmental damage, BP's insistence that everything is getting better and its numerous doubtful explanations merely act as salt on a not-yet-healed wound. For example, on Pointe à la Hache, about 45 minutes south of New Orleans, oystermen say their catches dropped after the spill and have been decreasing ever since. BP shot back by saying that depleted oyster beds could be due to a variety of factors other than the spill—including the divergence of fresh water from the Mississippi into coastal marshes.

ANALYSIS

THE BP OIL SPILL RAISES MANY QUESTIONS ABOUT ENVIRONMENTAL ethics and companies' responsibilities towards employees, nature, and the communities and other stakeholders dependent on the natural environment for economic survival. Environmental ethics is the study of human interaction with nature. In a business situation, environmental ethics is concerned with a company's responsibility to protect the environment in which it operates.

Businesses have traditionally shown indifference towards the environment and environmental protection was seldom seen as a priority. People saw the natural world as a free and unlimited good which could be exploited without doing any morally significant harm. Pollution could damage the environment, but the damage done was considered to be unimportant because the world was seen as such a large place. In recent decades, business leaders and policy makers have come to realize that resources aren't unlimited and to address the harms to people, animals, and ecosystems.

The petroleum industry repeatedly causes harm to the environment. Oil exploration and production involve risky processes but the industry thrives because it offers significant economic rewards. The industry is prone to what some describe as "incidents," especially in the drilling procedure. On the one hand there are accidents due to unanticipated malfunctions, failures, or side-effects of technological systems. On the other hand, there are those episodes which are a direct result of deliberate unethical and irresponsible behaviors that benefit the company at the expense of the environment, and the safety, health, and even lives of employees.

BP has been found guilty of the latter: deliberate disregard of warnings that imminent danger was looming. According to various sources, immediately after the explosion, BP, the rig operator Transocean, and the Obama administration were of the opinion that the disaster was an unpredictable event. However, interviews with workers, information gathered by researchers and testimony given to Congressional and Coast Guard hearings prove that there was in fact abundant evidence that an explosion could take place.

BP and its partners Transocean and Halliburton ignored the forewarnings without fearing much reprisal, as the Mineral Management Service (MMS) of the Department of the Interior had long ago ceded all immediate and important regulatory control to the industry itself. The US Department of Labor's Occupational Safety and Health Administration (OSHA) and the Department of Environmental Protection (DEP) also regulate specific aspects of the industry but are said to be more reactionary than proactive in enforcing safety and environmental protection laws. The extent of self-regulation became obvious when Captain Nguyen, the co-chairman of the Coast Guard Inquiry, questioned the rig safety measures, specifically regarding the blowout preventers: "So my understanding is that it is designed to industry standard, manufactured to industry standard, installed by industry, with no government oversight of the construction or the installation. Is that correct?" Interior Department regulator Michael Saucier replied, "That would be correct."

Further, instead of taking responsibility for the 11 deaths and the inestimable damage caused to the environment, BP blamed Transocean (now the world's largest offshore drilling contractor). At the same time, numerous industry experts and fellow oil executives accused BP of cutting corners in order to save time and money. One of the concerns was that BP was not sufficiently reactive when its crew experienced continuous and repeated problems related to powerful "kicks" of surging gas, which, according to employees, resulted in the job's falling behind schedule and costing BP millions of dollars in rental fees. During all of this the workers contended with stuck drilling pipes and broken tools. Moreover, the company used a well design that presented few barriers to high-pressure gas rising up, skipped a crucial $128,000 test of the quality of the cementing, and failed to install capping devices at the top of the well that could also have prevented gas from lifting a critical seal. Chairman of the House Energy and Commerce Committee, Henry A. Waxman, said that "BP has cut corner after corner to save $1 million here, a few hours or days there, and now the whole Gulf Coast is paying the price."

BP's negligence in failing to implement industry-wide safety standards against the loss of human life and extraordinary environmental damage is well-established. This case is also relevant to more controversial questions in business and environmental ethics. One question considers how societies should regulate potentially risky activities: in what circumstances should regulation be left to the industry and in what circumstances is government oversight required? As we saw above, industry determined and implemented rig safety measures with no government oversight. When pondering this question, we should keep in mind that government regulation can be costly and inefficient, especially in areas where considerable technological competence is required, and that industry may be more likely to endorse voluntary standards.

Second, there are questions of corporate social responsibility and sustainability: what are the responsibilities of companies to the community and to the environment when there are risks of substantial damage? On the shareholder account of corporate social responsibility, a company has an obligation to follow the law and widely accepted industry standards, but no further obligations to take actions that might harm the bottom line. On stakeholder and sustainability accounts, BP's obligations to the community and environment might go considerably further. For example, the use of Corexit was approved by the United States Environmental Protection agency at the time BP chose to use it. Did BP have an obligation nonetheless to look for less toxic alternatives to the cleanup? Does BP have moral obligations beyond its legal settlements to remediate the environmental damage?

Critics of BP and other drilling and mining companies say that businesses need to invest more in safety, training, and environmental remediation, rather than just trying to greenwash their operations by finding excuses for the harm caused. It is also argued that efforts should be made to make extraction operations less intrusive and more sustainable. Pressure to do so is mounting as human needs expand, the costs engendered by deteriorating ecosystems rise, and the environmental awareness of consumers increases. Companies, including BP, already address environmental challenges by adopting techniques such as environmental auditing and corporate environmental reporting. BP says that since the 1970s, no major BP oil or gas project has moved forward until independent experts have assessed the environmental impact. According to the company, these reviews are thorough and examine potential problems and the best ways to address them.

NOTE

1   Qtd. in Julia Bradshaw, "BP Settles 2010 Gulf Oil Spill Claims with US
     States for Record $18.7bn," *The Telegraph* (July 2, 2015).

DISCUSSION QUESTIONS

(1) BP was found responsible for the Deepwater Horizon oil spill. However,
    in the immediate aftermath of the disaster, the company blamed
    Transocean (the rig's owner) for the catastrophe. What were BP's
    arguments for this? What are some of the consequences of this denial of
    responsibility?

(2) The petroleum industry is strongly involved in self-regulation. What are
    the reasons for this? Might this arrangement suit certain parties? Which
    are these? What are the consequences?

(3) Do you think that it is BP's responsibility to reinvest in the environment
    since it already pays heavy taxes? Is this not the responsibility of the
    government?

(4) Who pays for the loss of income of communities in areas affected by
    human-made disasters such as the Deepwater Horizon oil spill? Can this
    loss be measured? What are the implications for future generations?

(5) Who are the actors involved in the Deepwater Horizon oil spill? Who
    has the power to assert their positions and stakes? Who has less or more
    power? Why?

FURTHER READINGS

"Deep Water: The Gulf Oil Disaster and the Future of Offshore Drilling. Report
     to the President" (2011).
Deepwater Horizon Study Group, "Final Report on the Investigation of the
     Macondo Well Blowout," Center for Catastrophic Risk Management,
     University of California at Berkeley (2011).
Elizabeth B. Kujawinski, Melissa C. Kido Soule, David L. Valentine, Angela K.
     Boysen, Krista Longnecker, and Molly C. Redmond, "Fate of Dispersants
     Associated with the Deepwater Horizon Oil Spill," *Environmental Science
     & Technology* 45.4 (2011): 1298–1306.
Lawrence C. Smith, Murphy Smith, and Paul Ashcroft, "Analysis of
     Environmental and Economic Damages from British Petroleum's
     Deepwater Horizon Oil Spill," *Albany Law Review* 74.1 (2011): 563–85.

9.

DAKOTA ACCESS PIPELINE: PROFITS V. PROTESTS

CYRLENE CLAASEN, TOM MCNAMARA,
AND IRENA DESCUBES

BACKGROUND

ON NOVEMBER 20, 2016, NATIVE AMERICAN PROTESTERS WHO call themselves "water protectors" were water-cannoned by police officers in sub-zero weather because they were showing their discontent about an ominous threat to their water sources, cultural sites, agricultural land, and property rights. Tressa Welch, an activist from the Fort Peck Indian Reservation who strongly opposes the Keystone XL pipeline, which will eventually connect Canadian tar sands to American consumption and export markets, participated in this protest. The said pipeline is expected to cross the Missouri river just outside of the reservation, 40 miles upstream of the tribes' multi-million dollar water treatment plant. The plant supplies clean water to communities throughout the region and an oil pipe leak would be catastrophic. Of Keystone XL, Ms. Welch had this to say: "Our people call it the black snake because it is evil."[1]

Before President Donald Trump's election in November 2016, Keystone XL was dead. In 2015, the US State Department denied TransCanada, the company involved, a key border-crossing permit. President Obama declared that the pipeline's approval would have destabilized the nation's global leadership on climate change action. But days after his inauguration, Donald Trump issued a memorandum encouraging expedited approval of the pipeline—an early confirmation of his abandonment of US climate leadership. On the same occasion, President Trump also signed a memorandum supporting the controversial Dakota Access Pipeline, a $3.7 billion pipeline which was stalled by the US Army Corps of Engineers (USACE) after protests were organized by the Standing Rock Sioux Tribe who feared drinking water contamination and damage to sacred burial sites.

Thus, with the intervention of the United States president, the underground Dakota Access Pipeline which belongs to Dakota Access, LLC, a subsidiary of Energy Transfer Partners (ETP), became fully operational on June 1, 2017 after months of legal bickering. The Dakota Access Pipeline is nearly 1,200 miles (1,900 km) long, spans the Bakken shale oil fields in North Dakota and continues through South Dakota and Iowa. Together with the Energy Transfer Crude Oil Pipeline in Texas, it forms the Bakken system. The channel transports 470,000 barrels of crude oil daily to a terminal in Illinois, where it can be shipped to refineries. The project transformed how oil is transported from North Dakota with new data confirming that pipelines presently transport more than three-quarters of the territory's oil. Before the Dakota Access Pipeline became completely active, about 25 per cent of North Dakota's oil left via railway. This percentage has dropped to 7 per cent.

When the shale fracking boom started around 10 years ago, North Dakota did not have many pipelines to get oil to the market. At its peak, in 2014, rail transport was roughly at 11 trains leaving with crude oil per day. However, this was much more costly. According to the North Dakota Pipeline Authority, since the Dakota Access Pipeline became operational, only one oil train departs North Dakota each day. In fact the entire oil industry is changing, as competition among pipeline companies is dramatically increasing.

However, these companies have serious challenges to overcome. One is the issue of pipe leaks and the consequential harm to the environment and people's livelihoods. A 2016 study confirmed that most pipeline leaks are largely preventable[2] and that ageing pipelines are often part of the problem. Based on data from the Pipeline and Hazardous Materials Safety Administration (PHMSA), an arm of the US Department of Transportation, the number of significant pipeline incidents related to old pipes grew 26.8 per cent from 2006 to 2015. In 2015 alone there were 326 such incidents—almost one per day. Opponents are of the opinion that pipelines may leak for years without anyone knowing and that companies prefer this method of transport only because it is more profitable.

These debates are taking place while the massive 2013 oil spill in North Dakota is still not fully cleaned up, reinforcing the uncertainty surrounding the future of the Dakota Access Pipeline. In June, a federal judge called for a new environmental review, saying that officials failed to fully consider the potential effects any oil spills could have on the Standing Rock Sioux tribe's fishing and hunting rights. Indeed, environmentalists and Native Americans accused the USACE of hastily approving each stage of the review process and ignoring federal regulations and established treaties with Native American tribes.

Pipeline protesters or water protectors found a sympathetic audience after news reports revealed that the pipeline was initially intended to cross the Missouri River at a different point, 10 miles upstream of Bismarck, the state capital. The pipeline was later rerouted to a half-mile upstream of the Standing Rock reservation, home to 8,200 people, 41 per cent of whom live below the poverty level. The people of Standing Rock rely on the Missouri River for drinking water, irrigation, and fish. Technically, construction sites are just north of the tribe's reservation, but the Sioux say that the government took this land from them illegally in an 1868 land treaty. Further, Native Americans are also accusing the government of approving pipeline construction without consulting them, as required by US law. President Trump is also accused of having personal interests in the project, as Kelcy Warren, Chief Executive of Dakota Access Pipeline, donated $100,000 to his election campaign. The founding partner of ETP, Marc Kasowitz, is also President Trump's personal lawyer.

Protesters were accused of starting fires and throwing petrol bombs at the police while the police were accused of using excessive force. Hundreds of people, many of them activists and journalists, were also arrested on charges of rioting and other felonies. According to reports, police even held some protesters in temporary cages. These allegations led the United Nations to speak out against the excessive force used against protesters (United Nations News, 2016). Clearly this has not helped much, though recently 84 congressional representatives caused much consternation and controversy when they asked US Attorney General Jeff Sessions whether those engaged in activism disrupting and damaging pipeline operations should not face terrorist charges under the US Patriot Act.

ANALYSIS

WHILE MANY ARGUE THAT THE DAKOTA ACCESS PIPELINE IS VIO-lating the rights of Native Americans, landowners, and farmers, and causes harm to the natural environment and agricultural land, ETP argues that the pipeline is an important economic mainstay of the US, as it contributes towards energy efficiency and independence. Other arguments in favor of the project are that the Dakota Access Pipeline creates jobs, frees up the railroads to allow for more grain exports, and that the pipeline method of transport is much safer for the environment and public in general. This point of view is supported by President Trump, who has backed the project from the outset.

Opponents, on the other hand, are of the opinion that the Dakota Access Pipeline and similar companies do more harm than good, as pipeline leaks often cause irreversible damage to the environment and people's livelihoods. Their claims have been backed up by the number of oil leaks taking place over the past decade and the lack of will from pipeline operators to clean up some of these leaks in a timely manner. In fact, during the Dakota Access Pipeline protests, a pipeline leak spilled 176,000 gallons of crude oil into a creek 150 miles from Cannonball, where Dakota protesters were camping out. This incident allowed the Sioux tribe's chairman, Dave Archambault II, to make an even stronger point about the threat of pipeline leaks to the environment and cultural heritage sites such as ancestral graves when he addressed the United Nations Human Rights Council in Geneva in an attempt to gain support for blocking the project by calling upon all parties to stop construction of the Dakota Access Pipeline. The tribe has been gaining more international support and vowed that they are not going to back down. Locally, more than 200 Native American tribes showed their support in the largest coming together of indigenous peoples in the US in decades. Other people and groups supporting the native tribes include hundreds of US military veterans who vowed to block completion of the pipeline,

Green Party presidential candidate Jill Stein, and Democratic presidential primary contender Bernie Sanders.

It is also important to keep in mind that landowners and farmers other than the Standing Rock Sioux tribe have also been raising their voices. For example, in 2016 the Iowa landowners filed lawsuits to prevent the state from using eminent domain to take their land to enable pipeline construction. Eminent domain is the right of the government or any of its agents to expropriate private property for private use. In addition, they also face the same issues as the native tribes—leaks are contaminating their water sources and their agricultural land. As a result they suffer great financial losses and have to engage in long and expensive court cases to get the pipeline companies to take responsibility for their actions. In the few cases where they do manage to obtain some compensation in an acceptable period of time, it is not enough to address the damage caused.

The issue at stake is to a great extent one of sustainability. The Native American Tribes, landowners, and farmers fear not only for their drinking water and the environment but indeed for their livelihoods. They are distressed because the long-term effects of continuous oil leaks into rivers, the water table, and land threaten their and their children's very existence. Dakota Access Pipeline and other such companies, however, encourage opponents to take into consideration the jobs they are creating, the taxes they are paying, and the eventual essential oil product which is used for energy consumption and pharmaceutical products (among other things), which they are making more easily accessible and available to the American people. These arguments do not always hold, though. For example, an economics expert has shown that the number of jobs projected by ETP (40 permanent jobs and between 8,200 and 12,000 temporary jobs) are more likely to be taken by out-of-state employers with their own skilled labor who will only subcontract some jobs to locals.

However, despite all the protests and accusations against the project, the Dakota Access Pipeline has been surviving so far. It has received support not only from the president of the United States, but also from other influential individuals such as the previously mentioned 84 congressional representatives asking for protesters to be criminally charged as terrorists.

Protesters and others against the Dakota Access Pipeline have also found alternative ways to affect the project and to hit where it matters.

For instance, opponents targeted the project's banks and investors, organizing global actions under the banner #DefundDAPL. The divestment campaign has racked up a series of victories even as the tribe's legal efforts to halt the pipeline have been foiled. As a result of this initiative, the financial giant ING, for example, has sold its stake in the $2.5 billion loan financing the Dakota Access pipeline. The Dutch banking and financial services company is the first of a group of 17 banks to divest from the loan that financed the project. ING's share in the loan was $120 million. The Norwegian bank DNB ASA also announced in 2016 that it would use its position as a lender of more than $342 million in credit to encourage a more constructive process to find solutions to the conflict that has arisen. More recently, Seattle, Washington's city council unanimously voted to not renew its contract with Wells Fargo partly because of its role as lender to the Dakota Access Pipeline.

ETP has reacted by filing a $300 million Racketeer Influenced and Corrupt Organizations (RICO) lawsuit against Greenpeace and other environmental groups for their activism against the long-contested North Dakota-to-Illinois project. In its 187-page complaint, ETP alleges that "putative not-for-profits and rogue eco-terrorist groups who employ patterns of criminal activity and campaigns of misinformation to target legitimate companies and industries with fabricated environmental claims and other purported misconduct" caused the company to lose "billions of dollars." The current lawsuit is seeking damages of up to $1 billion. ETP's legal team said in a press release that they planned to establish a website to keep track of information about the case, publish progress reports, and set the record straight when necessary. Greenpeace called the case nothing more than harassment by "corporate bullies."

All in all, it is anticipated that the need for oil will rather increase than decrease and that pipelines will stay the preferred means of transporting oil to dissemination points. This means that Dakota Access Pipeline might run out of capacity to transport North Dakota's vast reserves of crude in the future. The North Dakota Pipeline Authority estimated that production will again exceed the pipeline capacity. They say this will eventually result in additional transport needs out of the region. The market will decide whether that is met by a new pipeline project, an expanded pipeline project or the use of rail. However, as the protests against the industry increases, interested operators and pipeline companies would have to think of ways to avoid the backlash which results in stalled projects and a loss of revenue, at least in the short term.

This means that rather than attacking protesters and their supporters, Dakota Access Pipeline should address the issue of preventable leaks resulting from ageing pipelines. It would require considerable investment to modernize and secure old pipelines, but ignoring to do so would only create more problems for the project. Further, the Sioux people are also concerned, as they are not consulted when decisions directly affecting them are made. The tribe said in a public statement, "Americans know this pipeline was unfairly routed towards our nation and without our consent." This type of action by companies has been labeled environmental racism. It would thus also be in the interest of Dakota Access Pipeline and its owner, ETP, to employ a more consultative and less authoritarian manner to address the Sioux tribe and other stakeholders who raise concerns over the impact of the pipeline project.

NOTES

1   "Life on the Keystone XL Route: Where Opponents Fear the 'Black Snake',"
    The Guardian (May 2, 2017).
2   Mehdi Piri and Michael Faure, "Self-Regulation versus Public Regulation:
    An Analysis of Environmental and Safety Standard Setting in the Oil
    and Gas Pipeline Sector," in *Market Integration: The EU Experience and
    Implications for Regulatory Reform in China*, ed. Niels Philipsen, Stefan
    Weishaar, and Guangdong Xu (Berlin and Heidelberg: Springer, 2016).

DISCUSSION QUESTIONS

(1)   Which, in your opinion, are the most important ethical issues associated
      with the Dakota Access Pipeline and what could be the consequences if
      these are not addressed?
(2)   What are some of the political issues which influence the ethical
      character of the case?
(3)   Why do you think the present American administration does not invest
      more in clean energies?
(4)   What are some of the social issues resulting from environmental damage
      caused by leaking oil pipes?
(5)   Why do you think the Native American tribes gained so much
      international and local support?

FURTHER READINGS

M. Kat Anderson and Michael J. Moratto, "Native American Land-Use Practices and Ecological Impacts," Sierra Nevada Ecosystem Project: Final report to Congress, Assessments and Scientific Basis for Management Options (1996). University of California, Centers for Water and Wildland Resources.

"Dakota Pipeline: What's Behind the Controversy?" *BBC* (February 7, 2017).

Joe Heim, "Showdown Over Oil Pipeline Becomes a National Movement for Native Americans," *The Washington Post* (September 7, 2016).

"Keystone Pipeline Defiance Triggers Further Assault on Citizens' Rights," *The Guardian* (May 3, 2017).

Robinson Meyer, "The Legal Case for Blocking the Dakota Access Pipeline," *The Atlantic* (September 9, 2016).

"Trump Advisors Aim to Privatize Untapped Oil Reserves on Native American Reservations," *Reuters* (December 5, 2016).

10

ACTIONS SPEAK LOUDER THAN WORDS: REBUILDING MALDEN MILLS

DAVID MEELER AND SRIVATSA SESHADRI

BACKGROUND

FOUNDED IN 1906, MALDEN MILLS IS A PRIVATELY HELD TEXTILE mill located in Massachusetts. Like many other textile mills in the US, late in the twentieth century Malden Mills faced financial difficulty and eventually declared bankruptcy. If this were an average story of a bankrupt textile manufacturer in New England, Malden Mills would have folded long ago. But the owner, Aaron Feuerstein, spent millions of research dollars to develop entirely new fabrics, and re-opened the old mill right there in Massachusetts. By world-salary standards, this was an expensive move. The revolutionary new fabrics were Polartec® and Polarfleece®.

Polartec® and Polarfleece® are highly versatile and technical fabrics that hold little moisture, provide excellent insulation, offer low weight, etc. These fabrics are currently used by outdoor enthusiasts, extreme athletes, and various US Special Forces teams. Developing such a high-tech fabric might make you think that Malden Mills heavily emphasizes advanced research and development in their profit-making strategy.

When speaking at MIT's Industrial Development lecture series in 1997, Feuerstein said,

> You can have the best engineers, the best R&D guy, the best technical expert, figure out how to get better quality. But in the last analysis, it's the man on the floor who is going to get that quality for you. If he feels he's part of the enterprise and he feels he is treated the way he should be treated, he will go the extra mile to provide that quality.[1]

IN SHORT, AARON FEUERSTEIN IS COMMITTED TO THE IDEA THAT Malden's workers—white collar and blue collar alike—are the strongest asset the mill can have. A quick survey of any Fortune 500 company will reveal a publicly stated commitment to the value of their workers. For example, General Motors (whose devastating plant closing in Flint, MI was the subject of the film *Roger & Me*) states, "We are committed to developing and deploying employee skills, talent and potential effectively, improving the diversity of our workforce, influencing and shaping our performance to drive business outcomes and giving employees unmatched career opportunities. We see a clear link between our investment in human performance and our market performance and financial results." While many companies develop grandiose statements expressing a commitment to their employees, the fundamental difference between Malden Mills and other corporations, according to Feuerstein, "is that I consider our workers an asset, not an expense."[2] Malden Mills demonstrates its appreciation of workers with actions, not mere words.

Developing new materials and re-opening the mill in an area requiring some of the highest wages in the world is not the only commitment Malden Mills made to its employees and communities. In 1995, a fire broke out at Malden Mills. The largest fire in Massachusetts for over 100 years destroyed three of Malden's 10 large buildings, ruining Polartec's® dyeing and finishing operations. A perfect opportunity, many would say, to relocate operations overseas and take advantage of lower wages and more liberal environmental regulations. Not so for Aaron Feuerstein. By the day after the fire, Feuerstein had announced that he would immediately rebuild the plant in Massachusetts, and keep employees on full salary for three months.

Employees at Malden Mills repay this loyalty by going those extra miles. One building crucial to Polartec® was saved from the fire in part due to the efforts of 36 employees who helped fight the fire into the night.

Afterwards, makeshift operations were put in place to compensate for the production capacity lost in the fire. Feuerstein was focused not only on his employees' welfare; he was also concerned with the communities where his facilities are located, and the environmental impact his company has on the world. The new Polartec® plant was the first textile mill built in Massachusetts in over a century. In rebuilding, Feuerstein constructed the plant as a high-tech and environmentally conscious facility complete with heat-recovery generators. These ultra-low-NOx systems decreased the facility's emissions by 40 per cent—a savings equivalent to the annual emissions of 4,300 vehicles. During the rebuilding phase, Malden Mills set up an employee retraining center that included GED courses, English as a second language, and basic computer courses to prepare employees to work at the new state-of-the-art facility. When *60 Minutes* asked Feuerstein about his business choices after the fire, his reply was simple: "I think it was a wise business decision, but that isn't why I did it. I did it because it was the right thing to do."[3]

ANALYSIS

ONE OF THE MOST IMPORTANT ASPECTS WE SHOULD NOTE ABOUT the Malden Mills case is that at the time of the fire, it was privately owned. Without stockholders scrutinizing his business decisions, Feuerstein could do just about anything without fear of being sued. This is in sharp contrast to Henry Ford, whose stockholders sued him for continually reducing the sales-price of his Model T automobile. The Ford stockholders contended that the price could remain stable, and that by reducing the price Ford was giving away their profits. Feuerstein's decisions were obviously expensive. Construction costs, wages, and benefits are all higher in America, as is the expense of building environmentally friendly industrial facilities. But it was Feuerstein's money. He could do with it as he pleased.

In the months after the fire, Feuerstein was lauded as a model of executive heart. He was hailed for his courage and his honorable code of ethics. But the tale of Malden Mills is not a complete triumph. As a result of the fire, Malden Mills lost a great deal of international business supplying upholstery fabric, and eventually had to shut down its upholstery division. Try as he might, Feuerstein could not prevent a plant shutdown or the layoffs of approximately 400 workers. Rebuilding after the fire also left the company with an enormous debt, and Malden

Mills filed for Chapter 11 bankruptcy protection. Since large creditors then held a significant stake in Malden Mills, their voice would guide future business decisions. By the end of 2003, Malden Mills emerged from bankruptcy, and within six months Feuerstein was out and a new CEO took the reins. Within one year Michael Spillane, President and CEO of Malden Mills, had put together a new senior management team and dedicated his tenure to increasing profitability, in part, through cost controls. By mid-2005, GE Commercial Finance, owner of Malden Mills, was looking for a buyer.

NOTES

1   MIT News, "Malden Mills Owner Applies Religious Ethics to Business," https://news.mit.edu/1997/mills-0416.
2   Steve Wulf, "The Glow from a Fire," *Time*, January 8, 1996, p. 49.
3   60 Minutes, "The Mensch of Malden Mills," https://www.cbsnews.com/news/the-mensch-of-malden-mills/.

DISCUSSION QUESTIONS

(1)   Consider the actions of Feuerstein and his statement, "I think it was a wise business decision, but that isn't why I did it. I did it because it was the right thing to do." In hindsight, given that a small town lost a major employer when the upholstery division was shut down, employees lost jobs, the mill went into bankruptcy, the creditors got the raw end of the deal—in other words, everyone suffered in the long term—were Feuerstein's decisions socially responsible? Why or Why not?

(2)   Suppose that Malden Mills had been a publicly traded company in which you held stock. Upon hearing news of the fire and CEO's decisions, how would you react? How would your reactions change if you were an employee? A customer? Was Feuerstein favoring the interests of some stakeholders over those of others?

(3)   If, through the good luck of substantial market demand, the mill had survived, would you view the ethics of the decisions differently?

(4)   What if the good luck turned out to be an enormous contract to provide uniform clothing for military, police, or fire and rescue forces?

(5)   What if the good luck turned out to be extremely high demand for the products from gang members? (Note: It is legal to be a gang member.)

FURTHER READINGS

Kenneth Campbell, "Malden Mills Owner Applies Religious Ethics to
    Business," *MIT News* (April 16, 1997).
Charlie Rose, "Kidnapped/Puzzle Master/Malden Mills," *60 Minutes* (2003).
    Columbia Broadcasting System.
Matthew W. Seeger and Robert R. Ulmer, "Virtuous Responses to
    Organizational Crisis: Aaron Feuerstein and Milt Colt," *Journal of
    Business Ethics* (2001): 369–76.
Robert R. Ulmer, "Effective Crisis Management through Established
    Stakeholder Relationships: Malden Mills as a Case Study," *Management
    Communication Quarterly* (2001): 590–615.

11.

STUDENTS PROTEST UNIVERSITY INVESTMENTS: VANDERBILT'S AFRICAN LAND-GRAB

JOSHUA M. HALL

BACKGROUND

ON WEDNESDAY, JUNE 8, 2011, UK'S *THE GUARDIAN* REPORTED THAT numerous US universities including Harvard and Vanderbilt were invested in companies that were buying large tracts of African farmland and kicking off the indigenous farmers in order for their employees (mostly non-Africans) to grow cash crops to sell to Europe.[1] Harms associated with this land-grabbing include, in addition to the evictions themselves, corruption among African governments and among absentee African land owners, increased food prices, and accelerated climate change.

The article mentions several specific examples of this land-grabbing practice. In Tanzania, Iowa University and a US corporation named AgriSol Energy planned to expel 162,000 people from their refugee settlements, people who had been farming the land for 40 years. And in South Sudan, the Texas corporation Nile Trading and Development secured a 49-year long lease to all natural resources on 400,000 hectares of land (roughly half a million soccer fields in total size—a bit less than one-third the size of the land area of Connecticut), all for just $25,000. Altogether, the World Bank claims 60,000,000 hectares—the size of France—had been bought in this way in just the past three years alone.

The primary company in which Vanderbilt, Harvard, and the other US schools were invested is EmVest (formerly Emergent Asset Management), based in London (and with offices in South Africa), and directed by investor Susan Payne and (former oil company geologist) David Murrin, former employees of JP Morgan and Goldman Sachs. The name of the fund is The African AgriLand Fund, which controls 100,000 hectares of land, operates in Mozambique, South Africa, Swaziland, Zambia and Zimbabwe, and openly utilizes tax havens all over Africa. It has a total investment estimated at $540,000,000, and project an investment return of 25 per cent. Also problematic is EmVest's strategy for capturing investors, which is to make doomsday projections about impending war between China and the West over limited food supplies.

According to the Oakland Institute, at least one of the villages affected by EmVest's African AgriLand Fund did not legally consent to the transfer of land, was not notified of the transfer in writing, and was experiencing greater difficulties getting enough food after the transfer. Additionally, there were few local jobs created (contrary to EmVest's promises to invest in local economic infrastructure); these jobs were mostly seasonal and low-paying, and some workers complained of not receiving their earned wages.

Vanderbilt's investments in EmVest and other morally question-able companies led to the formation of an undergraduate organiza-tion, the Vanderbilt Responsible Endowment Campaign. In addition to the $26 million invested in EmVest (out of a total 2011 endowment of $3.3 billion), other problematic investments by Vanderbilt include an investment in a company that directly supported Apartheid in South Africa, and $145,000,000 in a hedge fund in the Cayman Islands (called Callao Partners Ltd Appleby Trust).[2]

The fight began when graduate students at Vanderbilt forwarded the *Guardian* article to Prof. Leslie Gill, Chair of the Anthropology Department, who then drafted a letter to Vice Chancellors Brett Sweet and Matthew Wright, requesting verification of the investment in EmVest. In support of this, a student also contacted Anuradha Mittal, director of the Oakland Institute, who encouraged them to begin the campaign. The group designed a proposal for an "Ethical Investing Policy," eventually secured a meeting with Chancellor Wright (who had visited

EmVest's site at Mozambique, but without meeting even a single local farmer). The group worked with Vanderbilt Students for Nonviolence to hold a teach-in in the administration building, submitted a letter to Chancellor Nicholas Zeppos, and constructed a tent city (from March to May of 2012) outside that building.

In response, an anonymous Trustee informed a student member of Vanderbilt Students for Nonviolence that the divestment had occurred (which remains the only official communication to that effect from the administration). The administration has still not, however, publicly acknowledged the divestment.

ANALYSIS

SOME HAVE ARGUED THAT WHAT ARE TERMED "LAND GRABS" ARE actually of benefit to the people of the global South, in that they facilitate economic development of unused land, and provide jobs and infrastructure for the local communities. In its mission statement, EmVest asserts that it aims to provide food security to communities, regions, and countries in a socially responsible, environmentally friendly, and sustainable manner.

As pointed out by the critics of land-grabbing, however, there is little to no empirical evidence of these alleged benefits, and significant evidence to the contrary. For example, one land grab in Malawi created only one permanent job and 200 seasonal jobs that paid only $0.70 per day.[3] Even if land grabs in general do in fact bring benefits to local populations, this case in particular raises several more fundamental issues regarding university ethics, including students' ethical obligations (including to themselves) and the ethical standards to which universities should be held.

Do undergraduate and/or graduate students have an ethical obligation to protest the investment decisions of their universities? Students not only share the same ethical obligations of all citizens, but are also members of the university and are likely better situated to learn about and take a stand against wrongdoings by their institutions. Since many ethicists hold that people have stronger obligations to perform duties that they are best qualified to do, students may actually have a greater responsibility than non-students to protest this sort of injustice.

On the other hand, might there be a competing ethical permission for students to protect themselves as vulnerable members of the institution?

Students do have particular vulnerabilities not equally shared by non-students. For example, many undergraduates at Vanderbilt (and elsewhere) are from lower socioeconomic backgrounds themselves and depend on scholarships to attend Vanderbilt. These protests could jeopardize their future academic and professional careers if they are pressured to leave, or unofficially blackballed by members of the administration. As anyone professionally involved in the academy is aware, even having a degree from a top-ranked US university is no guarantee of financial or professional success, unless there is also a functioning and supportive network in place.

And, lastly, in regard to students, might it be "inappropriate" for students to intervene, as Vanderbilt's Vice Chancellor Matthew Wright, for one, initially claimed? In response, the Oakland Institute's Anuradha Mittal asks, "Since when can universities decide what students should be involved in, and not be involved in? And you hope that institutions of higher learning would really contribute to the buildup of democratic societies, where people can question, especially when the actions of the university are having a huge socioeconomic and environmental impact somewhere else."

Some might feel that this case and all of its publicity scapegoats Harvard and Vanderbilt. After all, the investment portfolios of most major US businesses are highly diversified and complex, and include ethically problematic aspects of which most shareholders are unaware. But a contrasting perspective is that universities' endowments should not be governed to maximize their value. Rather, the social function of universities to educate the next generation of leaders and citizens who will have major impacts on global justice gives rise to special obligations to make sure that their investments meet ethical standards. This perspective raises important questions about the nature of the university, its purposes (including its moral purposes), and the responsibilities of its administrators, faculty, and students.

More troubling than the potential scapegoating (of universities such as Vanderbilt) is the possibility that this story thereby distracts from more pervasive issues of global capitalism. After all, the total of universities' investments is minuscule compared to the total investments from the US government and companies. Should we not be focusing our critical energies on the companies with the most power and influence in terms of the US's total investment portfolio? Perhaps we should be more concerned with the economic relationship between the global North and South as a whole, rather than fixating on the hypocrisy of the North's institutions of higher education.[4]

NOTES

1   See John Vidal and Claire Provost, "US Universities in Africa 'land grab,'" *The Guardian* (June 8, 2011).
2   Alexander Lavelle, "Aristotle, Justice, and Investment," unpublished manuscript.
3   Blessings Chinsinga, Michael Chasukwa, and Sane Pashane Zuka, "The Political Economy of Land Grabs in Malawi: Investigating the Contribution of Limphasa Sugar Corporation to Rural Development," *Journal of Agricultural and Environmental Ethics* (2013): 1075.
4   This case study has benefited enormously from Alexander Lavelle's unpublished paper "Aristotle, Justice, and Investment" and from an interview conducted with Anuradha Mittal from the Oakland Institute.

DISCUSSION QUESTIONS

(1)   Is the Oakland Institute correct that universities should be held to a distinct, more demanding ethical standard than other US businesses?
(2)   Vice Chancellor Matthew Wright argued that it is "inappropriate" for undergraduates to involve themselves in their school's investments? Is he right? If not, why not?
(3)   What ethical obligations do US undergraduate and graduate students have (including obligations to themselves) when deciding whether to protest unethical investments at their colleges and universities?
(4)   Do reasonably well-functioning global markets fairly determine land usage and agricultural policies? If not, how should these be determined?
(5)   Compare and contrast the ethics of student self-protection, and their possible obligation to hold their institutions accountable for their investment decisions. How should these be balanced?

FURTHER READINGS

Lorenzo Cotula, Nat Dyer, and Sonja Vermeulen, *Fuelling Exclusion? The Biofuels Boom and Poor People's Access to Land* (London: International Institute for Environment and Development, 2008).

Declaration on Land Issues and Challenges in Africa. Assembly of the African Union, Thirteenth Ordinary Session at Sirte, Libya, July 2009.

Ruth Hall, "Land Grabbing in Southern Africa: The Many Faces of the Investor Rush," *Review of African Political Economy* (2011): 193–214.

Phoebe Stephens, "The Global Land Grabs: An Analysis of Land Governance Institutional," *International Affairs Review* 20.1 (2011): 1–22.

"Voluntary Guidelines on the Responsible Governance of Tenure of Land and other Natural Resources, Zero Draft," Rome: Food and Agriculture Organization of the United Nations (2011).

Wendy Wolford, Saturnino Borras, Jr., Ruth Hall, Ian Scoones, and Ben White, *Governing Global Land Deals: The Role of the State in the Rush for Land* (New York: Wiley-Blackwell, 2013).

12

THE RANA PLAZA COLLAPSE

ALEX SAGER

BACKGROUND

ON APRIL 24, 2013, THE EIGHT-STORY RANA PLAZA IN BANGLADESH collapsed killing 1,129 people, many employed in garment factories serving international brands that included Benetton, the Children's Place, Joe Fresh, Mango, and Walmart. The collapse was one of a recent series of highly publicized tragedies in Bangladesh's garment industry, which directly or indirectly employs four million people and comprises 80 per cent of Bangladesh's $21 billion export market, making up 18 per cent of the country's GDP in 2013.

The collapse was in many ways predictable. The owners had added additional stories to a building without receiving a permit to do so. The building was not designed for industrial use, but much of the space had been leased to garment factories with heavy machinery. Despite police warnings to evacuate and employee protests at the new cracks that had appeared in the building, managers ordered garment workers to come to work.

The Rana Plaza Collapse exemplifies the political corruption and economic pressures that contribute to widespread labor abuses in Bangladesh's and many other developing countries' export sectors. It was preceded by the April 11, 2005, collapse of the Spectrum-Sweater factory in Savar that killed 64 people. The November 24, 2012, Dhaka garment factory fire killed 117 people and injured many more, because of the lack of emergency exits. Many more incidents go unreported in the international news. The avoidable deaths of workers is only the most extreme example of widespread, questionable labor practices in the developing world, which include slavery and indentured labor, child labor, physical and sexual abuse, exposure to hazardous chemicals, and low wages.

There have been a number of responses that address safety and working conditions in Bangladesh, including a National Action Plan to review fire safety and structural integrity for buildings with ready-made garment factories and a compact between the government of Bangladesh, the European Union, the United States, and the International Labor Organization to improve working conditions. The International Labor Organization has established a fund to compensate victims of the Rana Plaza collapse. As of June 2014, the fund had received less than half of the $40 million target and half of the companies associated with manufacturing in the Rana Plaza failed to contribute.

On May 23, 2013, international retailers and Bangladeshi trade unions released the *Accord on Fire and Building Safety in Bangladesh* calling for increased inspections, remediation, and training, as well as contributions from signatory companies. The *Accord* is a legally binding document, which requires companies to fix buildings likely not to meet safety standards and to continue to employ and compensate workers while repairs are taking place. Though many major international brands have signed the accord, Walmart, Gap Inc., and H&M refused. Walmart and Gap Inc. later joined a coalition of major North American apparel companies, retailers, and brands to form the Alliance for Bangladesh Worker Safety and created the Bangladesh Worker Safety Initiative.

It is too early to know the long-term effects of these initiatives, but there are some grounds for concern about their scope, efficacy, and broader effects. Though the Institute for Global Labour and Human Rights reports successes from a collaboration between Bangladeshi workers, the Institute, Gap and H&M in improving conditions, wages, and benefits for factories in the Ha-Meem and Windy Groups of factories, these groups comprise only a fraction of Bangladesh's garment factories. Even leaving aside widely recognized problems with corruption, the Bangladeshi government does not currently have enough staff to rigorously inspect all of its factories.

Inspections can also harm workers that they are designed to help. The *New York Times* reports that inspections organized through the Bangladesh Accord Foundation have led to the closing of some factories, leaving thousands of workers unemployed and uncompensated as repairs are made.[1] Factory owners and labor unions have asked international brands to pay wages, but so far have had limited success.

ANALYSIS

THE RANA PLAZA COLLAPSE CLEARLY INVOLVED NEGLIGENCE ON the part of the building owner, the garment factories leasing space, and the public officials expected to oversee safety compliance. Workers should not be subjected to easily preventable, immanent, life-threatening danger, a conviction expressed by the arrest and conviction of building owner Mohammed Sohel Rana and factory owner Bazlus Samad Adnan, who employed 1,700 people at the Rana Plaza. But the reason that this case is interesting for business ethics is that issues surrounding the collapse raises broader issues about safety, working conditions, and wages.

Working conditions in the developing world often appear unacceptable from the perspective of people in affluent, Western countries. Nonetheless, workers routinely accept risks and choose to labor for what seem like low wages because jobs in the export sector are better than other alternatives open to them. In fact, companies serving international brands often pay higher wages than local companies. Moreover, the only reason that developing world countries are able to attract business for their export sectors is because they offer plentiful cheap labor. Though many developed world consumers take pride in paying more for clothing made by unionized workers in their country, refusing to buy cheap foreign goods may very well slow economic development and harm the global poor. The imposition of safer worker conditions by international firms under pressure from consumers abroad may be welcome, but it can also be an imposition for workers who lose wages or their jobs when the companies they work for do not meet standards.

In 2014, Bangladesh raised the minimum wage 79 per cent to $68 per month without overtime (adjusted for purchasing power parity), cutting into profit margins and contributing to a slowdown in the garment industry. One consequence of the international focus on Bangladesh is that factory owners reported that export orders fell to rivals.[2] The disproportionate focus on Bangladesh after the Rana Plaza collapse is questionable, since there are similar labor practices in many countries, including major rivals such as China, Vietnam, Indonesia, and Cambodia.

How do we decide what just labor standards are? Should this question be largely determined by supply and demand on the market in which workers and firms negotiate wages and working conditions? Are there universal minimal standards that all ethical employers must respect? Should citizens decide labor practices through democratic processes? Are multinational corporations bound by the labor standards of the countries in which they operate or of the countries in which they are based? Or do they need to find some sort of compromise? Should countries comply with standards set by the International Labor Organization or another international body? What role should consumers play? These are complicated questions.

One concern that many people have about overseas labor is that it is exploitative. Though theorists have understood exploitation in various ways, a core idea is that exploitation occurs when one party is able to take unfair advantage of the other, usually because the exploiting party enjoys more power or possesses information that the exploited party lacks. Notably, exploitation is often mutually beneficial. For example, low-wage labor under unpleasant conditions is often better than the alternative of unemployment. Nonetheless, critics retort that it is exploitative because workers are not in a position to bargain for something better.

The challenge for any account of exploitation is to explain when an agreement is unfair. Broad accounts of exploitation hold that most agreements reached between parties with unequal bargaining power are unfair. One concern, though, is that this may entail that most employees are exploited, including relatively well-paid employees in developed countries. Narrower accounts of exploitation locate unfairness against a baseline of what would be determined under conditions of perfect competition: if workers are being paid less than they would in a free market, they are exploited. These accounts raise the opposite concern: if markets are reasonably efficient, then almost nobody can claim to be exploited.

Some business ethicists have preferred to distinguish questions of safety and working conditions from questions of wages. After all, even advocates of low-wage overseas labor condemn businesses that enslave workers, use physical violence to compel workers to meet quotas, or force children to work long hours. Regarding questions of safety, business ethics sometimes invokes rights such as the right to life or notions of human dignity. For example, Denis Arnold and Norman Bowie have argued from a Kantian perspective that respect for persons requires that employers guarantee minimal health and safety conditions and that they inform workers of any workplace hazards so that they can make rational decisions about accepting work.

Critics from libertarian market-based perspectives have responded that it is illegitimate to distinguish between wages and improvements to worker safety and health. The cost of a salary increase and the cost of a sprinkler system have the same effect on a company's bottom line. In contrast, they place the emphasis on worker choice and view the market as providing sufficient information to allow employees to choose rationally whether they wish to assume the risks.

This debate raises two issues. First, are market mechanisms the right tools for determining just labor conditions and wages? Libertarians contend that if workers have freely decided to sell their labor in a competitive market, then competition will lead employers to offer wages and working conditions that satisfy workers' preferences. Workers are usually the best judges of their needs and their tolerance for risk, and this should be respected. In response, critics contend that labor conditions should not be set solely by supply and demand; they prefer instead to invoke independent standards such as basic human rights, or to have these questions be determined by democratic processes.

A second, related issue concerns the extent to which imperfect and asymmetrical information, barriers to entry, monopoly power, and background political and social conditions impair the market from functioning efficiently. Libertarians who oppose regulation gain traction from the assumption that markets are fairly efficient in practice. Where this turns out not to be the case, the market should not be relied on to set just labor conditions, even if this would be best in an ideal world of perfect competition.

Leaving aside questions of safety and fair wages, who is responsible for labor abuses and workplace dangers? Often critics of overseas labor conditions place the primary responsibility and blame on multinational companies. For example, Kalpona Akter, executive director of the Bangladesh Center for Worker Solidarity, commented on the Rana Plaza collapse: "After the Tazreen fire, it was a cemetery, human bodies all over the floor. And now we have another one ... American companies, they know this is happening. We've told them: Remember these human faces. You killed these girls."[3]

Is Akter right that American companies are to blame for these tragedies? The answer to this question turns on whether or not American (and other) companies failed to meet the moral obligations they had to workers in the supply chain. In order to determine companies' obligations, it may also be necessary to determine other agents' moral obligations. Another complex question concerns how moral responsibility should be reassigned if some parties fail to fulfill their obligations. For example, presumably local suppliers and governments have obligations toward the safety of workers. In fact, H&M's reason for rejecting the Accord on Fire and Building Safety in Bangladesh was that it thought responsibility for safety standards rested in the factories and in the local government. A further concern is that foreign corporations or consumers are imposing their labor standards on the developing world with limited knowledge of local conditions, and that this is condescending and paternalistic.

The Bangladeshi government has labor standards in place, but they are often not enforced due to corruption or lack of capacity. If local companies fail to meet their obligations, do these obligations automatically fall on companies further up in the supply chain? To answer this, we need to determine what role multinational companies play and can play in working conditions. Did the fact that Bangladesh factories manufacture clothes for export to international brands play a significant role in the working conditions, or are workers poorly paid or mistreated because of vulnerabilities caused primarily by local conditions? How we answer this question will affect where we should direct our attention in identifying potential for reform. Should we think of overseas working conditions in terms of corporate social responsibility or as a question of government regulation and reform (keeping in mind that it might be both)?

Another question concerns the moral obligations of parties in a commodity chain. The fair trade movement places moral obligations on consumers with the conviction that they can pressure companies into improving conditions. One reason why many people focus on large, foreign companies is the conviction that they have the power and responsibility to change practices and conditions in companies that supply them. If we believe companies have some obligations, there are further questions. How much knowledge do companies need to acquire about their contractors, keeping in mind the many challenges of effectively monitoring practices abroad? What if contractors subcontract some work to other companies? When answering these questions, it is important to keep in mind that monitoring and compliance have costs that may impact vulnerable workers.

Another question concerns the type of measures that ought to be adopted and who should determine their content. Should labor standards be determined primarily by regulation or by voluntary compliance? The Accord on Fire and Building Safety in Bangladesh gives trade unions a major role in setting policies and also serves as a binding agreement. The International Labor Organization serves as an independent chair. One drawback to this sort of agreement is that companies may be reluctant to join. For example, Gap refused to be part of the Accord because it feared that it might result in lawsuits and that it would require them to fund safety upgrades. In contrast, the Bangladesh Worker Safety Initiative was founded by retailers and takes more of a corporate social responsibility approach. Though companies may be less reluctant to become involved in this sort of initiative, one concern is that it gives workers and unions limited power to help set the agenda and that it lacks independent monitoring.

Lastly, we can ask about the role of the global capitalist economy in putting pressure on production and arguably contributing to a race to the bottom. In recent years, textile companies' product life cycles have become shorter, with new collections appearing monthly and even weekly (as opposed to bi-yearly cycles in the past). Shorter lead times and last minute changes lead factories to subcontract to second- and third-tier suppliers over which there is limited control. Furthermore, buyers place enormous pressure on price, leading suppliers to frequently switch to new factories or new countries to meet demands. The result is that factories have no guarantee of work in the future; this removes the incentive to invest in safety and better equipment and motivates them to cut corners to meet demands. Addressing these concerns involves suppliers and buyers, but also requires structural changes in the industry and in consumer attitudes and demands.[4]

NOTES

1   Steven Greenhouse, "Bangladesh Inspections Find Gaps in Safety," *New York Times* (May 11, 2014).

2   Serajus Guardir, "Rising Wages Squeeze Bangladesh Garment Makers as Factories Await Upgrades," *Reuters* (April 13, 2014).

3   Qtd. in Sarah Stillman, "Death Traps: The Bangladesh Garment Factory
     Disaster," *The New Yorker* (May 1, 2013).
4   I'm grateful to Peter Jonker for his comments on this case study and his
     insights into the textile industry.

DISCUSSION QUESTIONS

(1) Is Kalpona Akter correct in claiming that American companies are
     morally culpable for the deaths of the people who died in the Tazreen fire?
(2) The economist Paul Krugman echoes the conviction of many of his
     colleagues that we should in fact praise cheap labor. Why do you think he
     believes this? Is he right? If not, why not?
(3) What moral obligations (if any) do consumers in the developed world
     have when deciding to buy clothing made abroad?
(4) Do reasonably well-functioning markets fairly set wages and working
     conditions? If not, how should these be determined?
(5) Compare and contrast the Accord on Fire and Building Safety in
     Bangladesh and the Bangladesh Worker Safety Initiative. What are the
     advantages and shortcomings of each?

FURTHER READINGS

Accord on Fire and Building Safety in Bangladesh, http://bangladeshaccord.org/.
Denis G. Arnold and Norman E. Bowie, "Sweatshops and Respect for Persons,"
     Business Ethics Quarterly 13.2 (2003): 221–42.
Bangladesh Worker Safety Initiative, http://www.bangladeshworkersafety.org/.
Jagdish Bhagwati, *In Defense of Globalization* (New York: Oxford University
     Press, 2004).
Institute for Global Labour and Human Rights, *Unprecedented Changes:
     Garment Workers in Bangladesh Fight Back and Win* (October 2014).
Naomi Klein, *No Logo: Taking Aim at the Brand Bullies* (New York: Picador,
     2000).
Paul Krugman, "In Praise of Cheap Labor," *Slate* (March 21, 1997).
Richard M. Locke, "Opening the Debate: Can Global Brands Create Just
     Supply Chains? A Forum on Corporate Responsibility for Factory
     Workers," *Boston Review* (May 21, 2013).
Lindsay Poulton, Francesca Panetta, Jason Burke, David Levene, and the
     Guardian Interactive Team, "The Shirt on Your Back: The Human Cost of
     the Bangladeshi Garment Industry," *The Guardian* (April 16, 2014).

13.

DISTRIBUTIVE JUSTICE: THE CASE OF CAFÉ FEMININO

KYLE JOHANNSEN

BACKGROUND

FAIR TRADE SOMETIMES GETS A BAD RAP. THOUGH THE LABEL IS meant to help conscientious consumers avoid supporting exploitive trade relationships with producers in the Global South, the idea of Fair Trade is commonly abused by companies seeking to take advantage of its marketing potential. By selling only a couple of Fair Trade certified products or by creating similar sounding labels, companies can market themselves as ethically minded without taking on the corresponding commitments that Fair Trade is supposed to embody. This phenomenon is frequently referred to as "fair washing." However, as an examination of coffee production in the Andean foothills of Northern Peru reveals, Fair Trade can sometimes yield significant economic and social benefits.

A number of Fair Trade coffee producers in that region operate under the brand name "Café Feminino." As the name suggests, producers are committed to improving local Peruvian women's socio-economic status. Money generated through the sale of their products is used to fund a number of development initiatives, including the creation of community spaces for women, workshops designed to develop women's leadership abilities, and a respiratory health initiative that targets the improvement of air quality in home kitchens.[1] Café Feminino imposes a unique requirement: members must be women who hold title to their coffee growing land. This has created a powerful incentive for female land ownership and a corresponding increase in women's economic independence.

In response to the crisis of falling prices and oversupply for coffee in the 1990s, Peruvian coffee cooperatives organized themselves under the umbrella cooperative CECANOR to gain fair-trade certification. Convinced that they produced a better product than the male members of CECANOR, female members created their own separate label in order to differentiate their product.[2] Though based in Peru, Café Feminino has extended its activities to benefit coffee producers in over 10 other countries through an extensive grants program. Examples include a respiratory health initiative in Columbia similar to the one in Peru, and an income diversification initiative in the Dominican Republic designed to increase women's economic independence.[3]

In addition to female ownership, other special features distinguish Café Feminino from other Fair Trade coffee labels. A second unique feature is that an extra two cents per pound on top of the standard Fair Trade premium goes directly to female producers who decide how to use it in their community. This means that, in total, Café Feminino secures 17 cents more per pound of coffee than is typically the case for coffee producers in the Global South. A third unique feature is Café Feminino's commitment to supporting women in the Global North. One of the ways it exercises this concern is by securing an extra two cents per pound to fund women's shelters in the communities where its coffee is sold. Another way is by encouraging its Northern business partners to be more inclusive of women. In particular, Café Feminino requires that a woman sign the contract between them on behalf of the partner.[4]

ANALYSIS

PROMOTERS OF FAIR TRADE ASSUME THAT EXISTING TRADE RELA-tions between businesses in the Global North and producers in the Global South are morally problematic, and that the right way to tackle the problem is via a consumer-driven approach. Given these assumptions, Café Feminino appears to be an exemplar of a socially responsible brand.

The benefits secured by Café Feminino for its members and other women in the rural communities of Northern Peru far exceed the benefits normally secured through North-South trade, and even those normally secured through Fair Trade as well. What's more, by focusing on a historically disadvantaged group (women in the Andean foothills of Peru), Café Feminino ensures that the benefits it secures impact those who really need them.

The assumption that there is something morally problematic with standard trade relations between businesses in the Global North and producers in the Global South is debatable, however. To fully evaluate this assumption requires reflecting on broader questions and theories of distributive justice, the branch of justice that examines the fair distribution of benefits and burdens. How one responds to cases like Café Feminino depends in part on whether one subscribes to a view of distributive justice that sees transactions in the free market as a just basis for distributing goods, or to a view that accords government a significant role in regulating the market and redistributing goods to remediate inequalities, or to a view that sees current economic institutions as instantiating structural injustice based on unequal power relationships between South and North.

According to most libertarians, economic transactions are only problematic in cases of theft or fraud. So long as the parties to a transaction did not acquire their holdings either directly or indirectly through theft or fraud, and so long as they do not commit theft or fraud against each other, then the outcome of their transaction is fair. It arguably follows that benefiting the less well-off by purchasing Fair Trade products is not a requirement of justice, but a matter of charity: possibly praiseworthy but not morally required.

A second, a very different sort of conclusion one might draw is that Fair Trade, even when conducted in accordance with the exceptionally high standards exemplified by Café Feminino, doesn't go nearly far enough. Instead, what's needed is a considerable degree of state level redistribution from those in the Global North to those in the South. There are a number of routes via which this conclusion might be reached. From a libertarian perspective focused on the historical injustices of, say, colonialism, it could be argued that current holdings are tainted by previous unjust transactions: the Global North has its current wealth in part because of past acts of theft and fraud against populations in the Global South. If so, then a considerable amount of redistribution may be needed for the sake of rectifying past injustice.

Redistribution could also be grounded in a liberal egalitarian perspective such as the one argued for by John Rawls. On his view, economic inequalities between citizens of the same society are only just when (a) they are consistent with equality of opportunity, and (b) they maximally benefit those who are worst off. If those with less did not have the same opportunities to attain wealth as those with more, and if the greater share of those who have more does not work to the benefit of those who have less, e.g., by incentivizing the use of productive talents that raise everyone's absolute position, then the inequality between them is unjust. Though Rawls himself did not extend his view to the global context, philosophers such as Charles Beitz and Thomas Pogge have argued from a Rawlsian perspective that it is clear that these inequalities should also be deemed unjust. The citizens of countries in the Global South do not have the same opportunities to acquire wealth as citizens in the North, and even if there's some sense in which existing inequalities benefit the global poor, it's highly doubtful that the benefit is maximal.

From another perspective, opting for state-level redistribution is almost as unsatisfying as settling for Fair Trade. It might be argued that the root problem is not an unequal distribution of wealth, but rather the global capitalist framework within which that inequality is situated. From a socialist viewpoint focused on the means of production, inequality is certainly a bad thing, but addressing it without also addressing the system of property underlying it is like treating the symptoms without providing a cure. A socialist might note that, first, global private ownership of the means of production has led to an unequal distribution of it between the Global North and South. While the North has various means of adding value to raw goods, e.g., advanced manufacturing facilities, the South largely does not. As a result, those in the Global South have no choice but to participate in exploitive trade relationships, as there are few productive options for them to choose from aside from producing and exporting largely unprocessed goods, for example, coffee.

A second point that someone with a socialist perspective might emphasize is that private ownership of the means of production among Southern producers puts them in competition with each other, thereby creating a race to the bottom. If a producer tries to raise her prices, she'll be undercut by the other producers she's in competition with. Private ownership is thus arguably responsible for sustaining the exploitive trade relations that Fair Trade is a response to.

Our discussion thus far presents a choice between two starkly opposed points of view. On the one hand, a libertarian proponent of the view that voluntary transactions are fair transactions would likely maintain that purchasing Fair Trade products, Café Feminino coffee included, does nothing to increase the amount of justice in the world. On this view, so long as Northern businesses don't defraud Southern producers, then all is fine as far as justice is concerned. In contrast, liberal egalitarians and socialists would likely maintain that Fair Trade falls dramatically short of what justice requires. If justice requires either large transfers of wealth from the better off to the worse off or common ownership of the means of production, then Fair Trade is arguably a distraction that diverts attention away from what we really ought to be concerned with.

Suppose we were to reject the view that voluntary transactions are always fair. However, suppose we also take for granted the background conditions we currently find ourselves in, i.e., conditions characterized by private ownership of the means of production and insufficient political will to implement a substantial international system of redistributive transfers. Though we might prefer either common ownership or a system of redistributive transfers, our moral analysis would be fairly superficial were we merely to lament the fact that this preference hasn't been satisfied. There remains an important, unanswered question about what Northern businesses and consumers owe to Southern producers in our present political and economic circumstances. And if we can agree that we have an obligation to benefit those in the South who are badly off, then we need to ask ourselves whether securing Fair Trade arrangements and buying Fair Trade products, especially in accordance with the more ambitious standards set by Café Feminino, would help us to fulfill that obligation.

There are at least two sides to this issue. One is whether Fair Trade would tangibly benefit socio-economically disadvantaged groups in the South. In this respect, Fair Trade seems superior to typical North-South trade relations, and the more ambitious form of Fair Trade exemplified by Café Feminino seems superior to standard Fair Trade. To fully assess the merits of Café Feminino-style Fair Trade, however, we would need to know what other feasible means of benefiting Southern producers are available to Northern businesses and consumers, and whether these means are more or less effective than Fair Trade. For example, does Fair Trade sometimes have negative effects that offset its positive effects? Paying a higher price to Fair Trade producers may disadvantage Southern producers who don't sell Fair Trade products. It may also remove some of the incentive for Southern producers to shift towards more lucrative forms of production. Would it be better for consumers to donate a portion of their earnings to reliable charities, rather than pay Fair Trade prices? Questions like these need to be answered before we can make a comprehensive assessment.[5]

The second side of this issue concerns the relationship between Fair Trade and the relevant background conditions themselves, e.g., ownership of the means of production. How would Fair Trade affect these conditions? Would it affect them in a positive way? These are complicated questions, but there are some things that can tentatively be said in reply. According to J.J. McMurtry, one of the problems with Fair Trade as it's normally practiced is that it leaves intact the structural conditions that create the need for Fair Trade in the first place.[6] For example, a Fair Trade label that increases wages and improves work conditions for female factory workers in the clothing industry benefits them, but it does so in a potentially temporary manner if it does not address the circumstances that make them vulnerable to exploitation. If their employers suddenly decided to pay less, these women would not have the economic independence necessary to refuse work. In this respect, however, Café Feminino is an important exception. Since the use of their label by any Peruvian producer is conditional upon female land ownership, Café Feminino has placed an important means of production into the hands of a disadvantaged group, thereby increasing their economic independence. Elevating the socio-economic position of women in this comparatively permanent way gives them a platform upon which to implement improvements on their own. It may also help to ensure that future measures taken to benefit the producers of Northern Peru, e.g., monetary transfers, have a greater chance of benefiting women, and not just those who have traditionally held a position of power in the area.

Though transferring ownership of one means of production to a disadvantaged group is admittedly a far cry from common ownership, it is nonetheless responsive to the socialist worry that lack of access to the means of production is the real issue. What's more, it's responsive to the liberal egalitarian view that the better off have an obligation to benefit the worst off. Across at least some of the perspectives discussed above, then, the sort of Fair Trade exemplified by Café Feminino arguably counts as a significant improvement in justice. Still, it's worth asking whether alternative approaches would bring us closer to that ideal.

NOTES

1   Café Feminino Foundation, http://www.coffeecan.org/our-work/peru.
2   Organic Products Trading Company, http://www.optco.com/cafe_
    femenino.htm.
3   Café Feminino Foundation, http://www.coffeecan.org/.
4   For a comprehensive description of Café Feminino, see J.J. McMurtry,
    "Ethical Value Added: Fair Trade and the Case of Café Feminino," *Journal
    of Business Ethics* 86.S1 (2009): 27–49, at 38–42.
5   Geoff Moore, "The Fair Trade Movement: Parameters, Issues and Future
    Research," *Journal of Business Ethics* 53.1/2 (2004): 27–49.
6   J.J. McMurtry, "Ethical Value-Added," 31–32.

DISCUSSION QUESTIONS

(1) Are voluntary transactions always fair? If not, what conditions must they
     satisfy in order to be fair?
(2) Assuming there's an obligation to benefit producers in the Global South,
     whose obligation is it? Is it a consumer obligation? A corporate obligation?
     A state obligation? A mixture of all three?
(3) Is Fair Trade the best feasible way for consumers to benefit producers in
     the Global South? What other options are available to them?
(4) Are current standards associated with the Fair Trade label high enough?
     What are the advantages and disadvantages of adopting higher standards?
(5) What lessons can we learn from the case of Café Feminino? Should
     Café Feminino be used as a model by other Fair Trade producers, or are
     the circumstances of different producers too dissimilar for any single
     approach to be generally applied?

FURTHER READINGS

Charles R. Beitz, *Political Theory and International Relations* (Princeton:
    Princeton University Press, 1979).
J.J. McMurtry, "Ethical Value-Added: Fair Trade and the Case of Café
    Feminino," *Journal of Business Ethics* 86.S1 (2009): 27–49.
Geoff Moore, "The Fair Trade Movement: Parameters, Issues and Future
    Research," *Journal of Business Ethics* 53.1/2 (2004): 73–86.
Thomas Pogge, *Realizing Rawls* (Ithaca: Cornell University Press, 1989).

Thomas Pogge, *World Poverty and Human Rights*, 2nd ed. (Malden: Polity Press, 2008).

John Rawls, *The Law of Peoples* (Cambridge, MA: Harvard University Press, 1999).

Eric St. Pierre, *Fair Trade: A Human Journey*, trans. Barbara Sandilands (Fredericton: Goose Lane Editions, 2012).

PART 3:
EMPLOYMENT
AND DIVERSITY

14. WANT THIS JOB? PROVIDE YOUR FACEBOOK USERNAME AND PASSWORD: THE CASES OF JUSTIN BASSETT AND ROBERT COLLINS

BRETT GAUL

BACKGROUND

DURING A 2012 JOB INTERVIEW, JUSTIN BASSETT, A NEW YORK CITY statistician, was asked to provide his Facebook username and password. While Bassett had expected to be asked the usual interview questions about his experience and references, he was taken aback by the unusual request to give the interviewer his Facebook login credentials. Rather than allow the interviewer to log into his account, Bassett refused to comply with the interviewer's request and withdrew his application.[1]

The case of Justin Bassett called attention to what had until then been a little-known practice. Prior to 2012 few people had heard of employers asking job applicants for their login credentials so that the employers could access a job applicant's private posts as part of a background check. The Bassett case was not the first of its kind, but because many people were unaware that some employers were asking job applicants for this information, the Bassett case circulated quickly on the Internet.

Some of the news stories about Bassett also referred to the case of Robert Collins, a Corrections Officer with the Maryland Department of Public Safety and Correctional Services. In 2010 Collins was returning to his job after he took a leave of absence following his mother's death. During a reinstatement interview, Collins was also asked for his Facebook login and password. "'I did not want to do it, but because I really needed my job and he [the interviewer] implied that this was a condition of recertification, I reluctantly gave him the password,'" Collins said.[2] When Collins asked the interviewer why he was logging on to his private account, he replied, "'I am looking through your messages, on your wall and in your photos to make sure you are not a gang member or have any gang affiliation.'"[3]

After his experience, Collins contacted the American Civil Liberties Union (ACLU) of Maryland. The ACLU of Maryland expressed concerns about the Division of Correction's requirement that job applicants and current employees seeking recertification provide their social media account usernames and passwords for background checks. In 2012 Maryland became the first state in the nation to prohibit employers from "requesting or requiring that an employee or applicant disclose any username, password, or other means for accessing a personal account or service through certain electronic communication devices" as a condition of employment.[4] Other states soon followed Maryland's lead and also outlawed this practice. According to the National Conference of State Legislatures, 25 states now have social media privacy laws that apply to employers.[5] Federal social media privacy bills have also been introduced in each United States Congress since 2012, but no bill gained enough support to become a law.[6]

ANALYSIS

THE CASES OF JUSTIN BASSETT AND ROBERT COLLINS RAISE SERIous privacy concerns. According to the Pew Research Center, as of 2017 almost 70 per cent of Americans use social media, up from 5 per cent in 2005.[7] Social media allows us to stay immediately connected with more people than at any previous time in human history. It also allows us to share personal thoughts, emotions, pictures, and information easily and instantly with those to whom we are connected. But is the information job applicants and employees post on social media—to use the words of George G. Brenkert—"job relevant"?[8] What right do employers have to view one's private social media activity on sites like Facebook? In states where asking for a job applicant's social media credentials has been outlawed, employers obviously have no legal right to make viewing a job applicant's private social media activity a condition of employment. But do employers have a moral right to view one's private social media activity? Even if employers have no such right, is it still prudent to ask for access to it anyway? To better understand this practice, it is helpful to consider it from the perspective of both employers and job applicants.

Employers may want to view a job applicant's social media activity because employing unethical people is ethically, legally, financially, and socially risky. Unethical employees can get employers in trouble with the law, cost them money in legal fees and lost business, and be bad for an employer's reputation. Brenkert argues that "the information to which the employer qua employer is entitled about the (prospective) employee is that information which regards his possible acceptable performance of the services for which he might be hired"—i.e., "job-relevant" information.[9] Conversely, employers qua employers are not entitled to know information that is not "job relevant."[10] However, Brenkert also argues that not only must a person have the ability to do a certain job, "but he must also be able to do it in an acceptable manner—i.e., in a manner which is approximately as efficient as others, in an honest manner, and in a manner compatible with others who seek to provide the services for which they were hired. Thus, not simply one's abilities to do a certain job are relevant, but also aspects of one's social and moral character are pertinent."[11] Employers may argue that viewing applicants' social media activity better enables them to determine applicants' abilities and character because social media activity provides evidence of who people really are. By viewing applicants' social media activity, employers may also see evidence of unethical or illegal activities that could lead them not to hire particular applicants and thus minimize risk. From an employer's perspective, then, where it is allowed by law, the practice of asking for a job applicant's social media credentials may be considered part of a thorough background check.

However, from the perspective of job applicants, the request to turn over their social media credentials may be viewed as a violation of privacy. According to Brenkert, "[t]o say that something is rightfully private is to say that A may withhold from or not share something, X, with Z. Thus to know whether some information, X, about a person or institution, A, is, or ought to be, treated as rightfully private, we must ask about the relationship in which A stands to Z, another person or institution."[12] Employers may be thought to have no moral right to access one's private social media accounts because social media activity is not "job relevant" and there is no relationship between the job applicant and the potential employer that justifies employer access to these accounts. Employers might like to know a great many things about their job applicants, but job applicants have the right to keep private information that is irrelevant to their ability to do the job. From this perspective, then, an employer's desire to know something does not outweigh a job applicant's interest in keeping certain kinds of information private.

Whether or not an employer asks job applicants for their private social media login credentials, many employers use publicly available webpages to screen applicants. According to a 2017 survey of more than 2,300 hiring managers and human resource professionals conducted by CareerBuilder, "70 percent of employers use social media to screen candidates before hiring, up significantly from 60 percent last year [2016] and 11 percent in 2006."[13] Additionally, 30 per cent of employers have personnel dedicated to researching candidates on social media.[14]

It is easy to focus on social media activity that employers might use as a reason *not* to hire a particular job applicant; however, the survey's results also indicate, perhaps surprisingly, that certain kinds of social media activity can actually *help* a candidate land a job. According to the survey's results, "more than 44 percent of employers have found content on a social networking site that caused them to hire the candidate. Among the primary reasons employers hired a candidate based on their social networking site were: candidate's background information supported their professional qualifications (38 percent), great communication skills (37 percent), a professional image (36 percent), and creativity (35 percent)."[15] However, even though 44 per cent of employers found social media content that led them to *hire* a candidate, a higher percentage of employers, 54 per cent, reported finding content on social media that led them *not* to hire a candidate.[16] Key content that counted against a candidate included:

- Provocative or inappropriate photographs, videos or information (39 percent).
- Information about them drinking or using drugs (38 percent).
- Discriminatory comments related to race, gender or religion (32 percent).
- Bad-mouthing their previous company or fellow employee (30 percent).

- Lies about qualifications (27 percent).
- Poor communication skills (27 percent).
- Criminal behavior (26 percent).
- Sharing confidential information from previous employers (23 percent).
- Unprofessional screen name (22 percent).
- Lies about an absence (17 percent).
- Posting too frequently (17 percent).[17]

According to the CareerBuilder survey, in addition to using social media sites, 69 per cent of employers are also using online search engines to research candidates.[18] Key content employers search for includes "information that supports their qualifications for the job (61 percent), if the candidate has a professional online persona (50 percent), what other people are posting about the candidates (37 percent) and for a reason not to hire a candidate (24 percent)."[19]

Even though viewing candidates' public and private social media activity and using online search engines can provide employers with useful information about candidates, using these tools can also be risky for employers themselves. For example, employers may learn details about applicants such as their age, race, national origin, color, religion, and whether they are disabled or pregnant. Under federal law, such details are protected and legally cannot be used in making hiring decisions. According to employment attorney Doug Hass, "'Once an employer knows this information, it can't unlearn it, and it can be accused of making a hiring decision based on that information.'"[20] For this reason, hiring managers must use social media and search engine results very carefully.

Employees must also use social media very carefully. Because many employees are at-will employees who can be fired at any time for any legal reason, they can easily be fired for social media activity that violates their employers' standards or that their employers find objectionable. But what about these employees' First Amendment right to freedom of speech? Generally speaking, the First Amendment right to freedom of speech means that people have the right to express themselves without fear of government interference or punishment. Put another way, just because employees have freedom of speech, that does not mean that their private sector employers cannot fire them for their speech. Freedom of speech protects individuals from consequences from the government; it does not protect them from consequences from their employers.

News stories of employees being fired for their social media usage are not unusual. For example, in June 2016, Christine McMullen Lindgren, a Bank of America employee in Atlanta, Georgia, was fired after posting racist remarks on Facebook.[21] More recently, in October 2017, CBS fired Hayley Geftman-Gold, a vice president and senior legal counsel at CBS in New York, for insensitive comments she posted on Facebook after a deadly mass shooting in Las Vegas, Nevada. Geftman-Gold wrote, "If they wouldn't do anything when children were murdered I have no hope that Repugs will ever do the right thing. I'm actually not even sympathetic bc country music fans often are Republican gun toters."[22] Although Geftman-Gold deleted and apologized for what she herself called an "indefensible post," those 35 words on Facebook had quickly damaged her career.[23]

For better or for worse, social media usage seems here to stay. Given its pervasiveness, employers will continue to be interested in viewing the social media activity of both job applicants and employees. For job applicants, employees, and employers, though, social media has the potential to help and the potential to harm. In the years since Robert Collins was asked to provide his Facebook credentials to keep his job with the Maryland Department of Public Safety and Correctional Services, it has been states, not the federal government, that have taken the lead in delineating social media user's legal rights to privacy. Twenty-five states have enacted social media privacy laws that prohibit employers from making access to private social media accounts a condition of employment. This is significant because outside of federally protected class status, laws in certain states which protect employees from retaliation for expressing their political views, and protections granted by the National Labor Relations Act which preserve the rights of employees to conduct conversations about the terms and conditions of their employment, employees—especially at-will employees—seem to have little legal protection from losing their jobs due to social media activity that employers find objectionable. In short, those who use social media do so at their own risk.

NOTES

1   Doug Gross, "ACLU: Facebook Password Isn't Your Boss' Business," *CNN* (March 22, 2012).

2   Ibid.

3   Ibid.

4   2012 Regular Session—Chapter 23 (Senate Bill 433) (2012).

5   National Conference of State Legislators, "State Social Media Privacy Laws" (May 5, 2017).

6   In 2012, during the 112th Congress, H.R. 5684, the Password Protection Act of 2012, failed to become a law. In 2013, during the 113th Congress, H.R. 2077, the Password Protection Act of 2013, failed to become a law. In 2015, during the 114th Congress, H.R. 2277, the Password Protection Act of 2015, failed to become a law. See https://www.govtrack.us/.

7   Pew Research Center, "Social Media Fact Sheet" (2017).

8   See George Brenkert, "Privacy, Polygraphs and Work," *Business and Professional Ethics Journal* 1 (1981): 19–35. The expression first appears on p. 24. Although Brenkert wrote this piece well before the advent of social media, his insights into employee privacy are still relevant.

9   Ibid., 24.

10   Ibid., 25.

11   Ibid.

12   Ibid., 23.

13   "Number of Employers Using Social Media to Screen Candidates at All-Time High, Finds Latest CareerBuilder Study," CISION PR Newswire (2017).

14   Lauren Salm, "70% of Employers Are Snooping Candidates' Social Media Profiles," CareerBuilder (June 15, 2017).

15   Ibid.

16   Ibid.

17   Ibid.

18   Ibid.

19   CISION PR Newswire, "Number of Employers Using Social Media to Screen Candidates at All-Time High, Finds Latest CareerBuilder Study."

20   Alexia Elejalde-Ruiz, "Using Social Media to Disqualify Job Candidates Is Risky," *Chicago Tribune* (January 11, 2016).

21   Ernie Suggs, "Bank of America Fires Employee over Racist Facebook Rant," *The Atlanta Journal-Constitution* (2016).

22   Brian Flood, "CBS Fires Vice President Who Said Vegas Victims Didn't Deserve Sympathy Because Country Music Fans 'Often Are Republican,'" *Fox News* (October 2, 2017).

23   Ibid.

DISCUSSION QUESTIONS

(1) Do you think a person's social media posts are "job relevant"? Why or why not?

(2) If during a job interview a hiring manager asked you for your Facebook username and password, would you provide them? Why or why not?

(3) From an employer's perspective, what are the advantages of viewing the social media activity of job applicants? What are the disadvantages?

(4) If you were responsible for hiring employees, would you ask for applicants' social media login credentials if the law in your state or province permitted it? Why or why not?

(5) What are the differences between not hiring job applicants because they refused to provide social media login information and firing employees because of their social media posts?

FURTHER READINGS

John F. Buckley IV, "Federal, State Legislation Banning Employer Requests for Social Media Information," *The Employment Lawyer Blog* (2016).

John R. Drake, "Asking for Facebook Logins: An Egoist Case for Privacy," *Journal of Business Ethics* 139.3 (2016): 429–41.

Kashmir Hill, "Why We Need a 'Password Protection' Act against Employers," *Forbes* (May 9, 2012).

Gray Mateo-Harris, "Politics in the Workplace: A State-by-State Guide," *Society for Human Resource Management* (2016).

David Matheson, "Unknowableness and Informational Privacy," *Journal of Philosophical Research* 32 (2007): 251–67.

National Conference of State Legislators, "Access to Social Media Usernames and Passwords," National Conference of State Legislators (2017).

Jonathan A. Segal, "Social Media Use in Hiring: Assessing the Risks," *Society for Human Resource Management* (2014).

15.

PROFESSIONAL MISCONDUCT WHILE OFF-DUTY

LUKE GOLEMON

BACKGROUND

CAROLYN STROM'S GRANDFATHER DIED IN JANUARY OF 2015 AFTER receiving palliative care from St. Joseph's Health Facility in Macklin, Saskatchewan. Strom, a registered nurse, took to Facebook and Twitter to decry what she took to be inadequate care at the facility in February of 2015:

> My grandfather spent a week in palliative care before he died and after hearing about his and my family's experience there, it is evident that not everyone is 'up to speed' on how to approach end of life care or how to help maintain an ageing senior's dignity. I challenge the people involved in decision making with that facility to please get all your staff a refresher on this topic and more. Don't get me wrong, 'some' people have provided excellent care so I thank you so very much for your efforts, but to those who made Grandpa's last years

less than desirable, please do better next time.... As an RN [registered nurse] and avid health care advocate myself, I just have to speak up. Whatever reasons/excuses people give for not giving quality of life care, I do not care. It just needs to be fixed.[1]

Although Strom did not work at the facility herself, members of the St. Joseph's Health Facility staff saw the post and felt shamed and attacked. Strom's status as an RN came up later during discussion of the post, and the Saskatchewan Registered Nurses Association (SRNA) was notified of the social media comments via a formal complaint, alleging professional misconduct.

After investigation, the SRNA concluded Strom was guilty of professional misconduct. They note the lack of outreach to the staff at the facility prior to the social media post as a key part of their decision: "Ms. Strom engaged in a generalized public venting about the facility and its staff and went straight to social media to do that."[2] Even though Strom stated she was venting from the perspective of an aggrieved granddaughter, the SRNA maintained she had overstepped the boundaries of what is acceptable for a registered nurse to say regarding her fellow nurses. The SRNA also concluded that while Strom was guilty of professional misconduct, her misconduct was not in any way malicious; she really was being sincere in attempting to improve the state of medical care at St. Joseph's Health Facility and healthcare for elderly persons more broadly. This appeared to factor into how harsh the penalty the SRNA decided to levy on Strom.

Strom appealed her verdict, but the judge dismissed the case. The costs of the case, including the appeal proceedings, were enormous: over $150,000. Strom's penalty was a $1,000 fine and one-sixth of the cost of the court proceedings—which added up to $26,000. A GoFundMe campaign set up by sympathizers raised $27,000 to cover her fine.[3]

ANALYSIS

STROM'S GUILTY VERDICT CAUSED SIGNIFICANT OUTCRY. MANY objected the punishment was excessive; $26,000 was an exorbitant fine for such a small infraction. Others did not see it as an infraction at all. Still others thought the first instance of holding someone accountable for activities ruled unethical after the fact can be controversial, but needs to be done. Broadly, there appear to be two issues at stake here. First, should the SRNA have sanctioned Strom? Second, were Strom's actions unethical in any way? Consider the former issue first.

Many have defended Strom from the SRNA's sanction on freedom of expression grounds, but freedom of expression usually concerns itself with interactions between the government and its citizens, not private entities and their interactions in the private sphere. Still, the moral principles undergirding freedom of expression carry some weight here. Worse cases have received leniency regarding freedom of expression in the past. To give one example, Bill Whatcott, a practical nurse, picketed Planned Parenthood clinics in Regina in 2002 and 2003. Although he was found guilty of professional misconduct, he won his appeal on the grounds of freedom of expression.[4] Because he situated his protest as a dutiful citizen rather than as a nurse, his appeal succeeded. It is unclear if this should hold for Strom. She did mention her credentials as a registered nurse, but did not try to situate herself as a nurse at St. Joseph's nor as a headline to tag the post as being from the perspective of a nurse rather than a granddaughter.

The SRNA assumed Strom's duties as a nurse in this case did extend to her comments on Facebook. Even if we agree with the SRNA on this point, it does not resolve the ethical issues. One serious concern is the inconsistency of the decision with two of the American Nursing Association's provisions in their code of ethics.

Provision three of the American Nursing Association's code of ethics states that "[t]he nurse promotes, advocates for, and protects the rights, health, and safety of the patient."[5] A nurse owes her clients—patients—a certain protection and advocacy. When on duty, for example, nurses *must* speak up on behalf of their patients if the system, visitors, circumstances, or even other medical professionals are endangering or are not properly caring for the patient in some way. Even when a medical professional is not working as such, their increased medical knowledge comes with an increase in obligations. For example, when a medical emergency occurs near an off-duty medical professional, she is often the best qualified among the bystanders to provide medical care; therefore, she ought to provide the emergency medical care over the other bystanders.[6]

As grounds for further concern, provision six states "[t]he nurse, through individual and collective effort, establishes, maintains, and improves the ethical environment of the work setting and conditions of employment that are conducive to safe, quality health care."[7] By the

SRNA's own principles, they appear to be committed to the permissibility of Strom's post if she was striving to improve the conditions of St. Joseph's workplace and attempting to protect and promote the rights and health of patients there. If anyone has the expertise to criticize these institutions, surely it is medical professionals. If this is right, then stifling Strom's speech by finding her guilty of professional misconduct violates ethical principles that all nurses should accept. Medical institutions certainly should not stand in the way of nurses fulfilling their ethical duty. Therefore, if Strom's post was within the realm of appropriately improving the quality of care for her clients (broadly construed), then she should not be found guilty of professional misconduct.

In response to the two concerns above, the SRNA can point out that Strom was not employed at St. Joseph's and therefore is unlikely to know details integral to improving the environment for patients. Considering she did not give specific recommendations for St. Joseph or its staff to follow, it is difficult to see how she is concretely improving the patients' environment there. Additionally, Strom may have hurt the environment of St. Joseph's by airing her grievances publicly first, rather than working with the staff at the facility.[8] Prospective patients might feel uncomfortable about going to St. Joseph's or stop going to St. Joseph's altogether. Especially considering the gravitas Strom lent her post by mentioning her medical credentials, those who read the post might seriously consider getting their healthcare elsewhere. Although these concerns appear to be strong enough to show Strom should have thought more about what she was going to do and perhaps pursue other alternatives, it is less clear if Strom should be found guilty of professional misconduct.

The above issues assume Strom was acting in the role of a registered nurse, but this too is contentious. Although she mentioned her role as a nurse, she neither worked at the facility nor did she engage in the sort of feedback a nurse would give if she had worked at the facility. The post itself was inspired by grief at the death of her grandfather, and many have complaints about how their elders' healthcare has been managed. Airing these sorts of complaints publicly may be neither nice nor fair, but it does not seem like professional misconduct. If Strom was playing *that* role, then accusations of professional misconduct miss completely. Nevertheless, concerns about how easily a professional can don and doff the role of their profession muddy the waters. Just because I do not intend for others to see me as a professional does not guarantee others will in fact see me as renouncing my role.

However, as noted before, medical professionals (and other professionals as well) receive additional duties in the course of receiving their training and knowledge, duties that extend beyond when and where one is employed or on-duty. If a certain sort of respect for fellow medical professionals is one of these duties, then Strom does seem to have done something wrong. It is possible, however, that the SRNA should not have sanctioned her and yet Strom is still blameworthy; the two issues appear somewhat independent.

NOTES

1 Victoria Dinh, "Facebook Post Leaves Prince Albert, Sask., Nurse Charged with Professional Misconduct," *CBC* (January 12, 2016).
2 "Nurse Who 'Vented' Online Found Guilty of Professional Misconduct," *CBC News* (December 3, 2016).
3 Ashley Martin, "Prosecution Draws Parallel between Registered Nurse Carolyn Strom's Case and Bill Whatcott's in Disciplinary Hearing," *Regina Leader-Post* (March 4, 2016).
4 Ibid.
5 American Nurses Association, "Code of Ethics with Interpretative Statements" (2015).
6 Ibid. One can also see this in the SRNA's "Standards and Foundations" statement, under "Standard IV: Service to the Public." Saskatchewan Registered Nurses Association, "Standards and Foundations" (2013).
7 Ibid.
8 While the SRNA now has guidelines developed from this case, at the time of the incident the guidelines only referred to one's own workplace.

DISCUSSION QUESTIONS

(1) Professionals certainly have obligations toward their clients, but do they also owe potential or ostensive clients (such as the patients of a medical facility where one does not work) anything beyond the norm?
(2) Should client-based professions require a certain code of conduct even when their members are not "on-duty"? Should it preclude them from conduct that would otherwise be appropriate?
(3) Do client-based professionals have a "whistle-blower" obligation?
(4) Is this obligation circumscribed in any way, such as by working within the system first?

(5) Medical professionals are not legally required to give aid while off-duty, ostensibly because they are not in the role of a medical professional at that time. What might we say about such roles on social media, where one's credentials are almost always visible on one's profile?

FURTHER READINGS

A. Firtko and D. Jackson, "Do the Ends Justify the Means? Nursing and the Dilemma of Whistleblowing," *Australian Journal of Advanced Nursing* 23.1 (2005): 51–56.

Pamela Grace, *Nursing Ethics and Professional Responsibility in Advanced Practice*, 3rd ed. (Sudbury, MA: Jones and Bartlett, 2018).

M. Johnstone, "Patient Safety, Ethics and Whistleblowing: A Nursing Response to the Events at the Campbelltown and Camden Hospitals," *Australian Health Review* 28.1 (2004): 13–19.

Daryl Koehn, *The Ground of Professional Ethics* (New York: Routledge, 2006).

S. Mansfield, et al., "Social Media and the Medical Profession," *The Medical Journal of Australia* 194.12 (2011): 642–44.

16

OBLIGATIONS, RESPONSIBILITY, AND WHISTLEBLOWING: A CASE STUDY OF JEFFREY WIGAND

BRIAN J. COLLINS

BACKGROUND

JEFFREY WIGAND IS ONE OF THE MOST FAMOUS "WHISTLEBLOWERS" in American history due to the portrayal of his story in the 1999 film *The Insider*. The film, starring Russell Crowe as Wigand and Al Pacino as CBS *60 Minutes* producer Lowell Bergman, details Wigand's struggle as he decides whether or not he will break his confidentiality agreement with former employer Brown & Williamson and expose the tobacco company's disturbing secrets.

The term "whistleblower" originates from a nineteenth-century British expression referring to the practice of unarmed police and merchants blowing an actual whistle to alert bystanders of crimes such as pickpocketing and shoplifting. When the expression "blowing the whistle" emerged in the American vernacular in the early twentieth century it had transformed slightly, now conjuring up an image of a referee putting an end to a match or stopping play to call a penalty. Though the expression simply meant to put a stop to something, it now carried with it a strong negative connotation that was used to brand individuals as "snitches" who "squealed" to authorities. However, beginning in the 1960s a young attorney and consumer advocate, Ralph Nader, helped to rehabilitate the word "whistleblower" back to its morally praiseworthy associations. Advocating for consumers and workers, Nader called for civic-minded "whistleblowers" in the government and private sectors to do their part by reporting fraud and generally poor policy and oversight. Nader's work, and the whistleblowers who stepped forward, helped lead to many consumer-protections laws such as the National Traffic and Motor Vehicle Safety Act (1966), which set new safety standards for vehicles and roadways, and the Wholesome Meat Act (1967), which set new regulations for the inspection of slaughterhouses and meat packing facilities.[1]

In 1970 the Occupational Safety and Health Act (OSH) was passed into law by Congress to act as whistleblower protection. It prohibits "employers from discriminating against their employees for exercising their rights under the OSH Act. These rights include filing an OSHA [Occupational Safety and Health Administration] complaint, participating in an inspection or talking to any inspector, seeking access to employer exposure and injury records, reporting an injury, and raising a safety or health complaint with the employer."[2] Legally, a whistleblower is anyone who reports illegal or unsafe activities or conditions within a business or organization.

This brings us back to the case of Jeffrey Wigand and Brown & Williamson. After completing his BA, MA, and PhD in biochemistry, Wigand began a career in the healthcare industry. For 17 years he worked in various roles for several healthcare companies such as Pfizer, Johnson & Johnson, and Biosonics. Then in 1989, somewhat surprisingly, Wigand accepted a lucrative offer from the tobacco company Brown & Williamson (B&W) (owned by British American Tobacco–BAT Industries). He was named the head of Research & Development to lead the department with an annual budget of $30 million and a staff of 243. Almost immediately there was tension between Wigand and his colleagues, as he felt that the level of testing and research was not up to par. Additionally, Wigand quickly began to feel that his scientific concerns over certain additives being used in the manufacturing process of tobacco products and his ethical concerns about marketing tobacco products to teenagers were not being taken seriously by company executives. Finally, after four years of increasing tension and disagreement, Wigand was fired on March 24,1993.

In order to keep his severance package, including medical benefits for his family, Wigand reluctantly signed a comprehensive lifelong confidentiality agreement with B&W that would forbid him from discussing *anything* about the company. However, in February of 1994 Wigand was sought out by Lowell Bergman, a producer at CBS's *60 Minutes*, to analyze some documents Bergman had obtained concerning Philip Morris (a competitor of B&W). This would be the beginning of a relationship that would eventually lead to Wigand breaking his confidentiality agreement and coming forward publicly as a whistleblower against B&W and the tobacco industry. Before coming forward publicly, Wigand worked privately (with his identity protected) with the Food and Drug Administration advising them on cigarette chemistry and some of the dangerous chemical additives. While Wigand remained hesitant to share everything he knew for fear of being sued by B&W and losing his family's medical benefits (on which one of his daughters depended to cover her medical expenses associated with spina bifida), he began to work with Bergman and *60 Minutes*. Then on November 29, 1995, Wigand gave a deposition in a case the state of Mississippi brought against the tobacco companies. Portions of this testimony were eventually published in *The Wall Street Journal* and on February 4, 1996, CBS finally aired the story and interview with Wigand. In these acts of whistleblowing, Wigand contended that B&W manipulated the nicotine and chemical additives in cigarettes, lied about their knowledge of the addictiveness of cigarettes, and failed to work towards developing "safer" cigarettes.

Wigand's decision to blow the whistle on B&W and the tobacco industry did not come without personal cost. In dealing with the pressure and stress, Wigand struggled personally with drinking, legal problems, and divorce. B&W engaged in a brutal smear campaign against Wigand and he received several death threats and faced other forms of intimidation severe enough to require a full-time bodyguard to help ensure his safety. Ultimately though, his actions helped lead to the Master Settlement Agreement (1998) between the four largest tobacco companies and 46 states. In this settlement the tobacco companies agreed to change marketing practices and pay over $200 billion dollars to help compensate for state-funded medical costs associated with smoking-related diseases.

ANALYSIS

WE NOW KNOW THAT CIGARETTES ARE ADDICTIVE AND DANGEROUS to health. Jeffrey Wigand helped bring these facts, and the tobacco companies' suppression of this information, into the open. This high-profile case is valuable because it provides a sort of arena where we can test and examine our concepts. We can use this case to frame questions about whistleblowing. For example: When is it morally *permissible* for someone to blow the whistle? When is it morally *required*? What is one supposed to do when other moral obligations are in conflict with whistleblowing (e.g., one's contractual obligations)?

One useful way of beginning to address these questions is to use Richard T. De George's well-known analysis of the morality of whistleblowing. De George offers five conditions that help determine when and under what conditions employees should blow the whistle. The first three of De George's conditions attempt to specify when the act of whistleblowing is morally justifiable and *permissible*.

Following Michael W. Hoffman and Mark Schwartz, we will call the first condition the "Harm Principle."[3] It states that the company, through its product or policy, must be doing or risking serious and considerable harm to employees or to the public. How does Wigand's case fare in relation to this first criterion? Brown & Williamson was aware of the harmful effects of smoking and knew that the nicotine in its cigarettes was addictive; they were manipulating the nicotine levels and other chemical additives in the tobacco for exactly these reasons. These circumstances appear to meet De George's "Harm Principle" perfectly. B&W products *and* policies were doing serious harm to people and, by covering up the information they had about addictiveness and the negative health effects of smoking, threatening even a greater number of people. So Wigand's case meets the first of De George's criteria for his act of whistleblowing to be morally justified and permissible.

De George's second and third conditions are closely related to one another; we'll call them the "Internal Reporting Principles." They state that once the serious harm or threat has been identified it must first be reported to an immediate superior. If the immediate superior does not effectively address the concern, then one can take the concern up the managerial ladder. De George contends that if these first three conditions are met, the act of whistleblowing is morally justified and permissible. In the case of Wigand and B&W, Wigand did report his findings to his superiors and attempted to move up the corporate chain when he was not satisfied with the responses he was receiving. Consequently, Wigand meets the first three of De George's criteria, thereby classifying his act of whistleblowing as morally justified and permissible. However, these criteria do not seem to take into account the fact that Wigand signed a contract that forfeited his right to speak publicly about information he had concerning B&W.

De George stresses that simply because an action is *morally permissible* does not mean that we must perform it. After all, whistleblowers face significant costs that need to be considered. De George offers two additional criteria that strengthen the moral status of whistleblowing from being merely permissible to being morally *obligatory*. We will call his fourth condition the "Evidentiary Principle." It states that the whistleblower must have documented evidence of the serious harm or threat that would convince a reasonable and impartial observer. This condition is offered with the idea that one need not come forward publicly without substantial evidence because without such support the individual would be taking a significant personal risk without a reasonable expectation that any advantage will be gained (i.e., that the harm or threat will be remedied). In Wigand's case he had documented scientific evidence that the nicotine in cigarettes was addictive and that the chemical additives being incorporated into the tobacco products had potential long-term health effects. In addition, Wigand had some evidence that the executives of B&W knew these things and were ignoring or even suppressing this information. However, given the money and power of the tobacco company and the circumstances of Wigand's daughter's medical condition, it is not immediately clear that the personal risk was outweighed by the chance of success. B&W did not have an explicit anti-retaliation policy and Wigand correctly feared that he would be met with hostility and backlash from his employer. Additionally, B&W was willing and able to threaten massive lawsuits against any media outlet showing even signs that they were considering investigating the story.

These questions concerning cost/benefit analysis relate to De George's fifth condition, which we will call the "Make a Difference Principle." This last criterion states that the individual must have good reason to think the chances that the whistleblowing will succeed in stopping the serious harm or threat outweigh the risk one takes in going public. Given the monetary resources and power of B&W, it does not seem immediately clear that Wigand's personal risk was outweighed by a reasonable expectation that any advantage would be gained. If Wigand's case meets De George's first three criteria but does not meet the fourth and/or fifth, then De George's analysis would be that whistleblowing would be morally justified and permissible but *not* something that Wigand was morally obligated to do.

NOTES

1   Ben Zimmer, "The Epithet Nader Made Respectable," *The Wall Street Journal* (July 12, 2013).
2   "The Whistleblower Protections Programs," United States Department of Labor (2015).
3   Michael W. Hoffman and Mark S. Schwartz, "The Morality of Whistleblowing: A Commentary on Richard T. De George," *Journal of Business Ethics* (2014): 771–81.

DISCUSSION QUESTIONS

(1)   If Wigand had not come forward, would he be morally responsible for future individuals addicted to and getting sick and dying from cigarette use?

(2)   How strong are contractual obligations? What are some examples when it would be morally permissible to break one's contract? What are some examples of when it would be morally impermissible to break one's contract?

(3)   Many people intuitively believe that employees ought to be loyal to their employers. Why do you think an obligation of loyalty might exist for an employee?

(4)   How much moral responsibility do the media have for making sure that morally justified acts of whistleblowing succeed in stopping the harm or threat?

(5)   Should the moral permissibility of whistleblowing depend on the motivations of the individual blowing the whistle? Do one's motivations affect the moral praiseworthiness of whistleblowing? What, if any, difference is there between moral permissibility, praiseworthiness, and obligation?

FURTHER READINGS

Marie Brenner, "The Man Who Knew Too Much," *Vanity Fair* (1996).

Michael W. Hoffman and Mark S. Schwartz, "The Morality of Whistle-blowing: A Commentary on Richard T. De George," *Journal of Business Ethics* (2014): 771–81.

17.

WHO JUDGES WHOM: THE ETHICS OF PERFORMANCE REVIEWS

MICHAEL KLENK

BACKGROUND

I WAS WORKING AS A MANAGEMENT CONSULTANT AT AN INTER-national business consulting firm for little more than a year when I heard that I might be in line for a promotion: the managing board had approved my manager's proposal to put me through the evaluation process. In that firm, as in many others today, performance appraisals are based on so-called 360-degree feedback (a form of multisource feedback). A senior manager in the firm was appointed as a facilitator to collect job performance evaluations based on questionnaires supplemented by interviews from my peers (those at the same organizational level), subordinates, superiors, clients, and myself, and to compile a performance report. I had a week to name three peers, two superiors, two clients, and two subordinates whom my facilitator would interview for about 20 minutes each. Interviewees were asked to report my strengths and weaknesses as a consultant and to assess my potential. Naturally, I nominated those I expected to provide positive feedback about me. Based on the interviews and questionnaires, the facilitator prepared a recommendation for the managing board, which would review all promotion reports and make a decision. The whole process took three months.

The 360-degree feedback process put me in a predicament. I had planned a career change from consulting to academia and was waiting for the outcomes of several open applications for doctoral positions. It was clear to me that, if I got a doctoral position, I would leave the firm shortly after a possible promotion. However, I did not dare to reveal this information to any of my colleagues because of the facilitation process. My gut feeling, bolstered by what I heard through the grapevine, was that the performance review would be handled with a view to my prospects of staying with the firm, rather than just past performance. I was also not sure how some of my colleagues and clients would think of my planned career move and whether it would negatively affect their ratings of me if I told them. There had been stories about personal grudges affecting people's behavior in the feedback process, and since I would only learn about the content of the feedback but not who gave it, I felt that extra care was needed in dealing with my colleagues, as anything could potentially affect their rating of me. Moreover, I knew that the managing board's debate about promotions would partly be a political matter: with only a limited number of possible promotions per job level (due to managerial and financial constraints), managers would negotiate with one another whether one of "their" employees would get the promotion if there were fewer spots than people eligible for a promotion. Proposing me for a promotion was politically risky for my manager to begin with (he would, perhaps, have to wait in line during the next promotion round) and the prospect of me leaving would very probably have discouraged him for standing up for me in the first place. So, I feared that revealing my (still tentative) career plans would harm my chances of being promoted.

For these reasons, I did not mention my changed career goals to anyone in the firm and also left my clients in the dark about my plans for the future. Eventually, the outcome of my facilitation process was positive, and I was promoted. Shortly after that, I also received an offer for a doctoral position and, two months after my promotion, I handed in my resignation.

The facilitation process also had an impact on my colleagues. Some felt the weight of their decision, which they knew would influence an outcome that was of significant financial and personal relevance to me.

Hence they suggested points of improvement privately to me but presented only positive points in the interview to increase my chances of getting the promotion. Others expected to be in line for promotion themselves soon, and so they wanted to be on good terms with me as they planned to nominate me as their peer-interviewee. Then there were those who may have been less favorably inclined, but I managed to steer clear of them in nominating my interviewees. I also knew that some colleagues hoped that I would stay with the company and on that basis gave positive feedback—the fact that I resigned shortly after the promotion, against the impression that I made during the interview, was a test not only of our professional but also our personal relationships.

More and more employees are set to face similar choices about what to reveal and what not to reveal, both as recipients and providers of performance appraisals, as 360-degree feedback as a means of performance appraisal is increasingly being used in organizational settings. Bracken, Timmreck, and Church estimate that up to 80 per cent of companies are using a form of multisource feedback today. Three primary reasons account for this trend. First, 360-degree feedback often accompanies the democratization and hierarchical flattening of organizations. Organizations that were once formed of formal and rigid hierarchies are slowly becoming democratic, flat, and open workplaces. Second, 360-degree feedback is thought to alleviate the problems that single-rater appraisal (where only one person assesses the employee, usually the manager) has with low rating objectivity and the resulting problems of low effectivity, discrimination, and fairness.[1] Third, "soft" criteria, such as innovativeness, seem increasingly relevant to assess job performance in many modern professions. For example, there are few objective criteria to measure the contribution of an individual consultant to a project's success and a consultant's performance may seem to be determined, at least in part, by the satisfaction of a client and one's supportiveness in a team. 360-degree feedback promises to capture these subjective criteria better than single-rater feedback.

ANALYSIS

THE CASE RAISES ETHICAL QUESTIONS, SOME OF WHICH ARISE IN all methods of performance appraisal and some of which are peculiar to performance appraisals based on 360-degree feedback. It will be helpful to begin the discussion with some observations about the ethics of performance appraisals in general and then to narrow down to the peculiarities of 360-degree feedback.

What should employers be looking at when making decisions about promotion and continued employment? A prevailing view is that it is fair to reward employees according to their performance on the job. Often, "performance" is understood in terms of (quantifiable) results, such as sales generated, or wedges produced, and it is assumed that employees have an equal opportunity to perform well according to the chosen measure. However, several considerations count against the view that objective, quantifiable criteria are a sufficient basis for making decisions about promotion and employment. First, quantifiable results do not exhaust performance in many jobs (particularly professional or managerial work). For example, in consulting, sales generated or utilization rate (the hours billed to a client divided by one's contract hours) are only part of the picture of a consultant's performance; subjective criteria such as supportiveness or innovativeness are relevant, too. Second, some people or groups of people might be at a systematic disadvantage in performing against a certain measure. Apart from complex issues to do with distributive justice, simple practical considerations indicate that equal opportunities to achieve quantifiable targets are sometimes missing. For instance, junior consultants do not fully control their utilization rate, as staffing depends on senior managers. Thus, companies might be morally required to look for more subjective, less quantifiable goals in measuring performance. Indeed, the rationale behind including interviews, rather than just questionnaires, in some 360-degree appraisals is precisely to gain information about softer criteria, too. With softer criteria, however, comes greater ambiguity and subjectivity in assessing a candidate's performance.

Can performance appraisals based on subjective criteria be fair? As Heilman and Haynes show, subjectivity in evaluating job performance opens the door for ambiguity and ultimately discrimination, inequality, and unfairness. For example, to be perceived as doing well in an area that is outside of one's gender stereotype (e.g., for a woman to be regarded as innovative) sometimes requires more effort and better results compared to a non-negatively stereotyped person. Rating distortions along these lines have long been documented in different performance appraisal methods. Discrimination based on demographic attributes such as age, race, or gender is without a doubt a serious legal and ethical issue for companies and they have a moral obligation to avoid it. Apart from discriminatory ratings, other causes curb the objectivity of performance ratings and thus make them unfair. The case illustrates—and research bears this out—that interviewees inflate ratings, restrict the range of ratings that they provide, or let global impressions of a person influence ratings on specific performance dimensions. Again, tying important outcomes such as a promotion or continued employment to such inaccurate methods seems arbitrary and unfair.

360-degree feedback has been hailed explicitly as a way to overcome inaccurate ratings. Indeed, as Bernadin and Tyler note, several lawsuits related to discrimination in performance appraisals lead to companies being ordered to replace single-rater methods with multisource methods on the assumption that this would increase the objectivity of the ratings. Thus, one should expect that 360-degree feedback offers not only a methodologically but also ethically preferable alternative.

Does 360-degree feedback deliver the promised advantages over single-rater systems when it comes to objectivity and thus fairness? There are reasons to be skeptical. While a conclusive assessment would be premature, there is considerable evidence that rating-objectivity is low for professional or managerial jobs, where performance is not well defined (as in the case above). As Sillup and Klimberg note, guidelines about how to interpret job performance criteria and training for the interviewees are required to ensure sufficient objectivity, but guidelines are often missing in practice. This leads to a more fundamental question.

What, if anything, justifies the use of performance appraisals in the first place? Banner and Cooke argue that employers can be justified in using performance appraisals on the grounds that performance appraisals yield economic benefit and help individuals to reach their own goals, but only if the performance appraisal is objective. However, given the problems with objectivity in the case of 360-degree feedback, the very justification of using the method is in question. In addition to unintentional rating distortions (biases such as gender bias or the tendency to rate people higher), there are intentional rating distortions, too. Intentional rating distortions occur when someone willfully rates higher or lower than what he or she perceives the correct rating to be, and they raise further ethical questions, which we will address below.

Perhaps performance appraisals are justified not because they accurately measure performance but because they help managers in leading the company. Indeed, managers often consider performance appraisals not (primarily) as a means to accurately measure performance but to pursue strategic goals (such as keeping people happy, managing people out, etc.). For example, according to former General Electric CEO Jack Welch, his company used performance appraisals to "cull" people ranked at the bottom relative to others, irrespective of their absolute performance.[2] Similarly, the managing board's final say on promotion decisions in the case above suggests that performance appraisals are a management tool and Longenecker and Ludwig provide compelling empirical data that managers often use feedback to pursue ulterior aims (such as keeping the team happy). They claim that this partly justifies the use of performance appraisals in a company—but only as a development tool, not a tool for making promotion and employment relevant decisions.

What kind of ethical problems does a company create for its employees by introducing 360-degree feedback? It seems that raters are dishonest when they intentionally distort their ratings (e.g., to dish out a favor), so is this a bad thing? Not all business ethicists view dishonesty in business as a problem. Albert Carr defends the permissibility of lying in business based on the argument that the only moral rule in business is the law. Like players in a game of poker, they do and should stick to the rules but strive to take advantage of other businesspeople by any legal means possible, suggesting that behavior that everyone expects is legitimate. Fritz Allhoff provides an argument in favor of the moral permissibility of bluffing. He argues that bluffing might be morally permissible for specific roles insofar as all involved parties rationally endorse bluffing, where "rationality" is understood as utility maximizing. For example, it might be permissible to bluff as an interviewee, but it would be impermissible to bluff in dealings with the facilitator outside of the facilitation process.

Irrespective of the soundness of these arguments, it is doubtful that they would legitimize lying or bluffing in the case of 360-degree feedback. First, it is not clear what the norms are about truth-telling in 360-degree feedback processes. For example, do colleagues in the "facilitation" game expect others to lie or bluff to them once they accept the role as a rater? Colleagues and clients in the 360-degree feedback probably do not expect the evaluated person to lie in normal business circumstances, so why would they change their expectations in an evaluation context? At the very least, the novelty of 360-degree feedback and the fact that it is deemed to be an instrument to measure performance objectively creates a moral hazard for people who mistake the rule that holds for 360-degree feedback in their company. Second, it is unclear which role(s) an employee has in a 360-degree process. Perhaps one need not tell the truth to one's colleagues insofar as they are one's raters (given that this might have strong adversarial effects on oneself), but with 360-degree feedback, every colleague might at some point become a rater. Does the role-change change whether colleagues should be truthful with each other? It is also doubtful that bluffing in the review process could be rationally endorsed. One might argue that bluffing would make it impossible to measure performance and thus frustrate the very purpose of performance appraisals.

A problem related to the multitude of roles introduced in the 360-degree feedback process (e.g., one as a rater, one as a colleague) is that it creates potentially conflicting moral obligations. Can a colleague have an obligation to report performance truthfully (to further the company's interest) but also an obligation to support a colleague who is a close friend, and if so, how is this to be resolved? Kerssens-van Drongelen and Fisscher argue that such dilemmas frequently arise in 360-degree feedback processes, and though they are optimistic, it is an open question whether 360-degree feedback can be designed to avoid such conflicting obligations (if indeed they arise).

Further ethical questions concern the unintentional rating inaccuracies in 360-degree feedback. As Murphy, Cleveland, and Mohler note, 360-degree feedback offers no discernible improvements over single-rater feedback when it comes to objectivity (and thus its resilience to biases). Moreover, 360-degree feedback seems to invite its own host of problems with biases. 360-degree feedback invites people to be agreeable and, as the case demonstrates, it can put pressure on employees to get along with their colleagues to have better chances in the feedback process. Whether someone finds someone else agreeable, however, is easily influenced by factors such as culture, upbringing, and, unfortunately, demographics. Ratings from several similarly-biased raters might indeed worsen rather than remove issues with objectivity, and it is conceivable that 360-degree feedback effectively reinforces cultural biases in a firm. Discrimination might thus still be a problem in 360-degree feedback. Moreover, agreeableness arguably belongs to "contextual performance" factors, which are not part of one's job description. Ethically, and legally, it is crucial for the criterion used to evaluate job performance to be related to job performance, and it would seem illegitimate to base decisions about promotion and employment on contextual performance factors.

The social nature of 360-degree feedback raises questions about its effect on company culture and employee privacy. Kantor and Streitfeld describe how Amazon's multi-rater appraisal system, which allows employees to submit anonymous, unsolicited feedback about each other, leads to a tough, highly competitive culture where feedback is sometimes used to settle personal grudges.[3] Collecting anonymous feedback seems required to protect people that give honest but negative feedback, but it invites politically motivated feedback, too. A related issue concerns privacy. Employees are arguably not obliged to inform their employers about private matters, such as future career plans, and thus this information should not play a role in performance evaluations. However, employees are bound to share some private information with their colleagues, and Sillup and Klimberg have suggested that this private information will eventually, and illegitimately, play a role in the feedback process. Even apart from potential effects on the performance appraisal, employers are set to gain more information about the employee than without the social nature of 360-degree feedback, and this might be worrisome in itself.

A final question concerns the extent to which different people have a right to have a say in one's performance evaluation process. The participation of people other than one's manager could be legitimized by the job-related information gained by adding their perspective (if that information would otherwise be missed, perhaps due to the complexity of the job). However, as Murphy, Cleveland, and Mohler point out, there is some doubt as to whether different sources add unique perspectives and so this justifying reason might be lacking. In that case, quite apart from the question of whether performance appraisals per se are permissible, one must ask what a company's legitimization is for giving different people a say in questions related to their employees' promotion and continued employment.

NOTES

1   Objectivity comprises the performance appraisal's accuracy, or the extent to which it measures what it is supposed to measure, and its reliability, or the extent to which results are independent of the person administering the performance appraisal.

2   Jack Welch, *Jack: What I've Learned Leading a Great Company and Great People* (London: Headline, 2001).

3   Jode Kantor and David Streitfeld, "Inside Amazon: Wrestling Big Ideas in a Bruising Workplace," *New York Times* (August 15, 2015).

DISCUSSION QUESTIONS

(1) To what extent does the legitimacy of 360-degree feedback used as a performance appraisal tool depend on the objectivity of its results?

(2) What are the obligations of interviewees and the person being evaluated when it comes to speaking the truth in the evaluation process? Does the 360-degree feedback process alter these obligations?

(3) On what basis can a company permissibly take the judgment of someone other than the employee's manager into account when making decisions about promotion and continued employment?

(4) What are the likely effects of using 360-degree feedback on a company's culture and under which conditions would these effects be a reason against using it?

(5) Under which conditions is agreeableness relevant for job performance and, if it is, would it be a permissible criterion for promotion and employment-related decisions?

FURTHER READINGS

Fritz Allhoff, "Business Bluffing Reconsidered," *Journal of Business Ethics* 45.4 (2003): 283–89.

David K. Banner and Robert Allan Cooke, "Ethical Dilemmas in Performance Appraisal," *Journal of Business Ethics* (1984): 327–33.

John H. Bernadin and Catherine L. Tyler, "Legal and Ethical Issues in Multisource Feedback," in *The Handbook of Multisource Feedback*, ed. David W. Bracken, Carol W. Timmreck, and Allan H. Church (San Francisco: John Wiley & Sons, 2001), 447–562.

David W. Bracken, Carol W. Timmreck, and Allan H. Church, eds., *The Handbook of Multisource Feedback* (San Francisco: John Wiley & Sons, 2001).

Albert Z. Carr, "Is Business Bluffing Ethical?" *Harvard Business Review* (1968): 146.

Madeline E. Heilman and Michelle C. Haynes, "Subjectivity in the Appraisal Process: A Facilitator of Gender Bias in Work Settings," in *Beyond Common Sense: Psychological Science in the Courtroom*, ed. Eugene Borgida and Susan T. Fiske (Malden, MA: Blackwell, 2008), 127–55.

Inge C. Kerssens-van Drongelen and Olaf A.M. Fisscher, "Ethical Dilemmas in Performance Measurement," *Journal of Business Ethics* (2003): 51–63.

Clinton Longenecker and Dean Ludwig, "Ethical Dilemmas in Performance Appraisal Revisited," *Journal of Business Ethics* (1990): 961–69.

Kevin R. Murphy, Jeannette N. Cleveland, and Carolyn J. Mohler, "Reliability, Validity, and Meaningfulness of Multisource Ratings," in *The Handbook of Multisource Feedback*, ed. David W. Bracken, Carol W. Timmreck, and Allan H. Church (San Francisco: John Wiley & Sons, 2001), 130–48.

George P. Sillup and Ronald Klimberg, "Assessing the Ethics of Implementing Performance Appraisal Systems," *Journal of Management Development* (2010): 38–55.

18.

FREE EXPRESSION IN THE WORKPLACE: THE FIRING OF JAMES DAMORE

NILS CH. RAUHUT

BACKGROUND

ON AUGUST 4, 2017, A DOCUMENT, TITLED "GOOGLE'S IDEOLOGICAL Echo Chamber," began circulating among Google employees and on the company internal communication forum Memegen. In the 10-page memo, the author, James Damore, writes that when it comes to diversity and inclusion, Google has created a politically correct monoculture that maintains its hold on company culture by shaming dissenters into silence. Damore argues that biological differences between men and women may explain why such a high percentage of men are working in tech and leadership and why a 50 per cent representation of women is so difficult to achieve. Since women, so Damore argues, have on average a greater tendency to "empathize" rather than "systematize," show higher rates of neuroticism (higher anxiety and lower stress tolerance) and are, on average, more agreeable rather than assertive, they are less likely to excel at coding than men who have been selected to strive for social status and who like things more than people.

James Damore had been a Google employee at the Mountain View campus of the company since 2013. Prior to his employment as a senior software engineer, Damore had studied molecular and cellular biology at the University of Illinois Urbana-Champaign and conducted research in computational biology at Harvard, Princeton, and the Massachusetts Institute of Technology. As more and more Google employees took notice of Damore's memo, the discussion spilled out onto the Internet. On August 5, "Google's Ideological Echo Chamber" was published by the Internet site *Gizmodo*.[1] Shortly thereafter, on August 7, James Damore was fired.

In a company-wide e-mail entitled "Our words matter," Sundar Pichai, the CEO of Google, explained the firing of James Damore as follows: "... we strongly support the right of Googlers to express themselves, and much of what was in that memo is fair to debate, regardless of whether a vast majority of Googlers disagree with it. However, portions of the memo violate our Code of Conduct and cross the line by advancing harmful gender stereotypes in our workplace. Our job is to build great products for users that make a difference in their lives. To suggest a group of our colleagues have traits that make them less biologically suited to that work is offensive and not okay. It is contrary to our basic values and our Code of Conduct."[2]

In response, James Damore filed charges against Google with the National Labor Relations Board (NLRB) for unlawful termination of his employment. On August 11, he wrote an op-ed article in the *Wall Street Journal* expressing his disappointment with Google's response to his memo: "Google is a particularly intense echo chamber because ... for many, including myself, working at Google is a major part of their identity, almost like a cult with its own leaders and saints.... In my document, I committed heresy against the Google creed by stating that not all disparities between men and women that we see in the world are the result of discriminatory treatment.... It saddens me to leave Google and to see the company silence open and honest discussion. If Google continues to ignore the very real issues raised by its diversity policies and corporate culture, it will be ... unable to meet the needs of its remarkable employees and sure to disappoint its billions of users."[3]

In January 2018, Jayme L. Sophir, a NLRB lawyer, wrote a legal memo on the Damore case. The memo comes to the conclusion that the firing of James Damore did not violate Federal Labor Relations Laws, since Google had made it clear that Damore was fired because he advanced stereotypes and not because he was drawing attention to workplace problems. His speech was, therefore, not protected by NLRB regulations.

In response to the publication of this legal memo, Damore withdrew his initial NLRB complaint and instead filed a new lawsuit against his former employer. In the new lawsuit, which he filed together with another former Google employee and three rejected job applicants, Damore accuses Google of gender, race, and ideological discrimination. Damore and his lawyer Harmeet K. Dhillon argue that Google defines and promotes diversity in such a way that Caucasian and Asian males are left out of consideration for certain categories of jobs. Moreover, the lawsuit also accuses Google of ostracizing, belittling, and punishing conservative white males for their heterodox political views and thereby creating open hostility for conservative thought.

ANALYSIS

THE FIRING OF JAMES DAMORE RAISES A WIDE RANGE OF MORAL and legal questions. Let us start with the most obvious one. To what degree do employees have a right to say what they truly believe in their workplace? From a legal perspective, all employees are covered by the First Amendment to the US Constitution, which protects individuals from the government regulating and curtailing free speech. However, it is important to realize that the First Amendment does not posit that employees of a private company have the right to express opinions or engage in political activity at work. Private employers have the power to discipline and terminate employees for statements made both in and out of the workplace. The only legal protection of speech at work is provided by the National Labor Relations Act (NLRA) and Title VII of the Civil Rights Act. In the first case, workers do have the right to express their beliefs if these beliefs are related to their working conditions. This statute has traditionally been linked to the right of employees to engage in activities that are related to collective bargaining and forming a union. It entails that workers have the right to talk about pay, promotions, and other work-related conditions. Title VII of the Civil Rights Act provides some protection of employee speech in cases where the statements are related to problematic employment practices in connection with race, color, sex, and national origin.

From a moral point of view, the situation looks different. It is fairly obvious that many employers, especially an employer like Google who wants to promote creativity and innovation, have a vested interest in fostering meaningful debate and discussion at work that allow for the expression of contrary points of views. In the past, Google has taken many steps to promote a climate of openness and dialogue among employees and between employees and upper-level management. Employees have the ability to search for information (even about different divisions) on the internal network. Employees are able and encouraged to make announcements and share information on the employee-only version of Google Plus. Google employees even have the possibility to openly confront executives with questions voted on by employees at weekly companywide meetings. Creating such an open and tolerant discussion climate in which employees can say what they truly believe—even if their beliefs run contrary to the status quo—is important for utilitarian and deontological reasons. Being able to say what you think without fear of repercussions contributes to creating a happy and satisfying workplace atmosphere, and open and inclusive work conversations can also allow communities to make progress on difficult issues. From a deontological perspective, meaningful and open dialogue that allows for the expression of contrary points of view is also an important factor in making employees think of themselves as autonomous agents rather than as passive subjects who work only as directed by someone else.

On the other hand, it is also undeniable that divisive employee speech at the workplace can negatively impact both workplace productivity and employee morale. Just imagine an employee who frequently attacks and challenges other colleagues over their habit of eating meat and persistently accuses them of being responsible for the abuse of animals in factory farms. It is clear that such a colleague, through the free expression of his heartfelt convictions, creates a problematic and less than ideal workplace atmosphere. This is the reason why it is useful for companies to clarify limits to free speech in their company code of conduct. In the case of James Damore, Google's employee code of conduct says the following: "Googlers are expected to do their utmost to create a workplace culture that is free of harassment, intimidation, bias, and unlawful discrimination." The question, of course, is whether Damore's publication of the memo "Google's Ideological Echo Chamber" should be seen as a violation of the employee's code of conduct. There are clearly passages in the memo that can be read as advocating discrimination and which can be seen as creating a hostile workplace environment for women. Damore might, however, respond to these charges by insisting that the overall intent of the memo was to suggest alternative views of how to increase women's representation in tech. He says at several points in the memo that he favors diversity, but that he objects only to the specific policies Google has chosen to increase diversity in its ranks. Moreover, Damore describes his motivation behind writing his memo as follows: "... open and honest discussion with those who disagree can highlight our blind spots and help us grow, which is why I wrote this document." Does this commendable motivation behind writing the memo provide a context that allows other Google employees to perceive Damore's misogynistic claims as a tolerable but misguided element in an open discussion?

Damore was prompted to write his memo after attending a diversity training workshop. This raises another set of questions: What strategies, training programs, and policies are most useful in increasing workplace diversity? James Damore says that he felt "silenced and marginalized" after attending the diversity training workshop. It seems pretty clear that this could not have been the intended goal of the diversity training. But how can companies make sure that the diversity training programs they develop and advocate do not have unintended consequences? Research on the effectiveness of diversity programs has yielded mixed results. Some studies show that diversity training is effective, others show it's ineffective and still others that it may actually lead to backlash.[4]

The case of James Damore also raises an interesting question about the role of science and free speech. Imagine, for example, a work colleague who is a flat-earther and who feels offended when you say at work that the world is round. In this case, it seems entirely reasonable to say that the belief that the earth is round should not offend anybody since it is a scientific fact. Expressing scientific truths might make people feel uncomfortable, but that is no reason for banning them from the workplace. What is interesting to notice is that James Damore probably sees himself to be in a similar position. He is a trained biologist and he might be thinking that by reporting biological differences between men and women in his memo he is merely saying what science has been discovering for some time, namely that there are important biological differences between men and women. The problem with this line of thought is that James Damore isn't using scientific results fairly. It is true that many of the differences between men and women described in his memo are confirmed by science, but there are many other biological differences between men and women (like the fact that men score higher on measures of anger and lower on co-operation and self-discipline) which Damore does not mention in his memo and which do not support his conclusion that men are biologically better suited to be software engineers than women. This suggests that Damore is not simply reporting scientific facts, but that he is selectively and illegitimately using scientific facts to support a contentious and controversial opinion. What's problematic here is not what science says, but how science is used.

Lastly, the case of James Damore raises interesting questions about reverse discrimination. Damore argues in his second lawsuit that Google's company policies to increase diversity among its employees amounted to open and illegal discrimination against Caucasian and Asian males. He argues in his lawsuit that Google's hiring practices negatively and disparately impact white male job applicants because non-male or non-conservative applicants will be hired over similarly situated Caucasian/Asian male applicants for any given position. Damore also contends that Google management created a work environment that was hostile for conservative employees. Damore said in a subsequent interview that "being conservative at Google was similar to being openly gay in the 1950s." An interesting question is whether this analogy is justified or whether it demonstrates instead that Damore conflates real and persistent discrimination with superficial and apparent bias.

NOTES

1   Kate Conger, "Exclusive: Here's the Full 10-Page Anti-Discrimination Screed Circulating Internally at Google," *Gizmodo* (August 5, 2017).
2   Sundar Pichai, "Our Words Matter," Message to Google Employees, e-mail (2017).
3   James Damore, "Why I Was Fired by Google," *Wall Street Journal* (August 11, 2017).
4   Alex Lindsey, Eden King, Ashley Membere, and Ho Kwan Cheung, "Two Types of Diversity Training That Really Work," *Harvard Business Review* (2017).

DISCUSSION QUESTIONS

(1)   If you had been the CEO of Google, would you have come to the same conclusion as Sundar Pichai that it is in Google's interest to fire James Damore for writing and publishing his memo?

(2) Suppose you had to write an employee handbook and explain what kind of speech will not be tolerated in the workplace: what would you write?

(3) What factors do you think are most important in making diversity-training programs effective?

(4) What role, if any, should biological differences between men and women play when it comes to selecting candidates for jobs or leadership positions?

(5) Does it make a difference whether the central claims in James Damore's memo were supported by scientific evidence?

FURTHER READINGS

David Brooks, "Sundar Pichai Should Resign as Google's C.E.O.," *The New York Times* (August 11, 2017).

James Damore, "Google's Ideological Echo Chamber: How Bias Clouds Our Thinking about Diversity and Inclusion," *Medium* (2017).

Kirsten Grind and Douglas MacMillian, "Google vs Google: How Nonstop Political Arguments Rule Its Workplace," *Wall Street Journal* (May 1, 2018).

Jeffrey Klein and Nicholas J. Pappas, "The Challenges of Regulating Employee Speech," *New York Law Journal* (December 21, 2017).

Douglas MacMillan, "Google Reins in Workplace Debate," *Wall Street Journal* (June 28, 2018).

Suzanne Sadedin, "A Scientist's Take on the Biological Claims from the Infamous Google Anti-Diversity Memo," *Forbes* (August 10, 2017).

Nick Wingfield, "The Culture Wars Have Come to Silicon Valley," *New York Times* (August 8, 2017).

19

DISTRIBUTIVE JUSTICE AND PRECARIOUS WORK

KYLE JOHANNSEN

BACKGROUND

PRECARIOUS WORK HAS BECOME THE NORM FOR YOUNG ADULTS in North America and elsewhere.[1] Where once it was normal to settle into a permanent position shortly after secondary school, it's now fairly typical to spend a few (often more than a few) years working part-time jobs while pursuing a post-secondary education. And for many, precarity doesn't end when one finishes one's degree. Becoming competitive in many industries now requires one to spend years working on a contractual basis, sometimes for the same employer and sometimes for different employers, all the while not knowing where or if one will be working months down the line.

Precarious work is tolerable when it serves as a stepping-stone to permanent, full-time employment. Knowing that the uncertainty about wages, geographic location, work conditions, etc., will pass and that the work one is currently doing will ultimately contribute to one's long-term professional wellbeing makes the hardship less hard. Unfortunately, though, precarious work often isn't like this. In academia, for example, many professors get stuck jumping from teaching contract to teaching contract, teaching more and/or being paid less than their permanent colleagues, and lacking sufficient time to do the research necessary to become competitive for tenure-track positions. Issues surrounding the precarity of sessional academic employment were recently highlighted and made publicly visible when thousands of college faculty and other college workers affiliated with OPSEU (Ontario Public Service Employees Union) went on strike on October 16, 2017.[2] Issues motivating the strike included lack of faculty control over course content and pedagogy, as well as a lack of job security and inadequate compensation.[3] The strike only ended when back-to-work legislation was passed on November 19, 2017.[4]

There is a large body of literature concerning both the demographics of precarious employment and the effects of precarious work on people who do it. The findings of this literature are concerning. With respect to demographics, young adults clearly make up a large proportion of the precarious workforce,[5] but a disproportionately large number of women, as well as members of racial minorities, find themselves precariously employed, too.[6] And with respect to effects, there is reason to believe that the precariously employed face higher levels of employment-related strain. Less control over work conditions, the need to balance the demands of multiple employers, effort spent securing references and applying for future contracts, and lack of support in the workplace: all of these things are commonly associated with precarious work, and the strain they cause can negatively affect workers' health.[7] In combination, the demographics of precarious work and its effects on workers raise issues of justice.

An additional concern associated with precarious work is the effect it has on the character of workers. Traditionally, the workplace was a place where workers could, and often would, form lasting, trusting relationships with their coworkers. For the precariously employed, however, there is little opportunity to develop such relationships. Though some forms of trust can be secured easily enough, e.g., the formal trust achieved via a contract, other forms of trust take time to develop, e.g., the informal trust between coworkers who have developed an unspoken reliance on each other to provide support where needed. The latter sort of trust goes hand in hand with cultivating a close relationship with one's coworkers, and forming close bonds is difficult when one is only temporarily employed. What's more, loyalty may not be an especially functional value in precarious employment. A sense of loyalty makes it difficult to let go of workers whose contracts have expired, and it makes it difficult for workers to leave a position for a superior contract at another location or establishment. All in all, precarity seems unconducive to, and may undermine, the cultivation of virtues such as trust and loyalty.[8]

Though it raises concerns, precarious work can have its benefits. The availability of part-time and contractual positions affords some people who would otherwise be unable to work the opportunity to do so. Good examples include students whose academic responsibilities preclude taking on a full-time job, as well as caregivers whose primary responsibility is child-care. What's more, the availability of certain forms of precarious work suits some people's lifestyle. For example, overseas contract work presents one with the opportunity to spend a year or two in a foreign country, and this has proven to be appealing for many young adults who would like to travel and experience the world before settling down. Lastly, it seems that some people prefer self-employment to other forms of employment, as it can afford one more rather than less control over one's work conditions than traditional employment. Being self-employed can yield a considerable amount of autonomy with respect to when one works, how much one works, etc.[9] What should we make of this medley of ostensibly negative and positive qualities?

ANALYSIS

OUR EVALUATION OF PRECARIOUS WORK DEPENDS ON A NUMBER of different factors. An important one is the definition we adopt. What exactly is meant by the term "precarious work"? The term is commonly used to refer to a number of different kinds of work: to self-employed work, migrant work, contractually limited work, and part-time work. Is there something that unifies all these kinds of work? Following Leah Vosko and the editors of *Gender and the Contours of Precarious Employment*, we should perhaps think of precarious work as "employment that lacks standard forms of labor security."[10] More concretely, we can say that precarious employment is characterized by things such as less compensation, fewer benefits, and lack of permanency.

Our evaluation also depends on the theoretical perspective we take. Comprehensively analyzing precarious work requires that we reflect on broader questions and theories of distributive justice: the branch of justice that examines the fair distribution of benefits and burdens. How one responds to precarious work depends in part on whether one subscribes to a view of distributive justice that sees transactions in the free market as a just basis for distributing goods, a view that accords government a significant role in regulating the market and redistributing goods to remediate inequalities, or a view that sees current economic institutions as instantiating structural injustice based on unequal power relationships between workers and employers.

According to most libertarians, economic transactions are only problematic in cases of theft or fraud. So long as the parties to a transaction did not acquire their holdings either directly or indirectly through theft or fraud, and so long as they do not commit theft or fraud against each other, then the outcome of their transaction is deemed fair. If one holds this sort of view, it arguably follows that there is nothing wrong with employers offering part-time work, short-term contracts, etc. So long as employees are working voluntarily, then precarious work is perfectly fair, from a libertarian point of view. Workers who don't like their wages or work conditions are free to leave and find work elsewhere.

Socialists, by contrast, would take the opposite position. From a socialist perspective, it seems that the rise of precarious employment is a predictable effect of a system where the means of production are privately owned. According to socialists (specifically Marxists), capitalist economies are built upon exploitation. Economic growth requires that some fraction of a business's earnings be reinvested back into it, and since providing workers with compensation equal to the full value of their labor would leave no resources for reinvestment, economic growth requires that some fraction of the value workers create be taken from them. In other words, economic growth requires exploiting workers. From this perspective, precarious work is best understood as contributing to the exploitation which capitalism requires. The features that characterize precarious employment, i.e., less compensation, fewer benefits, lack of permanency, etc., are made possible by the fact that workers lack ownership of the means of production, and these features function to allow capitalists to further cut costs and thereby expand their businesses. Socialists would thus likely see precarious work as another form of exploitation within an inherently exploitive system.

A second criticism that socialists would likely make of precarious work is that it further alienates workers from the product of their labor. Socialists maintain that in pre-capitalist societies, workers had a special relationship with what they produced. For example, craftsmen, by employing talents developed through years of training, would create a good that was uniquely their own. Such production was a source of fulfillment. By dividing labor and mechanizing production, capitalism turned workers into metaphorical cogs that lack the relationship they once had with what they produce. Instead of being uniquely responsible for the production of a small number of goods, individual workers in a capitalist society play a small role in the production of a very large number of goods. Finding fulfillment in the repeated pulling of a switch or pressing of a button on an assembly line is ostensibly more difficult than finding fulfillment in crafting an item. This problem, though not specific to precarious work, is arguably exacerbated by it. Though playing a small, repetitive role in producing a large number of goods is not very fulfilling, it's arguably easier to find fulfillment in a workplace where one is permanently employed. A permanent employee has a greater opportunity to develop the sense that she's a member of a larger team, and thus to take pride in what that team produces. For temporary workers, however, this sense of connection is more difficult to come by.

From a liberal egalitarian perspective, precarious work is a complex matter. According to the most significant liberal egalitarian in contemporary political philosophy, John Rawls, economic inequalities between citizens of the same society are only just when (a) they are consistent with equality of opportunity, and (b) they maximally benefit those who are worst off. If those with less did not have the same opportunities to attain wealth as those with more, and if the greater share of those who have more does not work to the benefit of those who have less, e.g., by incentivizing the use of productive talents that raise everyone's absolute position, then the inequality between them is unjust. From this perspective, precarious work can be but isn't necessarily unjust. Precariously employed workers seem to be worse off than other workers, by and large, but that in and of itself is not a source of injustice. What matters is whether the inequality between them and other workers is in their (precarious workers') benefit, and whether it is consistent with equality of opportunity.

With respect to equality of opportunity, a major consideration is whether any particular case of precarious work is transitional or not. Students working part-time jobs and contractual employment that reliably lead to permanent employment are both fine, from a liberal egalitarian perspective, because they don't reflect class hierarchy. Though students and contract workers find themselves in inferior working conditions by comparison with those in full-time permanent employment, this is relatively unproblematic so long as it's merely a phase in one's life. If those who enjoy full-time permanent employment were required to go through such a phase themselves, then there's no unfairness between them and their precariously employed colleagues. Precarious employment is just part of the training process, and anyone who works hard and has the requisite skills will secure better forms of employment, in time.

When precarious employment is not just a phase, the question to ask, from a liberal egalitarian perspective, is why? Is it because precarious jobs are the only kind available and there aren't opportunities for workers to develop their qualifications and obtain more stable employment? Is it because precarious employment suits workers' lifestyle? Or is it because those who are precariously employed lack marketable talents (as well as the natural capacity for those talents)?

In cases where precarious jobs are the only ones available to some workers, precarious employment constitutes a clear violation of equality of opportunity. Correcting this inequality might require any number of things, for example, improving access to post-secondary education so that training is easier to secure, or regulating precarious positions to ensure that workloads aren't excessive and that hidden costs (such as moving around and repeatedly applying for jobs) are compensated for or otherwise mitigated.

In cases where precarious employment is a lifestyle choice, liberal egalitarians have less cause for complaint. Inequalities in the distribution of resources that reflect lifestyle choices, e.g., the choice to be self-employed or the choice to work part-time in order to pursue other interests, do not reflect unequal opportunity. Still, liberal egalitarians would perhaps be concerned to ensure that the distribution of resources not become too unequal between those who've chosen precarious employment and those who've chosen full-time permanent work. After all, inequalities are supposed to work to the benefit of those who are less well off, even when the less well-off are less well off by choice. When navigating this problem, it is important to be conscious of the metric one employs. Rawls himself was concerned specifically with inequalities in the distribution of goods, and thus his theory ostensibly commits him to subsidizing citizens' lifestyle choices, i.e., to redistributing goods from those who choose to work harder and longer to those who've opted for a greater amount of leisure.[11] However, for those who include wellbeing in their metric, i.e., those who are interested in the distribution of satisfaction, it's less obvious that there is any significant inequality between those who prefer to work more and those who prefer either more leisure or less burdensome work. Those who work less may have fewer resources at their disposal, but that doesn't mean they're less happy. Some may very well be happier than those who've chosen to work long hours.[12]

In cases where precarious employment reflects a lack of natural capacity for marketable talents, liberal egalitarians like Rawls would ostensibly be concerned to ensure that any inequalities work to the benefit of the precariously employed. Resource inequalities traceable to a lack of natural ability do not reflect inequality of opportunity (on Rawls's understanding of it), but the state would have to ensure that the superior earnings of those with more natural ability maximally benefit those with less ability. The problem is that it's unlikely that lack of natural ability is ever a good explanation for why someone becomes stuck in precarious employment. Though some jobs require talents that some may lack the capacity to develop, e.g., accounting, engineering, etc., and others only require abilities that the majority of adults either possess or could possess, the fact that jobs of the latter sort are sometimes offered on a precarious basis has little to do with the talents they require. With the exception of seasonal work, the reason employers offer positions on a part-time or contractual basis is because it's cost effective for them to do so. As such, liberal egalitarians seem committed to eliminating precarity in cases like this, or at least to ensuring that mechanisms are in place that protect precariously employed workers' ability to transition to full-time permanent work.

NOTES

1   For extensive discussion of this trend, see Bessant et al. (2017).
2   "Ontario College Strike Begins Monday Morning as Employer Rejects Faculty Offer," *Business Insider* (October 15, 2017).
3   "College Faculty Union Launches Ad Campaign on Bargaining Issues," *Business Insider* (October 6, 2017).
4   "Labour Needs a Strong NDP to Tackle Precarious Work," Ontario Public Services Employment Union (November 19, 2017).
5   See Bessant et al. (2017).
6   See Vosko et al., eds. (2009).
7   See Lewchuk et al. (2011), 25–31.

8   For a discussion of precarious work's effect on character development, see Sennett (1998), especially chapter 1.

9   For a sympathetic look at precarious employment, see "In Praise of 'Precarious' Work," *Canadian Business* (October 24, 2012).

10   See Vosko et al., eds. (2009), 2.

11   See Kymlicka (2002), 72–75. In response to the claim that his theory requires subsidizing citizens' lifestyle choices, Rawls has suggested that leisure time be included among the list of primary goods his theory is concerned with distributing. With this inclusion, those who opt for more leisure would not be counted among the least well off. Whether Rawls's reply is adequate is an open question. See Rawls (2001), 179.

12   For discussion of labor burdens, including welfare in the metric of justice, see Cohen (2008), 101–07.

DISCUSSION QUESTIONS

(1)   Is capitalism an inherently exploitive system? Does economic growth require exploiting workers, or can exploitation be avoided through regulation?

(2)   How often is precarious work freely chosen by those who do it? Are those who find themselves "stuck" in precarious work responsible for their own situation?

(3)   Do you think that precarious employment is unfair to workers? If so, is it always unfair, or is it only unfair in certain cases? Are there certain conditions that, if met, suffice to make precarious employment fair?

(4)   How does citizenship affect the fairness of precarious employment? Does it matter whether a precariously employed worker is a foreign migrant or a citizen? Why or why not?

(5)   What does equality of opportunity require? Is precarious employment compatible with it? And is there a relationship between equality of opportunity and the distribution of natural talents and natural capacity?

FURTHER READINGS

Judith Bessant, Rys Farthing, and Rob Watts, *The Precarious Generation: A Political Economy of Young People* (London: Routledge, 2017).

Mark Cohen, "The Effect of Crime on Life Satisfaction," *The Journal of Legal Studies* 37 (s2): s325–s353.

Will Kymlicka, *Contemporary Political Philosophy: An Introduction* (Oxford: Oxford University Press, 2002).

Wayne Lewchuk, Marlea Clarke, and Alice de Wolff, *Working without Commitments: The Health Effects of Precarious Employment* (Montreal & Kingston: McGill-Queen's University Press, 2001).

John Rawls, *A Theory of Justice* (Cambridge, MA: Belknap Press, 1971).

Richard Sennett, *The Corrosion of Character: The Personal Consequences of Work in the New Capitalism* (New York: W.W. Norton & Company, 1998).

Leah F. Vosko, ed., *Precarious Employment: Understanding Labour Market Insecurity in Canada* (Montreal & Kingston: McGill-Queen's University Press, 2006).

Leah F. Vosko, Martha MacDonald, and Iain Campbell, eds., *Gender and the Contours of Precarious Employment* (London: Routledge, 2009).

20.

RELIGIOUS COMMITMENTS IN THE WORKPLACE

T.J. BROY

BACKGROUND

IN 2012, DAVID MULLINS AND CHARLIE CRAIG VISITED MASTERPIECE Cakeshop in Lakewood, Colorado to order a wedding cake for their wedding reception.[1] Because same-sex marriage was not yet legal in Colorado, the couple planned to marry in Massachusetts and then celebrate their wedding with family and friends in Colorado. Expert baker and owner of Masterpiece Cakeshop, Jack Phillips, refused to sell the couple a wedding cake due to his religious commitments. Phillips is a conservative Christian and believes marriage is intended by God to be between a man and a woman. For Phillips, baking a cake for a same-sex marriage would amount to an endorsement of a celebration which runs counter to his deeply held religious beliefs.

The Colorado Anti-Discrimination Act (CADA) makes it illegal for anyone to refuse access to goods and services in a place of public accommodation due to disability, race, creed, color, national origin, ancestry, religion, sex, marital status, or sexual orientation. When violations of the CADA are alleged to have occurred, the Colorado Civil Rights Commission investigates in order to determine whether or not a violation has in fact taken place. If the commission determines a violation has taken place, then remedial measures (excluding fines or monetary damages) can be ordered. Mullins and Craig filed a complaint with the commission, which found Phillips had violated the CADA when he refused to provide a cake for Mullins and Craig's wedding reception, and ordered Phillips to cease and desist discriminating against same-sex couples as well as remedial measures including staff training on the CADA and the preparation of quarterly compliance reports detailing the number of customers denied service and the reasons for such denial.

Phillips appealed all the way to the Supreme Court, which decided in his favor. The Court determined the Colorado Civil Rights Commission violated Phillips's rights under the First Amendment by displaying "clear and impermissible hostility toward the sincere religious beliefs that motivated [Phillips's] objection [to same-sex marriage]."[2] When considering other cases where bakers had refused to decorate cakes with messages critical of same-sex marriage or containing Bible passages used to support criticism of same-sex marriage, the commission ruled in those bakers' favor, noting that because the nature of the message was offensive, those bakers' had no obligation to provide the service. When dealing with Phillips's case, one commissioner called the invocation of religious belief to justify exemption to anti-discrimination law "one of the most despicable pieces of rhetoric that people can use."[3] The Supreme Court saw this language as evidence the commission was neither fair nor impartial toward Phillips.

Phillips believes his baking amounts to a form of artistic expression. Whereas in the other cases of bakers refusing to write messages on cakes, the objection was to the content of the message, Phillips's objection was to the exercise of his artistic abilities in baking and decorating the cake. Whether or not the cakes were decorated with text Phillips found objectionable, Phillips sees his baking the cakes as a form of expression. To force Phillips to provide cakes would then be a case of forced expression and so a violation of Phillips's free speech rights.

The Court did not rule that the only way to respect Phillips's First Amendment rights was to allow him to refuse service to same-sex couples. Rather, the Court ruled that the Colorado Civil Rights Commission violated Phillips's First Amendment rights in the way they treated him during the proceedings. This leaves open the possibility that a suitably neutral treatment of Phillips's case might reach the same conclusion, that he must serve same-sex and opposite-sex couples alike, and in so doing not violate his First Amendment rights.

There is little doubt that Phillips's religious beliefs are sincere. Phillips told Mullins and Craig that he would provide any other service (cookies, brownies, birthday cakes, etc.); his only objection was to a wedding cake for a same-sex wedding. Phillips also closes his bakery on Sundays, refuses to bake cakes containing alcohol, and refuses to make cupcakes for Halloween, all as a result of his religious beliefs.[4]

ANALYSIS

THIS CASE BRINGS TWO VALUES INTO TENSION. FIRST, PROFESsionals should have the right to adhere to their sincere religious beliefs. Second, clients should not be discriminated against on the basis of their sexual orientation. When these two values collide, how should we decide what to do?

One might think that sincere religious beliefs amount to a reason for granting exemptions to the law so long as no one is harmed by the exemption. For example, you might think the state has good reasons for restricting alcohol use by minors. It seems likely that a child taking a sip of wine as part of a religious ceremony will not undermine those reasons. So, it seems plausible that an exemption can be made to the law banning alcohol consumption by minors so that minors can participate in certain religious ceremonies. Is this what the *Masterpiece Cakeshop* case is like?

Whether or not you think the *Masterpiece Cakeshop* case is sufficiently similar to the communion wine case will likely depend on how you understand what it is to harm someone. One might think the only way to harm someone is by depriving them of some good. Should the only baker available refuse to bake cakes for a same-sex marriage, then it is plausible to say the same-sex couple was harmed. So long as there is another baker available, however, you might think no one is harmed by the baker refusing to bake the wedding cake. On the other hand, one might think there is another type of harm besides being deprived of some good. Someone might suffer dignitary harm if they are treated unequally relative to their fellow citizens. The disrespect inherent in treating someone less than others as a result of their sexual orientation might constitute a kind of harm. If you think there is such a category of harm, you would have good reason to consider the

Masterpiece Cakeshop case as distinct from the communion wine case. In the *Masterpiece Cakeshop* case, someone suffers dignitary harm. In the communion wine case, no one suffers dignitary harm. So, in the one case an exemption to the law is not permissible and in the other case an exemption to the law is permissible.

There are ways one might approve of some cases of a baker refusing services to a same-sex couple and yet disapprove of others. Take Phillips's argument that his baking a cake amounts to a case of expression. It seems reasonable to suppose that it would be permissible for a gay baker to refuse to print Leviticus 20:13 on a cake.[5] If this is right, then there is reason to think it would be permissible for a baker like Jack Phillips to refuse to print "Congratulations David and Charlie" on a cake for Mullins and Craig's wedding celebration. So, it might be that it is permissible for Phillips to refuse to print congratulatory messages on a wedding cake for a same-sex marriage and yet be impermissible for Phillips to refuse to sell a blank sheet cake to a same-sex couple. Plausibly, Phillips is expressing something by printing on a cake and not expressing something by ringing a transaction through a cash register.

If this analysis is correct, then it is plausible there would be some cases where a baker's right to free expression would outweigh the dignitary harm done to a same-sex couple and some cases in which the dignitary harm done to a same-sex couple would outweigh the curtailing of a baker's right to free expression. It might be that forcing a baker like Phillips to bake a custom cake is asking too much, that it amounts to a violation of the baker's First Amendment right to free expression. It might still be reasonable, however, to demand the baker sell a cake out of a catalogue of standard cakes rather than create a custom cake for a same-sex wedding. The larger the gap between the baker's serving a same-sex couple and his act being an act of expression, the less harm is done to the baker. In this sort of case, the dignitary harm done to the same-sex couple might be greater than the harm done to the baker, and so the baker ought to sell the standard, catalogue cake.

NOTES

1   *Masterpiece Cakeshop v. Colorado Civil Rights Commission* U.S. 548 (2018).
2   *Masterpiece Cakeshop v. Colorado*, 12.
3   Ibid., 13.

4   *Masterpiece Cakeshop v. Colorado* (Thomas, J., concurring), 10.
5   "If a man lies with a male as with a woman, both of them have committed
     an abomination; they shall surely be put to death; their blood is upon
     them."

DISCUSSION QUESTIONS

(1) How would you balance religious freedom and freedom of expression
     with the demands of anti-discrimination in this case?
(2) Is baking a cake a form of expression? How does that affect the analysis of
     this case?
(3) Is dignitary harm a sort of harm? How does that affect the analysis of this
     case?
(4) Does it matter for the analysis of the case whether or not bakers are
     professionals? Why or why not?

FURTHER READINGS

John Corvino, Ryan T. Anderson, and Sherif Girgis, *Debating Religious Liberty
    and Discrimination* (Oxford: Oxford University Press, 2017).
Haley Holik, "You Have the Right to Speak by Remaining Silent: Why a
    State Sanction to Create a Wedding Cake Is Compelled Speech," *Regent
    University Law Review* 28.2 (2016): 299–318.
Douglas Laycock, "The Wedding-Vendor Cases," *Harvard Journal of Law &
    Public Policy* 41.1 (2018): 49–77.
Brian Leiter, *Why Tolerate Religion?* (Princeton: Princeton University Press,
    2014).
Yossi Nehustan, *Intolerant Religion in a Tolerant-Liberal Democracy*
    (Portland: Hart Publishing, 2015).

21

GUESTS WITH AUTISM AND REASONABLE ACCOMMODATIONS AT DISNEY

KEVIN MINTZ

BACKGROUND

THE PLAINTIFFS IN *A.L. V. WALT DISNEY PARKS AND RESORTS US*[1] and *T.P. et al. v. Walt Disney Parks and Resorts US*[2] are suing under Title III of the Americans with Disabilities Act (ADA) and California's Unruh Civil Rights Act, which require that people with disabilities receive reasonable accommodations to allow for equal access to public facilities like theme parks. The plaintiffs are people with Autism Spectrum Disorder (ASD) and their families. ASD is a psychological diagnosis that encompasses a wide range of developmental difficulties. ASD can involve challenges in social environments like amusement parks and challenges in changing routine.[3] Walt Disney Parks and Resorts, US (Disney), a subsidiary of The Walt Disney Company, is responsible for the operation of the company's US amusement parks, the Disneyland Resort (Disneyland) in Anaheim, California, and The Walt Disney World Resort (Disney World) in Orlando, Florida.[4] Disney's magical worlds resonate with many people who have ASD, providing them with joy, comfort, and safety in a way that few other places do.[5] Accordingly, some of these plaintiffs are Disney's most avid fans.

They are suing Disney over the main disability accommodation procedure in place at the amusement parks. The Disability Access Service (DAS) allows all guests with disabilities whose condition prevents them from waiting in a standard queue to receive a return time that equals an attraction's current wait time minus 10 minutes. For example, suppose a DAS user requested a return time for *It's a Small World* at 2:00 p.m. on a given day when the standard wait time is 50 minutes. In this situation, a DAS user would be given a return time of 2:40 p.m.

The DAS, therefore, requires people with disabilities, including ASD, to wait a comparable amount of time for an attraction as other guests but grants flexibility as to where they wait. Guests must request the DAS at Guest Relations; it cannot be obtained or reserved in advance. At Guest Relations a "Cast Member" (Disney's term for theme park personnel) is required to ask someone requesting the DAS to explain why their disability requires this accommodation. It is at a Cast Member's discretion whether or not a guest receives access to the DAS.[6]

Both Disneyland and Disney World have different procedures for distributing DAS return times. In Disneyland, a DAS user must request a return time at one of several kiosks scattered throughout the park or at Guest Relations. Here, a return time is electronically linked to the user's admission ticket. At Disney World, guests receive return times at individual attractions. A DAS user can only request one return time at a time.[7] The DAS can be used in conjunction with Disney's Fastpass service, which gives all guests the opportunity to schedule a return time to wait in a line with a minimal wait time.

The plaintiffs in these cases (currently 54) allege that the DAS fails to accommodate their disabilities, which, they claim, preclude them from waiting an extended period of time for an attraction. They further claim that in addition to not being able to wait an extended period of time, their disabilities necessitate their visiting attractions in a very specific and regimented order. From their perspective, the DAS does not allow this to happen. They argue that not having shortened wait times or being unable to visit attractions in a specific order causes the symptoms of their ASD to be exacerbated. Specifically, they claim that because the DAS requires them to wait, they experience meltdowns involving socially inappropriate or even violent behavior that precludes them from enjoying Disney theme parks on an equal basis with those who do not have ASD. Meltdowns for people with ASD can involve extreme behaviors that go beyond simple tantrums. It is important to recognize that most of these plaintiffs are represented by and through a parent or legal guardian due to their significant limitations. These individuals are more often than not the primary caregiver for the individual with ASD, and, as such, frequently experience the negative consequences of their loved one's meltdowns firsthand.[8]

Disney instituted the DAS on October 9, 2013. Prior to that date, Disney offered the Guest Assistance Card (GAC) to accommodate people with disabilities. The GAC allowed guests who are currently served by the DAS to have unlimited access to alternative attraction entrances, usually an attraction's exit or its Fastpass line.[9] Disney publicly states that it instituted the DAS because the GAC procedure was subject to considerable abuse.[10] For example, according to some news reports, wealthy families were hiring wheelchair users to accompany them to Walt Disney World so that these families would have unlimited access to Fastpass lines.[11] This abuse presented tangible costs for Disney. The people who hired wheelchair users no longer had to pay Disney to use its VIP Tour Service, which also provides preferential access to theme park attractions. The minimum current cost of a VIP Tour can range from $2,975 to $4,375 per day, plus the cost of individual admission tickets.[12] From another perspective, the abuse of the GAC came with public relations costs for Disney in that it might reflect poorly on the company to have a system of disability accommodation that was subject to such abuse. Rather than seeking the reinstatement of the GAC, the plaintiffs in these cases are seeking a modification to the DAS procedure that would allow for both the shortening of wait times to accommodate their limitations and the ability to plan the routine that they would follow during their visit.

In September 2016, Disney gave this statement to the *Orlando Sentinel* regarding these cases: "Disney Parks have an unwavering commitment to providing an inclusive and accessible environment for all our guests, and we fully comply with all ADA requirements."[13] Courts have thus far agreed, but in August 2018 the 11th Circuit remanded A.L. back to the lower courts for further consideration,[14] and individual plaintiffs involved in *T.P. et al.* are awaiting final decisions.[15]

ANALYSIS

REGARDLESS OF WHAT THE COURTS ULTIMATELY DECIDE, THESE cases raise important questions about the extent to which a large corporation, like Disney, is responsible for promoting disability equality. In particular, these cases evoke long-standing debates among disability advocates and scholars over the merits of the medical model versus the social model of disability. The medical model of disability treats disabling conditions as individual pathologies. The purpose of accommodations from the perspective of the medical model is to *fix* or *cure* individuals in order to make them fit into existing social structures. The social model, in contrast, views disability as an interaction between an impairment and existing social structures that do not adequately accommodate the impairment and, as such, *create* disability. The aim of accommodations under the social model is to minimize the effect that social barriers have on the day-to-day experiences of someone with an impairment such that it does not disable them.[16]

There are strong arguments in favor of both models being useful to provide reasonable accommodations for people with disabilities. There are features of the DAS that align with both models of disability. From one perspective, Disney does recognize that physically waiting in line is a socially constructed obstacle that should be accommodated either for legal or ethical reasons. This is reminiscent of the social model. From another perspective, however, one could also argue that by making people with ASD wait a comparable amount of time as other guests, Disney is treating their individual limitations as conditions that have to be *fit* into the protocol of waiting an extended period of time for an attraction. A more ardent defender of the social model would argue that, much like how stairs disable those who cannot walk, extended wait times disable those with ASD by causing meltdowns. This perspective would place a burden on Disney to develop procedures that minimize wait times for those with ASD in order to diminish the likelihood of a meltdown.

Relatedly, the concept of universal design[17] encourages the construction of accessible products and environments for a wide variety of customers from the outset, minimizing the need for individualized accommodations. Adopting a universal design perspective would encourage Disney to develop a procedure for waiting that minimizes wait times for all guests, regardless of disability. Developing such a procedure would not only minimize the need to provide specialized accommodations for people with ASD, but might also make it easier for guests with small children to enjoy the park by minimizing the incidents of tantrums while waiting for an attraction. It is also significant to acknowledge that the process of requesting the DAS from a Cast Member has the potential to result in what Jonathan Wolff calls "shameful revelation," in which a person with a disability feels stigmatized because of the procedures in place to request accommodations.[18] Universal design would not completely eliminate the need for individual accommodations, but it would minimize the risk of guests with ASD or their loved ones experiencing shameful revelation by reducing the need to request individual accommodations.

According to the courts' positions on these cases thus far, the ADA can be interpreted as supporting a number of perspectives on what constitutes a reasonable accommodation. An individual corporation's choice about how to best meet the requirements of the ADA requires that stakeholders make important and difficult choices about how the need or (hopefully) desire to accommodate those with disabilities is to be prioritized against other concerns, such as maximizing profit. The answer to this question will vary based likely on corporate culture and other factors, particularly cost. For example, if wealthy Disney patrons opted to misuse the GAC instead of paying for the VIP tour, this would provide Disney with a justification for examining how the GAC could be reformed to minimize this loss in revenue while still taking into consideration the needs of customers who have disabilities requiring accommodation in the waiting process. The DAS, or whatever accommodation procedure Disney chooses to adopt, must meet several potentially conflicting ethical criteria. First, the procedure must be designed to be administered efficiently from Disney's perspective. Second, it must be designed so as to minimize the instances of non-disabled guests abusing the procedure. Third, it must provide guests with disabilities, including ASD, with equal access to an enjoyable experience on par with that of other guests.

The remainder of this discussion will focus specifically on criterion three. Disney and the plaintiffs in these cases disagree on the kind of equality that is at stake in the ADA's equal access requirement. This disagreement mirrors disagreements among egalitarians over what the precise scope of social equality is and how disability fits into that scope. With the DAS, Disney seems to be asserting that, for its purposes, disability equality is best achieved through simple equality;[19] in essence, every guest regardless of disability status has an equal opportunity to enjoy attractions by having to wait an equal amount of time. From one perspective, this promotes fairness because, with the exception of where they wait, guests with and without disabilities are being treated in the same way.

Critics of simple equality, most notably John Rawls, point out that in some instances, treating all people the same way can have outcomes that perpetuate ethically problematic inequalities. Rawls is mostly thinking about access to the job market, where simple equality might not be sufficient to correct injustices in the distribution of jobs, because of its inability to correct for broader inequalities in education and the like.[20] He accordingly favors fair equality of opportunity whereby people are given resources and opportunities which not only eliminate discrimination but work toward the remedying of morally arbitrary inequalities that affect, among other ends, the distribution of income and wealth.

Applying fair equality of opportunity in these cases, it seems that these plaintiffs would be entitled to arrangements that mitigate the negative effects that having a meltdown might have on their ability to enjoy Disney's amusement parks on an equal basis with others. This does not necessarily equate to shortened wait times, however; Disney could, for example, maintain the DAS and allow for the construction of quiet areas in the amusement parks where people with ASD and their companions could go to either prevent or recover from a meltdown safely and comfortably. There are two main difficulties in applying fair equality of opportunity in this case. First, Rawls has been criticized for not taking issues of disability into account when formulating his view.[21] This is because his theory of justice as fairness assumes an ideal society where people are more or less equal in their physical and mental capacities, meaning that no one in this ideal society has a disability. As such, it is unclear whether the plaintiffs in these cases would have a claim to fair equality of opportunity as Rawls conceives of it.

Equally significant, however, Rawls specifically intends fair equality of opportunity to apply to the institutions which comprise the basic structure of society. He defines the basic structure of society as "the way in which the major social institutions distribute fundamental rights and duties and determine the division of advantages from social cooperation…. Taken together as one scheme, the major institutions define men's [or individuals of any gender] rights and duties and influence their life prospects, what they can expect to be and how well they can hope to do."[22] On this definition, it is unclear as to whether Disney is a part of the basic structure of society. This is because, as a corporation, Disney does not distribute rights and duties in the same way that a more political institution, such as a legislature, might. A case could be made that Disney does influence many people's life prospects, especially those of people like the plaintiffs in these cases. However, making this claim requires a considerable expansion of what Rawls had in mind when he formulated his account of fair equality of opportunity. As such, it seems appropriate to consider other conceptions of equality that might be better suited to thinking about how to accommodate the plaintiffs in these cases.

Another approach to equality that Disney might appeal to is equality of access to advantage. Advocated most strongly by G.A. Cohen, this framework holds that the aim of equality is to provide all people with access to benefits that correct for disadvantages arising from circumstances outside of an individual's control.[23] Equality of access to advantage would seem to frame accommodation requests in terms of the assumption that having ASD and not being able to wait in lines or deviate from routines are disadvantages over which none of the plaintiffs have control. As such, this view seems most compatible with the argument that the plaintiffs are making in these cases, specifically that shortened wait times are a reasonable accommodation for how the uncontrollable symptoms of ASD manifest themselves at a Disney amusement park. This view is subject to at least two major objections.

The main objection is that Cohen makes an inappropriate distinction between those people with disabilities who become disabled through no fault of their own, and those who become disabled through risky behavior. Although this seems irrelevant in the case discussed here, in that people with ASD are not responsible for their diagnosis, it is an important objection to consider when extending an accommodations procedure to all people with disabilities. It would seem unfair, for example, for Disney to offer the DAS only to those people who were born disabled and not to those with spinal cord injuries from preventable car accidents.[24] With this in mind, the ADA does make mention of the notion of equal benefit and equal enjoyment of goods and services,[25] which seems to parallel Cohen's notion of equal access to advantage, making it intuitively appealing in this case.

Alternatively, Disney could adopt an equality of capability approach in trying to evaluate its accommodation procedure. Advocated most strongly by Amartya Sen and Martha Nussbaum, equality of capability holds that people should be allowed to develop the capacities necessary to live a flourishing human life.[26] Nussbaum's iteration of equality of capability in particular is relevant here because among other capacities she deems necessary for human flourishing is the capacity to use one's imagination.[27] Disney's magical worlds offer one of many venues through which people develop and use their imagination, but for people with ASD especially, Disney might provide the primary way through which to realize this capacity. On this interpretation of Nussbaum, Disney has an obligation to maximize the opportunities people with ASD have to enjoy the parks. In all likelihood, this would mean taking proactive measures to minimize the effect of these plaintiffs' limitations on the enjoyment of the parks. The limitation of this approach to equality would be that it is unclear why a corporation should have an interest in promoting human flourishing. A similar question could be applied to the ideal of equality more generally except that, unlike human flourishing, the notion of equality is central to the ADA, which makes it a concern for all American corporations.

Related to questions of disability equality are questions about the rights of those who care for Disney guests with ASD. Writers focusing on the ethics of care, like Eva Feder Kittay, argue that the caregivers of people with disabilities have the right to have their care responsibilities recognized as work worthy of similar respect paid to other professionals.[28] With that in mind, it is worth considering whether Disney has obligations to the caregivers of those with ASD when they visit the parks. For example, if a meltdown can cause physical or emotional injury to a caregiver, does Disney have ethical obligations to help prevent these meltdowns because of safety concerns?

The questions raised here are only a sample of those which could be considered in light of these cases. The answers to these and other questions have implications not only for Disney and these plaintiffs but for any corporation trying to effectively serve customers with varying kinds of disabilities.

NOTES

1   Pacer Monitor, *A.L. et al. v. Walt Disney Parks and Resorts U.S., Inc.*, Pacermonitor.com.
2   Pacer Monitor, *T.P. et al. v. Walt Disney Parks and Resorts U.S., Inc.*, Pacermonitor.com.

3   Centers for Disease Control, "Autism Spectrum Disorder (ASD)," Cdc.gov.

4   "Company Overview of Walt Disney Parks and Resorts U.S., Inc.,"
     Bloomberg.com.

5   Ron Suskind, *Life, Animated: A Story of Sidekicks, Heroes, and Autism*
     (Glendale, CA: Kingswell, 2014).

6   Anne Macklin, "Disney Parks Disability Access Service Card Fact Sheet,"
     Disneyparks.com.

7   Ibid.

8   See, for example, Anne Conway, "Disney Autism Order—2016,"
     Deadline.com.

9   ThisYouNeed.com, "Disneyland Guest Assistance Card" (2013).

10   Macklin, "Disney Parks Disability Access."

11   Lisa Belkin, "Disney World Scam: Wealthy Moms 'Rent' Disabled Guides
     to Skip the Lines (and Shame Humankind)," *Huffington Post* (May 16,
     2013).

12   Walt Disney World, "Private VIP Tours."

13   Paul Brinkmann, "Disney Wins 45 More Autism Lawsuits, but Appeals
     Are Filed," *Orlando Sentinel* (September 26, 2016).

14   Plainsite, *A.L. et al. v. Walt Disney Parks and Resorts*, Plainsite.org.

15   Pacer Monitor, *T.P. et al. v. Walt Disney Parks and Resorts U.S., Inc.*

16   Joseph Shapiro, *No Pity: People with Disabilities Forging a New Civil
     Rights Movement* (New York: Times Books/Random House, 1993), 41–73.

17   National Disability Authority, "What Is Universal Design,"
     Universaldesign.ie.

18   Jonathan Wolff, "Fairness, Respect, and the Egalitarian Ethos," *Philosophy
     & Public Affairs* 27.2 (Spring 1998): 97–122.

19   Michael Walzer, *Spheres of Justice: A Defense of Pluralism and Equality*
     (New York: Basic Books, 1983), 13–17.

20   John Rawls, *A Theory of Justice, Revised Edition* (Cambridge, MA:
     Harvard University Press, 1999), 62.

21   Martha Nussbaum, "Disability and the Social Contract," in *Frontiers of
     Justice: Disability, Nationality, Species Membership* (Cambridge, MA:
     Harvard University Press, 2006), 96–154.

22   Rawls, *A Theory of Justice*, 62.

23   G.A. Cohen, "On the Currency of Egalitarian Justice," *Ethics* 99.4
     (July 1989): 917–20.

24   Elizabeth Anderson, "What Is the Point of Equality?" *Ethics* 109.2
     (January 1999): 287–337.

25 United States Department of Justice, "Americans with Disabilities Act Title III Regulations," ADA.gov.

26 Amartya Sen, *The Idea of Justice* (Cambridge, MA: Harvard University Press, 2009), 234.

27 Nussbaum, *Frontiers of Justice*, 76.

28 Eva Feder Kittay, *Love's Labor: Essays on Women, Equality, and Dependency* (New York: Routledge, 1999), 50–52.

DISCUSSION QUESTIONS

(1) From an ethical (as opposed to a legal) perspective, do you think the DAS is a reasonable accommodation procedure for those with ASD? If you think it is reasonable, how do you think Disney could best respond to the concerns of the plaintiffs in these lawsuits? If you think it is not an ethically reasonable accommodation, what alternatives could Disney consider and how might you go about evaluating which alternatives are best?

(2) Independent of legal requirements, what do you think is the strongest ethical argument for Disney to provide accommodation for people with ASD? What are some counter-arguments to this position and how would you respond to them?

(3) What conception of equality, if any, should Disney use to decide upon a disability accommodation procedure? Consider simple equality, fair equality of opportunity, equality of access to advantage, and equality of capability in formulating your response. Justify your answer. If you think equality shouldn't be a consideration, what other factors should Disney consider and why?

(4) How should Disney prioritize the needs of customers with disabilities against factors like the prevention of potential abuse?

(5) Should the experiences of caregivers of those with ASD be a consideration when evaluating whether the DAS is an ethically reasonable accommodation? If so, why and how should Disney factor those experiences into their decisions about accommodation procedures?

FURTHER READINGS

Lisa Belkin, "Disney World Scam: Wealthy Moms 'Rent' Disabled Guides to Skip the Lines (and Shame Humankind)." Huffingtonpost.com. http://www.huffingtonpost.com/2013/05/14/skipping-lines-at-disney_n_3275836.html. (Accessed October 22, 2017.)

Kimberley Brownlee and Adam Steven Cureton, *Disability and Disadvantage* (New York: Oxford University Press, 2009).

Eva Feder Kittay, *Love's Labor: Essays on Women, Equality, and Dependency* (New York: Routledge, 1999).

Karen Klugman, *Inside the Mouse: Work and Play at Disney World, the Project on Disney*, ed. Stanley Fish and Fredric Jameson (Durham, NC: Duke University Press, 1995).

Martha Craven Nussbaum, *Frontiers of Justice: Disability, Nationality, Species Membership* (Cambridge, MA: Harvard University Press, 2007).

Ron Suskind, *Life, Animated: A Story of Sidekicks, Heroes, and Autism* (Glendale, CA: Kingswell, 2014).

22.

WOMEN'S AUTONOMY AND FETAL PROTECTION

SARA DE VIDO

BACKGROUND

FETAL PROTECTION LAWS CONSTITUTE "AN ARRAY OF LEGISLATION
that purports to promote the protection of fetuses."[1] Illustrative examples are fetal homicide laws (laws separately criminalizing the killing of
a fetus during an attack on a pregnant woman), policies aimed at coun-
tering the abuse of drugs, statutes regulating maternal conduct, and
laws that authorize the confinement of pregnant women to protect the
health of the fetus. According to the study conducted by the Guttmacher
Institute, a research and policy organization based in the United States,
as of October 1, 2017, 24 states and the District of Columbia consider
substance use during pregnancy as child abuse; 23 states and the District
of Columbia require health care professionals to report suspected prenatal drug use, and 7 states require them to test for prenatal drug exposure if they suspect drug use; 19 states have either created or funded
drug treatment programs that specifically target pregnant women, and
17 states and the District of Columbia provide pregnant women with

priority access to state-funded drug treatment programs; 10 states prohibit publicly funded drug treatment programs from discriminating against pregnant women.[2]

In some cases, courts have interpreted existing legal provisions aimed at the protection of children to include the fetus in their scope of application. For example, the Alabama Supreme Court in 2018 expanded the protection granted to the "child" by the Alabama Code 197, Section 26-15-3.2, commonly referred to as "the Chemical Endangerment Statute,"[3] to include both viable (able to survive outside the womb) and non-viable fetuses. The original purpose of the legislation was to protect children from being exposed to drugs in clandestine methamphetamine labs, but these developments significantly broadened the application of the law. The Supreme Court partially confirmed the decision of the lower Court of Criminal Appeals (which considered the statute as applicable to viable fetuses only), and further ruled that the viability distinction was irrelevant. The Court argued that it was illegal for any pregnant woman not only to use substances, but also to enter places where such substances are manufactured or sold. The case, *Ex parte Ankrom and ex parte Kimbrough*,[4] concerned two women, Amanda Kimbrough and Hope Ankrom, who were convicted under the statute. Amanda was sentenced to 10 years in prison after her premature infant died soon after birth and she was tested positive for methamphetamine. She also admitted to having used drugs a few days before going into labor. Hope was arrested, three weeks after giving birth to her healthy child, for having tested positive for cocaine. The three-year prison sentence was suspended, and the woman was placed on probation.[5] A law aimed at punishing anyone putting children at risk was used to criminalize the behavior of pregnant women.

Fetal protection policies, related to fetal protection laws, were adopted by some corporations, usually those operating in male-dominated sectors, in the 1980s and 90s to protect female employees' offspring. One famous case in that respect is *United Automobile Workers v. Johnson Controls Inc.* (JCI), decided in 1991.[6] JCI, a battery manufacturer, continued a fetal protection policy begun by its predecessor, which consisted in advising female workers of the risks deriving from the fetus being exposed to lead. In 1982, the company decided the voluntary program was not sufficient and that it had a "moral requirement" to protect female employees' offspring.[7] The presumption was that all female workers, unless proven otherwise, were able or likely to bear children. No provision was addressed to male workers. According to the policy, the company would not hire women for high-lead exposure jobs. Women were transferred to other jobs apparently without loss of pay or benefits, although the new positions did not allow for overtime pay.[8]

On March 20, 1991, the Supreme Court,[9] reversed the Court of Appeals ruling. In addressing the question of "whether an employer, seeking to protect fetuses, may discriminate against women just because of their ability to become pregnant," the Supreme Court concluded unanimously that the policy was clearly discriminatory on the basis of sex, because fertile men were still allowed the choice of taking risks by applying for particular jobs.[10] The Court considered the statutory "bona fide occupational qualification" (BFOQ), by which employers are permitted to make hiring decisions that in other contexts would constitute discrimination, so long as the discriminatory policy is "necessary to the normal operation of that particular business or enterprise." In this case, the BFOQ provision prohibited an employer from discriminating against a woman because of her capacity to become pregnant "unless her reproductive potential prevents her from performing the duties of her job."[11] The policy could not be justified under the BFOQ statute. However, the Court clearly indicated that the employer's policy might prevail where there is proof that the damage to fetuses is female-mediated only and where the cost of compensation for any harms done to fetuses would constitute a threat to the employer's business.[12]

Much as they agreed that the policy was discriminatory, the Supreme Court judges differed significantly on the scope of statutory BFOQ. Five of the judges were in favor of considering the employer's justification only if it related to the essence of the business, whereas the other four judges deemed that avoiding injuries to third parties (also the fetuses) was part of the normal operation of the business.[13] Some employers later used the Court decision to justify not providing job accommodations to pregnant employees.[14]

ANALYSIS

FETAL PROTECTION LAWS POSE MANY ETHICAL ISSUES, WHICH I will deal with by taking different perspectives: the fetus's, the woman's, the man's, the physician's, and the company's.

Let us start with the fetus. Exposure to lead can have severe consequences on a woman's health, but the effects on health were relevant, at the time of *Johnson Inc.*, only insofar as they affected a potential pregnancy. A "fetal protection law" is not about the protection of the pregnant woman. It is therefore necessary to consider the legal and ethical status of the fetus.

In the *Vo v. France* judgment, for example, the European Court of Human Rights argued that "the potentiality of that being and its capacity to become a person [...] require protection in the name of human dignity, without making it a 'person' with the right to life" enshrined in the European Convention.[15] It continued, saying that "the unborn child's lack of a clear legal status does not necessarily deprive it of all protection under French law,"[16] and that, in the case at issue, the interests of the mother and the child clearly coincided. The case concerned the negligent behavior of a French doctor who ruptured the amniotic membrane of the applicant, causing the termination of her pregnancy. The right to life in the European Convention of Human Rights is granted to "everyone" (Article 2), whereas the American Convention on Human Rights, adopted by numerous countries in Central and South America, grants protection "in general, from the moment of conception" (Article 4.1). Does the latter constitute an international recognition of the personhood of the fetus? The Inter-American Court of Human Rights, in a landmark case on in-vitro fertilization, *Artavia Murillo v. Costa Rica*, interpreted Article 4.1 by saying that the "direct subject of protection is fundamentally the pregnant woman, because the protection of the unborn child is implemented essentially through the protection of the woman," and that "it is not admissible to grant the status of person to the embryo."[17] It further argued that the words "in general" in Article 4.1 of the American Convention mean that "the protection of the right to life under this provision is not absolute, but rather gradual and incremental according to its development, since it is not an absolute and unconditional obligation, but entails [an] understanding that exceptions to the general rule are admissible."[18]

Turning to national jurisprudence, the US Supreme Court, in the famous *Roe v. Wade* case (1973), was "persuaded" that "the word 'person', as used in the Fourteenth Amendment, does not include the unborn,"[19] but found that there was a legitimate interest in potential life "at viability" identified between the 24th and 28th weeks, because "the fetus then presumably has the capability of meaningful life outside the mother's womb."[20] The Alabama court, in the aforementioned case, included both viable and non-viable fetuses in the notion of "child."

Can medical technology help the courts? Is viability a useful scientific concept or is it more a legal "fiction"? At one end of the spectrum are those who believe that moral status begins at conception. At the other end are those who reject prenatal personhood altogether. For instance, Alejandro Madrazo contends that prenatal personhood is "a vehicle for justifying restrictions on women's sexual and reproductive rights and, more specifically, for trumping the right to choose."[21] In an attempt to find some middle ground, Margaret Little elaborated a "gradualist" perspective to respond to the question of whether or not the fetus has a moral status. She acknowledged that "at some point late in pregnancy, the fetus [deserves] the very strong moral protection due to newborns." There is no agreement about prenatal personhood among scholars, let alone among activists, courts, and religious authorities.[22]

The second perspective to consider is that of the woman, and pertains to her autonomy.[23] When women entered the labor market, in particular during the twentieth century, they faced severe discrimination. Unhealthy work conditions were used as a justification to limit female employment, endorsing the paternalistic view that women were in need of constant protection and incapable of determining their own interests.[24] Fetal protection policies were not interested in the individual right to health and reproductive health of the woman, but in the health of the fetus, which was considered worthy of protection. The policies were addressed to women capable of bearing children. The assumption was that a woman *must* intend to become a mother. Another issue is that women continued to be employed in other traditionally female-dominant positions—such as waitressing and nursing—which also had the potential to cause damage to a fetus. Fetal protection policies, it could be seen, only emerged with regard to "male" jobs. Furthermore, in practical terms, the interest of the company was not actually in the well-being of the fetus, but rather in avoiding financial liability for exposing the unborn to dangerous substances. In 1995, in *Pizza Hut of America v. Keefe* (900 P.2d 97, 1995), the Colorado Supreme Court argued, for example, that a separate liability could be conceived for the injuries to the child, independently of any injury suffered by his or her mother, caused before birth by the employer.

In the case of state fetal protection laws, it is the behavior of the mother—in cases of drug addiction, for example—that is criminalized and punished. In the view of one of the judges, Chief Justice Malone (as expressed in *Ex parte Ankrom and ex parte Kimbrough*), the law opened up the possibility of a woman committing a felony even if a criminalized act were committed without knowledge or intent. The judge considered that this application of the law raised "profound concerns" in terms of respecting individuals' rights to due process.[25] What about the case of a woman who is unaware she is pregnant, is arrested, and found to be suffering from the effects of drugs? Any expectant mother can fear prosecution. When can the state replace the autonomous decision of a pregnant woman who is not aware of the risks to her fetus? Women forced to receive medication to protect their fetuses, women prosecuted for the use of substances, women who are unable to work because of these laws—all these situations have a key aspect in common: the health of their fetuses is paid more attention than their own rights and autonomy. One might argue that these laws are a form of discrimination against women because they are based on the conviction that women are reproductive objects and are the ones who must be blamed for any harm to their fetus. Fetal protection laws can also be considered a form of gender-based violence against women, as recently defined by the UN Committee on the elimination of discrimination against women in its General Recommendation No. 35 (2017), meaning a form of violence—mainly (but not only) psychological violence—committed by the State through laws that perpetuate "the subordinate position of women with respect to men and their stereotyped roles."[26]

A third perspective to consider is that of the healthcare professional, or rather of the healthcare professional in relation to the pregnant woman. The relationship between patient and health professional may be impaired by fetal protection laws. As it has been argued, medical staff become "the primary detectives and enforcers of state fetal protection statutes, often with the support of the police, prosecutors, and even judges."[27] Are physicians sufficiently trained to enforce fetal protection laws? Can a woman trust a doctor who is entitled to report her behavior to the authorities? One related question is whether these laws discourage unhealthy and dangerous behaviors or rather encourage women to avoid health services and eventually to interrupt their pregnancies. As pointed out by Chief Justice Malone in *Ex parte Ankrom and ex parte Kimbrough*, the chemical-endangerment statute "will now supply women who have, either intentionally or not, run afoul of the proscriptions of the statute a strong incentive to terminate their pregnancy." Even without resorting to abortion, a woman could be induced to avoid regular medical check-ups, which are important during pregnancy, at the expense of the fetus's health.

Another perspective to consider is that of men. Fetal protection policies were not aimed at protecting men from harmful consequences on their reproductive health. Should it not be considered a form of discrimination against men who do not benefit from the protection against harmful substances in the workplace? What about fathers who are disabled or who die because of exposure, for example, to lead? With regard to fetal protection laws such as the chemical-endangerment statute, could a man be prosecuted for exposing a pregnant woman to *methamphetamines*? According to the interpretation of the Alabama Supreme Court, it appears so, although in the case of *Ex parte Ankrom and ex parte Kimbrough* the Court only addressed maternal behavior. Furthermore, what happens if, in such a case, the man was not aware of the pregnancy? And who should bear the burden of proving whether or not prior awareness existed?

From a business point of view, how should companies tackle similar situations? In the *UAW v. Johnson Controls* judgment, Justice Scalia contended that a "substantial risk of tort liability" would be an acceptable BFOQ exception.[28] What constitutes a "substantial risk of tort liability"? Does the risk of being sued by a pregnant woman for exposure of her fetus to chemical substances fall under this category? Would it be possible to argue that company policies demonstrate the same structural discrimination that exists in society as a whole, suggesting that only women are in need of protection, and that, for this reason, others are responsible for deciding what is better for them?

We should also consider another possibility: to shift the focus from a general prohibition addressed to certain categories of persons to the adoption of measures to prevent damages to women's and men's reproductive health. There are alternatives to fetal protection laws and policies, such as strategies that are capable of "maximizing women's employment choices and reproductive health, and at the same time of minimizing risks for the fetus."[29] Increased maternal leaves; prenatal care; research on workplace hazards; support to women before, during, and after childbirth—including enrollment into treatment programs—could help avoid criminalization of women's behavior. Otherwise, fetal protection laws risk criminalizing the behavior of any fertile woman engaged in activities that could potentially harm a fetus simply because she might get pregnant sooner or later.

NOTES

1 Goodwin (2014), 787.
2 Guttmacher Institute, "Substance Use During Pregnancy," https://www.guttmacher.org/state-policy/explore/substance-use-during-pregnancy
3 Chemical Endangerment of Exposing a Child to an Environment in which Controlled Substances Are Produced or Distributed, Ala. Code § 26-15-3.2.
4 No. 1110176, 2013 WL 135748. Goodwin (2014), 788.
5 Suppé (2014), 55.
6 *UAW v. Johnson Controls, Inc.*, 886 F.2d 871, 875 (7th Cir. 1989) *(en banc)*, cert. *granted, 110* S. Ct. 1522 (1990), *rev'd and remanded, 11* S. Ct. 1196 (1991).
7 O'Brien et al. (1991), 151.
8 Ibid., 152.
9 *United Automobile Workers v. Johnson Controls*, 499 U.S. 187 (1991), International Union, United Automobile, Aerospace & Agricultural Implement Workers of America, UAW, No. 89–1215 (1991).
10 O'Brien et al. (1991), 172.
11 *UAW v. Johnson Controls*, para. 1207.
12 O'Brien et al. (1991), 183.
13 O'Brien et al. (1991), 182.
14 Feldmeier (2008).
15 *Vo v. France*, Appl. No. 53924/00, July 8, 2004.
16 *Vo v. France*, para. 86.
17 *Artavia Murillo et al. v. Costa Rica Judgment*, November 28, 2012, paras. 222 and 223 (Preliminary objections, merits, reparations and costs).
18 *Artavia Murillo et al.*, para. 264.
19 *Roe v. Wade*, 410 U.S. 113 (1973), 156.
20 *Roe v. Wade*, 163–64.
21 Madrazo (2014), 344.
22 Qtd. in Nelson (2013), 115.
23 In terms of right to reproductive autonomy, see Nelson (2013), 70.
24 Blan (1994), 29.
25 *Ex parte Ankrom*, 84.
26 General recommendation No. 35 on gender-based violence against women, updating general recommendation No. 19 CEDAW/C/GC/35 (July 14, 2017).

See also the book project *Violence against Women's Health*, by Sara
De Vido, vawh.wordpress.com.

27   Goodwin (2014), 812.
28   *UAW v. Johnson Controls* (US Supreme Court), paras. 1216–17.
29   Blank (1994), 154.

DISCUSSION QUESTIONS

(1)   Fetal protection policies and fetal protection laws have been adopted
      in order to protect fetuses from certain harmful behaviors by pregnant
      women. Should the interest of the fetus prevail over a pregnant woman's
      autonomy? Always, never, or only in certain circumstances?
(2)   Why might fetal protection laws and policies be considered a form of
      discrimination against women? What about a form of gender-based
      violence against women?
(3)   Do you think that a law could be designed to effectively and
      simultaneously protect *both* pregnant women and their fetuses? What
      would such a law include?
(4)   Do some of your own research on the effects of drugs on pregnant women
      and their fetuses, as well as on the health effects on the same individuals
      of alcohol and of coffee. Compare the two situations, and comment on
      the assumption that certain drugs are ethically worse than others. What
      about driving "risky" means of transportation, such as motorcycles?
      Should those sorts of behaviors by pregnant women be regulated too?
(5)   Concerning other unhealthy behaviors, such as eating junk food, do
      you think that the State should guarantee healthy food to all pregnant
      women?

FURTHER READINGS

Robert H. Blank, *Fetal Protection in the Workplace: Women's Rights, Business
      Interests, and the Unborn* (New York: Columbia University Press, 1994).
Jessica M. Boudreaux and John W. Thompson, "Maternal-Fetal Rights and
      Substance Abuse: Gestation without Representation," *Journal of the
      American Academy of Psychiatry and the Law* 43.2 (2015): 137–40.
John P. Feldmeier, "Fetal Protection Policies in the Workplace: The Response
      to *UAW v. Johnson Controls*," *Politics & Policies* 23.4 (1995): 657–87.
Michele Goodwin, "Fetal Protection Laws: Moral Panic and the New
      Constitutional Battlefront," *California Law Review* 102 (2014): 781–876.

Chancey B. Herbolsheimer, "Fetal Homicide Laws: The Policing of Women's Bodies," *Inquiries Journal* 8.10 (2016).

Alejandro Madrazo, "Narratives of Prenatal Personhood in Abortion Law," in *Abortion Law in Transnational Perspective: Cases and Controversies*, ed. Rebecca J. Cook, Joanna N. Erdman, Bernard M. Dickens (Philadelphia: University of Pennsylvania Press, 2014), 327–46.

Erin Nelson, *Law, Policy and Reproductive Autonomy* (London: Hart, 2013).

Christine N. O'Brien et al., "Employer Fetal Protection Policies at Work: Balancing Reproductive Hazards with Title VII Rights," *Marquette Law Review* 74 (1991): 147–229.

Rachel Suppé, "Pregnancy on Trial: The Alabama Supreme Court's Erroneous Application of Alabama Chemical Endangerment Law in *Ex parte Ankrom*," *Health Law & Policy Brief* 7.2 (2014): 49–75.

Elizabeth Wicks, *The State and the Body* (Oxford and Portland: Hart, 2016).

23.

GENDER-BASED DISCRIMINATION: GLASS CEILINGS AND SEXUAL HARASSMENT

SARA DE VIDO

BACKGROUND

THE HASHTAG #METOO IS THE VOICE OF A GLOBAL MOVEMENT against sexual harassment. On October 15, 2017, the 44-year-old actress and activist Alyssa Milano tweeted, "If you've been sexually harassed or assaulted write 'me too' as a reply to this tweet."[1] The tweet was launched a few days after the allegations of sexual harassment and abuses committed by the famous Hollywood producer Harvey Weinstein, reported by the *New York Times* and the *New Yorker*. Thousands of women replied to the Tweet and the message spread worldwide. Women told stories of sexual harassment and other sexual crimes of which they have been victims over the years. They reported episodes of sexual harassment in the workplace, in classrooms, in restaurants, during job interviews.[2] The reaction to the movement was mixed. On the one hand, dozens of female celebrities started to reveal cases of sexual harassment and rape by famous producers, photographers, and actors, breaking the silence that surrounded their world. On the other hand, another famous actress,

Catherine Deneuve, joined 99 other French women in a letter that was published on *Le Monde*: "we defend the liberty to disturb," (the word used is *importuner*, meaning to disturb, to annoy, and not *harceler*, which is to harass) "which is fundamental for sexual liberty."[3] As women, they said that they do not adhere to a feminism that "leads to hate with regard to men and sexuality." Deneuve later apologized to all victims of sexual violence; while adhering to her original statement, she declared that she did not condone sexual abuse or misconduct. Conservative positions have developed across the world, and especially in the US, blaming the #MeToo movement for accusing men without respecting their due process rights, and in the end damaging women and causing a drawback in the long battle for equality.[4]

On International Women's Day, the UN mandates on women's rights supported the #MeToo movement, calling it as a "transformative, liberating and empowering" movement. A few days later, the Special Reporter on violence against women (VAW), Dubravka Šimonović, clearly endorsed the #MeToo movement in her statement to the Commission on the status of women:

> It is my firm conviction that these powerful few words #Metoo should guide the discussions of this year's session of the Commission. Our challenge now is to find ways and construct the means to support this and similar movements, with the aim of achieving a change that will put a lasting end to tolerance of the violence against women.[5]

What emerges from the statement is the attempt to change attitudes that normalize sexual harassment, that consider it as a "normal" practice in the relationship between women and men. Even though sexual harassment might be addressed to both women and men, it disproportionately affects women, because it is connected to the stereotyped roles of women in society.

These issues are particularly pressing in business where women encounter difficulties in rising through the ranks of corporations, in getting promotions and benefits *because they are* women. This phenomenon is called the "glass ceiling." An interesting case in that respect has involved Novartis Corporation, the world renown pharmaceutical and healthcare company, and Alcon Laboratories Inc., one of its divisions. The lawsuit began in March 2015 and was settled in 2016. Novartis had already faced a discrimination case, which led to a $253 million verdict against the corporation in 2010. In the most recent case, Elyse Dickerson, on behalf of herself, and Susan Orr, on behalf of herself and other similarly situated women, sued Alcon Laboratories, Inc. for gender discrimination.

The two women were Global Directors at Alcon. According to the individual and collective action complaint,[6] Dickerson was Alcon's first female Global Director and managed one of Alcon's largest product portfolios, whereas Orr was the primary driver in the acquisition of a potential blockbuster medication.[7] Nonetheless, the two directors were paid less than similarly situated men and faced discrimination with regard to career-enhancing opportunities.

Susan Orr eventually resigned. Elyse Dickerson fought gender discrimination from within. In response, the company retaliated by starting an investigation to find possible reasons to fire her. During a global webcast watched by the company's employees around the world, she asked what the management was doing to change the gender gap in the leadership of the Alcon division.[8] She did not get an answer.

Dickerson asked for redress under Title VII of the Civil Rights Act of 1964 as amended, and to be reinstated to the job she would be doing without Novartis's discriminatory practices. She also asked for $10 million in damages.[9] Orr sought redress, both on her behalf and on behalf of many women in similar situations, for violations of the Equal Pay Act of 1963. She asked for $100 million damages, including, but not limited to, back pay, liquidated damages, and reasonable attorneys' fees and litigation costs.[10] She additionally sought redress under the Civil Rights Act of 1964.

The complaint filed by the two women emphasizes the company's "boys' club atmosphere."[11] An example of this attitude is the fact that the company refused to fire a male senior marketing manager who, during a meeting, undid his belt buckle and said "let me introduce you to the newest member of the team."[12] Another example of the "club" is the organization of "breakfast clubs" to which female employees were hardly ever included.[13] These behaviors led to diminished compensation and fewer career-enhancing opportunities for women. Plaintiffs demanded a trial by jury. After less than one year, Novartis agreed to pay $8.2 million to settle the collective class action lawsuit filed by female employees who complained of discrimination regarding pay and promotional opportunities. The settlement was far less than the $110 million initially sought. Elyse Dickerson did not accept the settlement. A motion filed by the defendant to sever the claims brought by the woman and transfer the venue of those claims to the US District Court for the Northern District of Texas was granted on April 21, 2016.[14]

ANALYSIS

THE WIDESPREAD PHENOMENA OF THE GLASS CEILING AND SEX-ual harassment in the workplace comprise discrimination based on gender and against women *because they are* women or because they affect women disproportionately. Women's rights have been recognized at the international level, starting from the nineties. Yet, discrimination in the workplace is still pervasive. How is this possible after adopting so many legal instruments? What is relevant in the analysis of discrimination in the workplace is that it is no longer a problem of discrimination *de jure*, meaning a discrimination clearly proscribed by law, but a discrimination *de facto*, that is, rooted in society.

The principle of non-discrimination on the basis of gender is encapsulated in several international legal instruments—see for example Article 2 of the Universal Declaration of Human Rights of 1948, and Article 2(2) of the International Covenant on economic social and cultural rights of 1966—and is included in national constitutions.

Article 1 of the United Nations Convention on the elimination of all forms of discrimination against women (CEDAW)—which the United States has not yet ratified—defines "discrimination against women" as "any distinction, exclusion or restriction made on the basis of sex which has the effect or purpose of impairing or nullifying the recognition, enjoyment or exercise by women, irrespective of their marital status, on a basis of equality of men and women, of human rights and fundamental freedoms in the political, economic, social, cultural, civil or any other field." Article 11 of the same Convention clearly focuses on equality in the field of employment. States parties shall take all appropriate measures to eliminate discrimination against women in the workplace and grant equal rights to men and women, including:

> [...] (b) The right to the same employment opportunities, including the application of the same criteria for selection in matters of employment; [...] (c) The right to free choice of profession and employment, the right to promotion, job security and all benefits and conditions of service and the right to receive vocational training and retraining,

including apprenticeships, advanced vocational training and recurrent training; (d) The right to equal remuneration, including benefits, and to equal treatment in respect of work of equal value, as well as equality of treatment in the evaluation of the quality of work.

According to the *Oxford English Dictionary*, the term "glass ceiling" was first used in 1984 to identify an invisible upper limit in corporations that prevents women from getting promotions, pay raises, benefits, and from rising in the ranks. Gay Bryant, in her book *The Working Woman Report*, defined it as follows:

> Throughout the corporate world—faster in some industries, slower in others—the door to real power for women has opened. But it is just ajar. Women may already be in middle management, but the steps from there up to the senior hierarchy are likely to be slow and painstakingly small. Partly because corporations are structured as pyramids, with many middle managers trying to move up into the few available spots, and partly because of continuing, though more subtle, discrimination, a lot of women are hitting a "glass ceiling" and finding they can rise no further.[15]

In 1987, in a report on the corporate glass ceiling by Ann Morrison, Randall White, Ellen Van Velsor, and the Center for Creative Leadership, the glass ceiling was defined as a "transparent barrier, that kept women from rising above a certain level in corporations [...]. [T]he glass ceiling applies to women as a group who are kept from advancing higher *because they are women* [emphasis original]."[16] The authors demonstrated that although women constituted an important part of the workforce in the US, it was difficult in the nineties to find women at the top of America's largest corporations. The US Department of Labor's 1991 *Report on the Glass Ceiling Initiative* further defined glass ceiling as "those artificial barriers based on attitudinal or organizational bias that prevent qualified individuals from advancing upward in their organization into management-level positions."[17]

The situation has not improved much over the years despite laws and policies aimed at achieving gender equality, but not *de facto*, in what actually happens in business. In the US, only 5.8 per cent of CEOs in companies listed in the S&P 500 index are women, according to a report published in 2017.[18] The situation is similar in other countries. In the

European Union, women are outnumbered by men in leadership positions in the corporate sector. On average, according to data collected by the European Institute for Gender Equality, in October 2017 women accounted for 25.3 per cent of board members in the largest publicly listed companies in the EU Member State.[19] France was the only State with a percentage above 40 per cent. The European Commission put the issue of women in leadership positions high on the political agenda in its 2010 Strategy for Equality between Women and Men.[20]

The glass ceiling is the product of the "unequal power relations between women and men." Over the years, international, regional, and national bodies have committed to breaking the glass ceiling through laws and policies. In the European Union, the European Commission has proposed a Directive on improving gender balance among directors of companies listed on stock exchanges.[21] It provides for quantitative objectives for Member States and emphasizes the importance of boards setting transparent selection criteria for candidates. However, is the system of "quotas" efficient in dealing with the glass ceiling? Is there not a risk of reverse discrimination against men?

Research indicates that quotas can only be a temporary answer to the problem, because they do not address the systemic causes and effects of gender discrimination.[22] A broader range of actions is required, including the eradication of gender stereotypes regarding leadership skills and the role of women in society. Furthermore, States must adopt measures that allow both women and men to reconcile family and work life. Measures only addressed to women are themselves a form of discrimination against women, because they take for granted the traditional role of a woman in the society, as vulnerable subject rather than actor of change.

Gender inequality and the glass ceiling are closely connected to sexual harassment, which often occurs in the workplace. Sexual harassment is a practice that is centuries old, as one author has argued, "at least, if we define sexual harassment as unwanted sexual relations imposed by superiors on subordinates at work."[23] African-American women were exploited in the US without legal protection, and free women employed in domestic service "commonly faced sexual advances by men of the households in which they worked."[24] Helen Campbell reported in 1887 on women wage-workers and noted the common understanding that "[h]ousehold service has become synonymous with the worst degradation that comes to woman."[25] In her pioneering work *Sexual Harassment of Working Women* (1979), Catharine MacKinnon argued that sexual harassment was a form of discrimination based on sex and that the unequal power relations in the workplace mirrored the ones existing in the household.[26]

The US Equal Opportunity Employment Commission defines workplace sexual harassment as "unwelcome sexual advances or conduct of a sexual nature which unreasonably interferes with the performance of a person's job or creates an intimidating, hostile, or offensive work environment," and includes several practices "from persistent offensive sexual jokes to inappropriate touching to posting offensive material on a bulletin board."[27] The Council of Europe Convention on preventing and combating violence against women and domestic violence, adopted in 2011 and entered into force in 2014, defines sexual harassment as any form of "unwanted verbal, non-verbal or physical conduct of a sexual nature with the purpose or effect of violating the dignity of a person, in particular when creating an intimidating, hostile, degrading, humiliating or offensive environment" (Article 40).

The workplace is sometimes an environment in which offensive sexual "jokes" and inappropriate touching take place. Similar behaviors can have severe consequences on the well-being and psychological health of a person, inducing him/her to leave their jobs. Though this may not at first glance appear to relate to the glass ceiling, sexual harassment has systemic effects that limit women's opportunities in the workplace.

NOTES

1   However, MeToo without the hashtag was coined by activist Tarana Burke in 2006.
2   R. Mellen, "The Women of the #MeToo Movement," for *Coming Forward*.
3   "Nous défendons une liberté d'importuner indispensable à la liberté sexuelle," *Le Monde* (January 9, 2018), www.lemonde. fr/idees/article/2018/01/09/nous-defendons-une-liberte-d-importuner-indispensable-a-la-liberte-sexuelle_5239134_3232. html?xtmc=deneuve&xtcr=1.
4   See, for example, the *American Conservative*, online.
5   62nd Session of the Commission on the Status of Women (CSW), Statement by Ms. Dubravka Šimonović, Special Reporter on violence against women, its causes and consequences, March 12, 2018.

6   *Elyse Dickerson and Susan Orr v. Novartis corporation and Alcon laboratories Inc.*, US District Court for the Southern District of New York, No. 1:15-cv-1980 (hereinafter, complaint).

7   Para. 2 of the complaint.

8   Para. 57 of the complaint.

9   Para. 9 of the complaint.

10 Para. 10 of the complaint.

11 Para. 20 of the complaint.

12 Para. 26 of the complaint.

13 Para. 28 of the complaint.

14 *Dickerson et al. v. Novartis Corporation et al.*, No. 1:2015cv01980– Document 78 (S.D.N.Y. 2016).

15 G. Bryant, *The Working Woman Report*, 19.

16 A. Morrison, R. White, E. Van Velsor, *Breaking the Glass Ceiling: Can Women Reach the Top of America's Largest Corporations?* (New York: Perseus Publishing, 1992; repr. 1994), 13.

17 *Report on the Glass Ceiling Initiative*, US Department of Labor (1991).

18 The Boston Consulting Group, *Proven Measures and Hidden Gems for Improving Gender Diversity* (September 12, 2017).

19 European Commission, *Report on Equality between Men and Women in the EU* (2018), 31.

20 European Commission, "Gender Equality," http://ec.europa.eu/justice/gender-equality/files/strategy_equality_women_men_en.pdf.

21 2017 Report, 29.

22 T.A. Thomas, "Reconsidering the Remedy of Gender Quotas," *Harvard Journal of Law and Gender* (2016).

23 Reva B. Siegel, "Directions in Sexual Harassment Law," in *A Short History of Sexual Harassment*, ed. Reva B. Siegel and Catharine MacKinnon (New Haven: Yale University Press, 2004), 3.

24 Ibid.

25 Qtd. in Ibid.

26 C.A. MacKinnon, *Sexual Harassment of Working Women: A Case of Sex Discrimination* (New Haven: Yale University Press, 1979).

27 FindLaw, "Sexual Harassment at Work," https://employment.findlaw.com/employment-discrimination/sexual-harassment-at-work.html.

DISCUSSION QUESTIONS

(1) What is the glass ceiling? Why do you think the metaphor of the glass is (or is not) accurate?

(2) Has the #MeToo movement helped women to report episodes of sexual harassment in the workplace? How? Do you think that without Twitter the movement would have had the same impact on society?

(3) If you were asked to elaborate a code of conduct for a corporation to stop sexual harassment, what would you recommend?

(4) If you were asked to help a corporation to counter the glass ceiling, which measures would you recommend?

(5) How do you think it is possible to dismantle gender stereotypes that are centuries old?

FURTHER READINGS

Robert C. Bird, "Precarious Work: The Need for Flextime Employment Rights and Proposals for Reform," *Berkeley Journal of Employment and Labor Law* 37 (2016).

Gay Bryant, *The Working Woman Report: Succeeding in Business in the 80s* (New York: Simon and Schuster, 1984).

European Commission, *Report on Equality between Women and Men* (Brussels, 2017).

Glass Ceiling Commission, *A Solid Investment: Making Full Use of the Nation's Human Capital* (1995).

Catharine A. MacKinnon, *Sexual Harassment of Working Women: A Case of Sex Discrimination* (New Haven: Yale University Press, 1979).

Ann M. Morrison, Randall P. White, and Ellen Van Velsor, *Breaking the Glass Ceiling: Can Women Reach the Top of America's Largest Corporations?* (New York: Perseus Publishing, 1992; repr. 1994).

Reva B. Siegel, "Directions in Sexual Harassment Law," in *A Short History of Sexual Harassment*, ed. Reva B. Siegel and Catharine MacKinnon (New Haven: Yale University Press, 2004).

Janet Sigal, "International Sexual Harassment," *Annals of the New York Academy of Science* 1087 (2006): 356–69.

Tracy A. Thomas, "Reconsidering the Remedy of Gender Quotas," *Harvard Journal of Law and Gender* (2016).

24

WOMEN AND ADVERTISING

SARA DE VIDO

BACKGROUND

VIOLENCE AGAINST WOMEN IS STILL A WORRYING AND WIDESPREAD phenomenon. Intimate partner violence (IPV) or domestic violence, which includes different types of violence perpetrated by a current or former partner, represents the most severe form of violence against women in every society. According to the 2014 report prepared by the National Intimate Partner and Sexual Violence Survey (NISVS), administered by the US Centers for Disease Control and Prevention, nearly 1 in 5 women (19.3 per cent) and 1 in 59 men (1.7 per cent) have been raped in their lifetime; 1 in 4 women (22.3 per cent) have been the victim of severe physical violence by an intimate partner, while 1 in 7 men (14.0 per cent) have experienced the same.[1] In Europe, a survey conducted by the European Union Agency for Fundamental Rights in 2014 showed that one in three women (33 per cent) has experienced physical and/or sexual violence since she was 15 years old, and that 22 per cent of all women who have a (current or previous) partner have experienced physical and/or sexual violence by that partner since the age of 15.[2] The report is based on 42,000 interviews with women living in the 28 EU Member States. At the international level, 35 per cent of women worldwide have experienced either physical and/or sexual intimate partner violence or non-partner sexual violence, according to a global review of available data prepared by the World Health Organization.[3]

Despite these disturbing statistics, business frequently produces and promotes products with images that objectify women, or portray their domination or violence against them. Media can influence consumer behavior and have the power to shape people's perception toward gender.[4] One major ethical concern is that advertisements and products depict and encourage, directly or indirectly, violence against women. A sample of recent ads from major companies illustrates this point.

In 2013 a web advertisement promoted Ford's Figo small car, the Indian version of the Fiesta. The ad, produced by the Indian advertising agency JWT, features three voluptuous women in a car trunk with their mouths gagged and their hands tied. Sitting in the front seat, the former Italian Prime Minister, Silvio Berlusconi, who has been involved in numerous sex scandals, smiles while making a V-sign. The caption reads, "Leave your worries behind with Figo's extra-large boot." Ford replied that it had not authorized the ad's publication, which was "contrary to the standards of professionalism and decency within Ford and our agency partners."[5]

Another example is the online ad created by Dolce & Gabbana in 2007 and soon after banned from Italian publications. It shows a woman wearing black lingerie and stilettos held down by a half-naked man. Three men are standing around them and are looking at her. The image was criticized for simulating a "gang rape" for the purpose of promoting fashion. What is striking is the element of domination, of the strength of the man over the woman.

Other ads emphasize the domination of men over women that "evoke"[6] rather than show episodes of violence.[6] A Marc Jacobs ad published in 2008 shows disembodied women's legs sticking out of a shopping bag. It is unclear whether or not the legs are attached to the body. A Blender's ad shows a naked female body hanging in pieces from the ceiling like meat in a butcher shop. A Calvin Klein ad depicts an elegantly dressed woman lying on the floor. An ominous male shape is approaching: is she waiting for him or is something bad about to happen? Belvedere, a Polish vodka brand, used a comedy video portraying a woman trying to wiggle out of a smiling man's grasp (supposedly her partner). The sentence accompanying the message can easily be read as sexual innuendo: "Unlike some people ... Belvedere always goes down smoothly." The ad was removed and Belvedere sent a donation to a women's charity.

Even examples that are meant to be "positive" can elicit a problematic message. Italy's football team Fiorentina joined the campaign to protect women from violence in November 2014. In a photo posted on Facebook, the footballers (all men) stand with their arms crossed over their chest; they create a sort of "barrier" in order to protect some women, their arms alongside their body, standing in line. The caption reads: "In difesa ci siamo noi" ("we are your defense").[7] Messages posted on Facebook by several women were extremely positive, but some women's associations did not agree. The photo shows women as vulnerable and defenseless persons, unable to save themselves from violence without the intervention of men.

The above examples are different in various ways, but they all represent women as weaker, and more vulnerable, than men. The question, then, is whether, and to what extent, media influence violence against women, and to provide an analysis from an international human rights legal perspective.

ANALYSIS

ONE ISSUE IS THAT ADVERTISEMENTS MAY INFLUENCE ATTITUDES that encourage violence toward women and reinforce sexist institutions. Radical feminists have argued that misogynistic images in advertising and entertainment create cultural support for men's violence.[8] Depicting women as objects (for example as "parts" of a body), or in prostration of some kind, or as vulnerable subjects, can lead "men to be more accepting of violence towards women and less sympathetic towards women's viewpoints and feelings in the sexual and non-sexual arena."[9] The objectification of women's bodies in advertisements results in dehumanization, and it is the first step in justifying violence against them.[10]

In her research on pornography, Catharine MacKinnon emphasized the "social hierarchy of men over women," in particular the presence of "so many distinctive features of women's status as second-class," including the servility and the display, and the requisite presentation of self as a beautiful thing.[11] She then posited that "male sexuality is apparently activated by violence against women and expresses itself in violence against women to a significant extent."[12] On her account, ads showing violence encourage violence by virtue of the representation of male domination over women. This position is reflected in the work of Jean Kilbourne, who argued in 1999 that "male violence is subtly encouraged by ads that encourage men to be forceful and dominant and to value sexual intimacy more than emotional intimacy."[13]

In some computer games that are so interactive they look like real life, that simulate sexual acts, murders, and violence, sex can be viewed as "largely a spectator sport for its participants."[14] If it is entertainment, it gradually permeates society, becomes something that is part of our culture, and is therefore accepted and not questioned.

> Decades of critiques by media studies scholars have not produced a significant reduction in negative representations of women in media and entertainment. If anything, today's girls grow up with a more amplified and widespread circulation of pornography, soft porn, graphic "entertainment" violence, and dead bodies.[15]

Feminist arguments are supported by meta-analyses that have investigated the relationship between media violence and aggression. For example, a group of psychologists from the American Psychological Society have demonstrated that "exposure [of young people] to violent scenes may activate a complex set of associations that are related to aggressive ideas or emotions, thereby temporarily increasing the accessibility of aggressive thoughts, feelings, and scripts."[16] A recent report prepared by the Commission on Media Violence established by the International Society for Research on Aggression (ISRA) contends that if the violent content of a movie or an ad is seen as "fun" or "normal," then "aggression concepts will be classically conditioned with positive feelings [...] such as seeing aggression as a more acceptable response to provocation."[17] Watching a violent ad does not automatically lead men to assault women; it is not a simple "cause-and-effect" relationship. However, although findings vary according to the samples' ages, the research paradigm, and participants' gender-role orientation, empirical work supports the thesis that exposure to media and ads is a risk factor for increased aggression in both the short and the long run.

Furthermore, even if social scientists still dispute the extent—if any—of the effects of some forms of advertising, many feminists contend that such ads constitute harm in themselves independently of their effects. Even if violent media cannot be shown to contribute to violence or discrimination, images that demean, degrade, or depict violence against women are still morally objectionable because their content is offensive.

If we grant that violence in the media can contribute to violent behavior or that violent media is in itself offensive, we are faced with an ethical conflict between freedom of expression and censorship. Should freedom of expression protect media's and advertising agencies' use of violent or degrading images? Or should measures be taken to eliminate or reduce images that encourage violence? If so, which images warrant censorship? Only images that explicitly depict violence or images that can be interpreted as having violent meanings? What about images that objectify women or include sexist representations? Who answers these questions? How should laws and polices be enforced? Is law the instrument for prohibiting certain images which encourage violence, or should companies voluntarily comply with certain standards?

It is useful to turn to international human rights law in order to understand whether or not it has a role in answering these questions. The UN Convention on the Elimination of All Forms of Discrimination against Women (CEDAW), adopted in 1979 by the UN General Assembly, is the first international legal instrument aimed at protecting women, although it does not contain the definition of violence against women.[18] Even though the Convention does not include provisions on media, States parties are required to take all necessary measures in order to "modify the social and cultural patterns of conduct of men and women" (Art. 5). Media can contribute to changing social and cultural patterns. In 1995, the Beijing Platform for Action, a non-binding act, stressed the fact that "images in the media of violence against women, [...] as well as the use of women and girls as sex objects, including pornography, are factors contributing to the continued prevalence of such violence, adversely influencing the community at large, in particular children and young people."[19] Accordingly, one of the actions recommended is raising awareness of "the responsibility of the media in promoting non-stereo-typed images of women and men, as well as in eliminating patterns of media presentation that generate violence, and encourage those responsible for media content to establish professional guidelines and codes of conduct."[20] The objectification or "commodification" of women has also been emphasized in the non-binding observations prepared by the CEDAW Committee regarding the implementation of the Convention in several States parties.[21] Furthermore, the Commission on the Status of Women encouraged media "to the extent consistent with freedom of expression, [...] to improve public awareness of violence against women and girls, to train those who work in the media and to develop and strengthen self-regulatory mechanisms to promote balanced and non-stereotypical portrayals of women."[22]

Guidelines for media are also mentioned in the Inter-American Convention on the Prevention, Punishment and Eradication of Violence against Women, adopted in 1994, in which States parties agree to undertake actions "to encourage the communications media to develop appropriate media guidelines in order to contribute to the eradication of violence against women in all its forms, and to enhance respect for the dignity of women" (Art. 8, letter g). The Council of Europe Istanbul Convention on Preventing and Combating Violence against Women and Domestic Violence, adopted in 2011 and entered into force on August 1, 2014, includes among States' obligations a provision on media: "Parties shall encourage the private sector, the information and communication technology sector and the media, with due respect for freedom of expression and their independence, to participate in the elaboration and implementation of policies and to set guidelines and self-regulatory standards to prevent violence against women and to enhance respect for their dignity" (Art. 17). In its recommendations in 2011, the Committee of Ministers of the Council of Europe posited that "Media organizations should be encouraged to adopt self-regulatory measures, internal codes of conduct/ethics and internal supervision, and develop standards in media coverage that promote gender equality."[23]

The international community has clearly taken a position against gender-based violence; the same position is confirmed by numerous judgments rendered by regional courts of human rights. Instead of asking States to adopt new legislation, however, international legal instruments—both binding instruments such as conventions and non-binding ones such as the Beijing Platform—have promoted a self-regulatory regime introduced and accepted by media. For example, in 2011 a group of both unions (including the International Federation of Journalists) and employers (including the European Broadcasting Union) adopted a "Framework of Actions on Gender Equality in the Audiovisual Sector in Europe," which affirms that "European social partners support fair and balanced gender portrayal while defending the fundamental principle of freedom of creative expression for film and broadcast creative content."[24] Few concrete guidelines are provided, however. Furthermore, in the BBC "Advertising & Sponsorship Guidelines," effective as of June 22, 2015, there is no explicit prohibition of advertisements encouraging, directly or indirectly, violence against women.[25] A clearer example of a code of conduct addressing gender issues is the "Canadian Code of Advertising Standards," which includes an entire section on "Gender Portrayal" and stresses that "caution should be taken to ensure that the overall impression of an ad does not violate the spirit of gender equality even though the individual elements of the ad may not violate any particular guideline."[26]

NOTES

1   Matthew J. Breiding, et al., "Prevalence and Characteristics of Sexual Violence, Stalking, and Intimate Partner Violence Victimization— National Intimate Partner and Sexual Violence Survey, United States, 2011," Surveillance Summaries, Centers for Disease Control and Prevention, September 5, 2014 / 63(SS08); 1–18.

2   FRA. 2014. *Violence against Women: An EU-wide Survey* (Luxembourg: Publication Office of the EU, 2014).

3   World Health Organization, Global and Regional Estimates of Violence against Women (2013), 2.

4   Roger Crisp, "Persuasive Advertising, Autonomy, and the Creation of Desire," *Journal of Business Ethics* 6.5 (1987): 413–18. Robert L. Arrington, "Advertising and Behavior Control," *Journal of Business Ethics* 1.1 (1982): 3–12.

5   Dean Nelson, "Ford Criticised for Indian Advert with Women Stuffed in the Boot," *Telegraph* (March 24, 2013).

6   See Women and Advertising, Huffington Post, and also Dominic Green, "15 Recent Ads That Glorify Sexual Violence against Women," *Business Insider* (May 18, 2013).

7   ACF Fiorentina, "In difesa ci siamo noi," online.

8   Ana J. Bridges and Robert Jensen, "Pornography," in Renzetti et al., eds., *Sourcebook on Violence against Women* (Thousand Oaks: Sage, 2011), 137.

9   Barrie Gunter, *Media Sex: What Are the Issues?* (Abingdon: Routledge, 2002). Experiments were conducted as early as the 1980s.

10 Skyla Seamans, "We're Not Buying What You're Selling: Violence against Women in Advertisements," *Violence against Women in the Media*, Susan B. Anthony Women's Center at MCLA Newsletter (2010). See also the documentary by Jean Kilbourne, *Killing Us Softly* (1979).

11 Catharine MacKinnon, "Sexuality, Pornography, and Method: 'Pleasure under Patriarchy,'" *Ethics* 99.2 (1989): 316–17.

12   Ibid., 334.

13   Jean Kilborne, *Can't Buy My Love: How Advertising Changes the Way We Think and Feel* (New York: Touchstone, 1999), 272.

14   MacKinnon, 327, note 15.

15   Joanne Clarke Dillman, *Women and Death in Film, TV, and News* (New York: Palgrave, 2014), 82.

16   Craig A. Anderson et al., "The Influence of Media on Youth," *Psychological Science in the Public Interest* 4.3 (2003): 81–110, at 95.

17   Barbara Krahé, Chair, ISRA Commission on Media Violence, "Report of the Media Violence Commission International Society for Research on Aggression (ISRA)," *Aggressive Behaviour* 38.5 (2012): 335–41, at 338.

18   A definition introduced in the "UN Declaration on the Elimination of Violence against Women," adopted by the UN General Assembly on December 20, 1993. A/RES/48/104.

19   "Beijing Platform for Action. 1995," Chapter IV: "Strategic Objectives and Actions," Par. 118.

20   Ibid., para. 125, letter j.

21   For example, "Report on Italy. 2011." CEDAW/C/ITA/CO/6. Para. 22; and "Report on Norway. 2012." CEDAW/C/NOR/CO/8. Para. 21.

22   UN Commission on the Status of Women (2013). "Report on the Fifty-seventh Session" (March 4–15, 2013). E/2013/27, E/CN.6/2013/11. Part B (vv).

23   Recommendation CM/Rec(2013)1 of the Committee of Ministers to member States on gender equality and media, adopted by the Committee of Ministers on July 10, 2013 at the 1176th meeting of the Ministers' Deputies.

24   UNI Global Union, "Framework on Gender Equality in the Audiovisual Sector" (January 8, 2014), uniglobalunion.org/news/framework-actions-gender-equality-audiovisual-sector.

25   BBC Editorial Guidelines, "Advertising and Sponsorship Guidelines for BBC Commercial Services," http://www.bbcworldwide.com/advertising.aspx.

26   The *Canadian Code of Advertising Standards* sets the criteria for acceptable advertising in Canada. Created by the advertising industry in 1963 to promote the professional practice of advertising, the *Code* is the cornerstone of advertising self-regulation in Canada.

DISCUSSION QUESTIONS

(1)   If you were asked to write a code of conduct for media regarding gender issues, which guidelines would you elaborate? Would these guidelines

only prohibit clear images of violence or also discriminatory images that emphasize domination of men over women?

(2) One possible instrument to avoid sexist advertisements is to establish a gender committee in the newsroom. How would this committee balance freedom of expression, on the one hand, and prohibition of violence against women, on the other hand?

(3) In her famous 1985 book *This Sex Which Is Not One*, Luce Irigaray posited that "the feminine occurs only within models and laws devised by male subjects. Which implies that there are not really two sexes, but only one. A single practice of the sexual." Watching contemporary ads, is it correct to say that there is only a single practice of the sexual?

(4) Compare Chapter IV of the Beijing Platform for Action with the Council of Europe Istanbul Convention. What are the main differences between the two instruments? Which one creates states' obligations?

FURTHER READINGS

Hilary Charlesworth and Christine Chinkin, *The Boundaries of International Law* (Manchester: Manchester University Press, 2000).

Council of Europe Convention on Preventing and Combating Violence against Women and Domestic Violence (Istanbul, 2011), online.

Sara De Vido, "States' Due Diligence Obligations to Protect Women from Violence: A European Perspective in Light of the 2011 CoE Istanbul Convention," in *European Yearbook on Human Rights 2014* (Antwerp: Intersentia Nwv, 2014).

Alice Edwards, *Violence against Women under International Human Rights Law* (Cambridge: Cambridge University Press, 2011), chapters 1, 2, 3, 4.

Erving Goffman, *Gender Advertisements* (New York: Harper & Row, 1979).

Luce Irigaray, *This Sex Which Is Not One*, trans. Catherine Porter (Ithaca: Cornell University Press, 1985).

Catharine A. MacKinnon, "The Roar on the Other Side of Silence," in *In Harm's Way: The Pornography Civil Rights Hearings*, ed. Catharine A. MacKinnon and Andrea Dworkin (Cambridge, MA: Harvard University Press, 1998).

Jennifer Siebel Newson, Documentary "Miss Representation" (2011; updated 2014).

Women's Media Center, *The Status of Women in US Media 2015*, online.

PART 4:
BUSINESS
PRACTICES

25.

THE ETHICS OF BLUFFING:

ORACLE'S TAKEOVER

OF PEOPLESOFT

PATRICK LIN

BACKGROUND

ON JUNE 6, 2003, ORACLE AMBUSHED PEOPLESOFT WITH AN UNSO-licited $5.1 billion cash offer to buy the rival technology company. This set the stage for the two Silicon Valley giants—both operating under the leadership of giant-sized egos—to play out a tale about power, drama, and deceit.

First, to introduce the players: Larry Ellison is Oracle's chairman, a swash-buckling personality known for his extravagant financial gestures, such as his financing of the yacht-racing team that won the America's Cup in spring 2003. Equally aggressive is Craig Conway, PeopleSoft's CEO at the time of the takeover attempt, who had once described Oracle, his former employer, as a "sociopathic company."

Just days before Oracle's hostile takeover bid, PeopleSoft had announced its agreement to buy another rival, J.D. Edwards, for $1.7 billion in stock—a deal which would make it the world's second-largest business software company behind SAP. PeopleSoft rejected Oracle's

$16-per-share offer as too low to be taken seriously and therefore simply a marketing ploy or distraction.

For more than a year, Oracle and PeopleSoft fought in the courtroom and the boardroom. Oracle successfully fended off an antitrust trial that examined whether the proposed takeover would be anti-competitive and harm the industry as well as customers. Shortly afterwards, PeopleSoft's board of directors announced a surprising vote of no-confidence in Conway, and he was fired in October 2004.

Over the course of that year, Oracle had changed its acquisition price several times, eventually tendering what the company called its "best and final" offer of $24 per share. PeopleSoft again rejected this offer, calling Oracle on its bluff. Finally, in December 2004, after more than twelve offers, PeopleSoft accepted Oracle's bid of $26.50 per share; the merger was completed in 2005.

It turned out that Oracle was not the only party that had bluffed in this bitter battle. Back in June 2003, PeopleSoft had implemented a "poison pill" plan stipulating that, should the company be taken over, its customers would be entitled to a refund of up to five times the licensing fees they had paid to the company. This tactic would commit the company to costly future obligations, and was intended to dissuade Oracle from its takeover ambitions. It took less than a year for PeopleSoft to let this policy expire.

A different kind of bluff had been played out in the AOL-Time Warner merger, another high-profile deal announced on January 10, 2000. The financial community was puzzled and shocked that a scrappy New Economy start-up such as America Online was capable of making a bid for Time Warner, a decades-old media empire, in a deal originally worth $165 billion. Many considered AOL's stock to be severely overvalued, but AOL had convinced Time Warner otherwise.

The AOL-Time Warner merger was cleared by regulators in early 2001, but the impending stock market crash, led by overvalued dot-com and technology companies, forced AOL-Time Warner to write off $99 billion in losses in 2002—leading some to observe that AOL had successfully "bluffed" Time Warner into believing that AOL's 30 million dial-up Internet subscribers were worth more than Time Warner's much larger, better established, and more iconic global business.

ANALYSIS

IN THE ORACLE-PEOPLESOFT CASE, THE INCENTIVE TO BLUFF IS easy to understand. Not only were the two companies fierce adversaries, but there was also personal animosity between the two company chiefs. As a result, the usual niceties of negotiation—such as trust and honesty—were replaced by a no-holds-barred fight. If all is fair in love and war, and business is war (at least in this case), then bluffing seems a rather innocuous tactic compared to some other tactics that could have been employed.

Workforce negotiations also offer key opportunities for bluffing, since these relationships can be acrimonious. Some employee unions are quick to threaten a strike (or suggest that a strike is strongly possible) if their demands are not met. On the other side, a company may be bluffing when it refuses to negotiate further, insisting that its last offer was the best it could do or that it would be forced into bankruptcy or layoffs without more employee concessions. If one side has been bluffing, we would expect that a strike can be averted in last-minute negotiations—hiding the bluff by finding some token area of agreement or another face-saving reason.

But as the AOL-Time Warner deal shows, a negotiation need not involve adversaries. If "hype" or exaggeration counts as bluffing, then untold numbers of dot-com companies may have bluffed their way into key relationships and millions of dollars in private funding, ultimately unable to deliver on their sales and revenue forecasts. We might ask, however, whether a company that believes its own hype can be fairly accused of bluffing, as compared to a company that knowingly puts forward an exaggeration.

It is not just soulless corporations that bluff: ordinary individuals do it too. Any situation where one can claim "This is my final offer" or present a "Do this, or else" threat provides a potential opportunity to bluff. From negotiating salaries to buying cars, many of us likely have experience of bluffing our ways into better deals, such as by feigning an inability to accept a low offer, or afford a high price, when the given amount would in reality have been perfectly satisfactory.

It is important not to conflate bluffing with lying, since not all cases of bluffing involve the explicit making of false statements. Bluffing in poker, for example, does not; it simply involves misleading other players by taking an action that conceals the strength or weakness of one's cards—for instance, by betting a lot of money when one has a weak hand. Depending on how AOL made its case to Time Warner, they might not have made a false statement—perhaps they merely provided overly optimistic forecasts. PeopleSoft implemented a poison-pill policy that could be renewed after a given date, but it didn't seem to make any (false) warranty that it would renew it. On the other hand, when Oracle made what it called its "best and final" offer, the company appears to have been making a false statement, given that the offer was subsequently raised. But it is possible that company executives simple changed their minds.

These situations highlight how difficult it can be to identify even a failed bluff, let alone to discern whether a bluff is in progress.

DISCUSSION QUESTIONS

(1) What exactly is bluffing—how should we define it? When it comes to bluffs that involve making false statements, where is the line between bluffing and lying, if one exists at all?

(2) How else might one bluff in business without making an explicit claim or threat that one has no intention of carrying out? Does creating doubt in the other party's mind, when a decision has already been made in one's own mind, count as a bluff?

(3) Since the two are often compared, what are some relevant similarities and differences between poker and business? If bluffing (and even lying) were allowed under the rules of a game, can we consider business to be a game in which bluffing is also allowed—or even necessary?

(4) Does the creation of "hype" by making exaggerated claims count as bluffing? Why doesn't story-telling count as bluffing?

(5) If bluffing is so pervasive and is often conducted by people we would consider to be otherwise ethical, does that suggest that it is morally permissible?

(6) Could we argue that a bluff (at least in the form that involves making false statements) is simply a lie made under mitigating circumstances—such as when another party has bluffed first, or when one believes a car dealer to be earning an unfairly high profit? Or does this seem like an attempt to rationalize unethical behavior?

(7) Can we distinguish between false-statement bluffs and outright lies by considering the intentions behind the statements made? If intentions are different, are they morally relevant?

FURTHER READINGS

Norman E. Bowie, "Does It Pay to Bluff in Business?" *Ethical Theory and Business* 3 (1993): 443–48.

Thomas L. Carson, Richard E. Wokutch, and Kent F. Murrmann, "Bluffing in Labor Negotiations: Legal and Ethical Issues," *Journal of Business Ethics* 1.1 (1982): 13–22.

Daryl Koehn, "Business and Game-Playing: The False Analogy," *Journal of Business Ethics* 16.12–13 (1997): 1447–52.

26.

CITIBANK AND COLLATERALIZED DEBT OBLIGATIONS

TOM MCNAMARA AND IRENA DESCUBES

BACKGROUND

FOUNDED IN 1812, CITIBANK IS NOW PART OF CITIGROUP, ONE OF the largest financial institutions in the world, with almost $2 trillion in assets. The bank has a storied past, with notable achievements including funding the first trans-Atlantic telegraph cable in 1866, establishing one of the first foreign exchange offices for converting currencies in the late 1890s, and assisting in the financing of the construction of the Panama Canal in 1906. The company's operations even encompassed the exploration of space through Citigroup's involvement in a partnership that launched heavy-lift space vehicles.

But one of the company's more notorious activities, and one which would play a part in its almost going bankrupt, was its involvement in something known as collateralized debt obligations (CDOs). CDOs are complex financial contrivances originally designed to help commercial banks improve their financial positions by allowing them to remove loans from their balance sheets. CDOs usually comprise a mixture of commercial loans and other financial assets, all pooled into one tradable instrument. The different sorts of assets that go into a CDO usually have different levels of quality, meaning that they must have different levels of reward for the investors who buy them. The solution is to cut the CDO into slices, or "tranches," with each having a different credit rating. The top slices are rated "AAA" and would therefore provide a lower rate of return, but with a very low chance that investors would lose their investment. For those with greater fortitude and higher appetite for risk, a bottom slice can be bought which carries with it a greater chance of default, but which also provides a correspondingly higher rate of return. Ominously, these lower slices are often referred to as "toxic waste."

During the run-up to the Great Financial Panic of 2008, the toxic lower tranches were largely backed by questionable loans. In the early 2000s the United States, like many developed nations, experienced a housing bubble, with the price of an average home increasing by almost 100 per cent between 2000 and 2006. Many housing mortgages were bundled into CDOs and sold to investors who saw this as a way to speculate and make money from the housing boom without necessarily having to buy a house. As the housing mania raged, lending standards slipped. So called "NINJA" loans ("No Income, No Job, No Assets") became more and more common. Experts assured us that none of this was cause for alarm. An authority no less than Alan Greenspan himself, former Chairman of the Federal Reserve ("The Fed"), had assured Americans that there was nothing to worry about. He was adamant that a speculative bubble in housing was impossible, due to the fact that a national housing market was really just a collection of smaller local markets. "Even if a bubble were to develop in a local market, it would not necessarily have implications for the nation as a whole," Greenspan assured the public.[1] Times were good and Citigroup, like the rest of Wall Street, was making money.

To understand how the crisis occurred, some knowledge of history and policy changes is needed. The entity that we now know as Citigroup came about in 1998 through a merger of what was then called Citicorp and the Travelers Group Inc., creating, at the time, the largest financial services company on the planet. Citicorp was primarily involved in banking activities, and the Travelers Group was an insurance company that also sold investors mutual funds. This was seen by many as a match made in heaven, since there was very little overlap between the two companies and a great potential for the cross-selling of products, as well as "synergies." There was just one small problem with this arranged marriage: technically, it was illegal.

After the Great Crash of 1929, several laws were put in place to limit the types of speculative activities that banks could take part in. One of the most well-known and effective of these laws was the Glass-Steagall Act of 1933, which separated commercial from investment banking and made it illegal for a bank to own an insurance company and an insurance company to own a bank. Citigroup lobbied for Congress to overturn the Glass-Steagall Act, allowing the merger to go through. Most notably, Citigroup was supported by then Fed Chairman Alan Greenspan, by the Secretary of the Treasury at the time, Larry Summers, and by his immediate predecessor, former Secretary of the Treasury Robert Rubin. (Rubin would join Citigroup as a senior executive in 1999.)

In November of 1999, Congress passed the Financial Services Modernization Act (FSMA), cynically referred to by many as the "Citi-Travelers Act." Passage of the FSMA (effectively, the repeal of Glass-Steagall) is seen by many as the first step in the undoing of the legislation that had maintained relative financial stability in the US for 80 years, unleashing what would become known as "casino capitalism."

By the summer of 2007, cracks in the financial system were starting to show, in part because of the merger of commercial and investment banking. The strategy of giving mortgages to just about anyone who wanted one with no questions asked, and then bundling them into a CDO and selling them off to someone as soon as possible in order to get them off your books, was starting to show its problems. An early warning sign was the fact that during this period Citigroup was forced to buy back $25 billion of its own CDOs, due to poor investor demand. Citigroup responded by creating new CDOs to buy back the old CDOs, thus creating an even bigger, and more fragile, house of cards.

By the fall of 2008, all the steam had run out of the market and everything came to a crashing halt. The run up to the financial crisis of 2008 (followed by the subsequent Great Recession of 2008) saw the creation of the largest speculative bubble in history, greater even than the one experienced in Japan in the late 1980s or the Great Crash of 1929 in the US. The fallout for Citigroup was devastating. Caught short, illiquid, and under billions of dollars of bad debt, the bank was virtually insolvent. In the immediate aftermath the US government invested $45 billion and took control of 36 per cent of the company in an effort to stop the bleeding and restore confidence. Millions of people lost their jobs and their homes, and trillions in profits were wiped out because of the collapse in house and stock prices. Between 2008 and 2009, the US economy shrank by almost 4 per cent. The Federal Reserve has estimated that it will take at least until the year 2023 for the US economy to return to its pre-crisis rate of growth. This extended subpar performance is expected to result in between $6 trillion and $14 trillion in lost economic output.

Investor lawsuits and official investigations would soon follow. In July of 2014, Citigroup announced that it had reached a comprehensive settlement with the US Department of Justice and several other Federal and State government agencies over various activities related to the company's issuance of CDOs between 2003 and 2008. Citigroup agreed to pay $4.5 billion in fines and charges, as well as provide $2.5 billion in "consumer relief," an act of penance in which the company provided financing for the construction of affordable housing, and reduced the principal on certain residential loans it had made.

ANALYSIS

BUSINESS ETHICISTS THINK ABOUT THE ETHICS OF THE CITIGROUP case by analyzing the actions of the company and its senior managers, and the rules and regulations that enabled the financial crisis, and by assessing the distribution of harms and benefits in the aftermath of the crisis.

The most straightforward ethical objection to Citigroup's behavior is that it was criminal. Even Milton Friedman, who believed a company's responsibility was to maximize profit for shareholders, insisted that actions follow the basic rules of society: law and ethical custom. A shareholder lawsuit filed in 2009 claimed that Citigroup knowingly engaged in deception and fraud, hiding tens of billions of dollars in toxic assets by repacking them as new CDOs. In 2011, Citigroup settled the lawsuit for $590 billion without admitting any wrongdoing.

Citigroup's actions also raise questions about the responsibilities of managers and regulators. Words like "crisis" and "panic" are often associated with the financial collapse of 2008, implying a certain randomness or unpredictability to events. But critics would counter that managers and regulators should have foreseen the impending threat to the economy from an unsustainable increase in asset prices, and from lax oversight and enforcement. For example, the former chairman of Citigroup, Robert Rubin (who as Treasury Secretary championed the

1998 merger that brought Citigroup into existence) testified that he wasn't aware of any problems with CDOs until the fall of 2007. Senior managers at best failed to meet their ethical responsibilities to properly oversee Citigroup's investments and at worse abetted reckless and possibly criminal behavior. (Another concern exemplified by Rubin is the possibility of conflicts of interest due to the "revolving door" of people moving between senior positions in the public and private sectors.)

Another set of ethical questions concern the distributions of burdens resulting from the crisis. The people who had taken out sub-prime NINJA loans to buy houses were commonly blamed for causing the crisis. "These people should live up to their responsibilities and pay their bills" and "People should be held accountable for their poor life decisions" were recurring refrains. What was usually overlooked was the fact that on the other side of every irresponsible borrower was an irresponsible lender. Why was it that people with "no income, no job, and no assets" were being held to a higher standard than the bank presidents who lent them huge sums of money without due diligence?

Furthermore, rather than paying for their "poor life decisions," many on Wall Street were handsomely rewarded for them. About $140 billion in compensation was paid out by major US financial firms only one year after the worst financial crisis in living memory. This was estimated to be even larger than the amount earned by Wall Street in 2007, the year when the speculative bubble reached its peak. In 2009 the average yearly salary in the financial industry was about $143,400. That same year, official unemployment hit a high of 10 per cent, with a broader measurement of unemployment used by the Bureau of Labor Statistics reaching an astounding 17 per cent.

Another criticism of the handling of the aftermath of the crisis was the immediacy with which banks such as Citigroup were in effect given blank checks, while the average Americans who lost their jobs or homes were seen as getting very little in the way of help. "Wall Street got bailed out, Main Street got left out" was a popular cry.

By the end of 2008, while the ashes of the financial crash were still smoldering, the US government made available over $240 billion in aid to prop up faltering banks, mainly through the Treasury Department's Troubled Asset Relief Program (TARP). According to Senator Elizabeth Warren, when one includes "secret" loans that the Fed made available to Wall Street banks, the cost of the bailout was much higher. In a Senate hearing, Senator Warren noted, "The biggest money for the biggest banks was never voted on by Congress. Instead, between 2007 and 2009, the Fed provided over $13 trillion in emergency lending to just a handful of large financial institutions. That's nearly 20 times the amount authorized in the TARP bailout."[2] In just one single lending scheme, the Fed handed out $9 trillion, with almost 70 per cent going to only three banks: Citigroup, Morgan Stanley, and Merrill Lynch. In another handout to Citigroup, the government stood ready to guarantee over $300 billion worth of toxic assets that the bank was holding.

In total, Citigroup would go on to receive an estimated $2 trillion in bailouts from the US taxpayer. And while the bank paid back all of the money it received in bailouts, many would argue that the bailouts themselves violated principles of justice. Disgruntlement resulted not only from the idea that harm caused by the crisis fell mainly on individuals losing their homes and jobs, while government assistance went mainly to Wall Street. It also came from the idea that the bailouts and the invocation of the "too big to fail" slogan violated principles of free competition central to a capitalist economy. As noted economist Joseph Schumpeter argued, at the heart of free market capitalism is the concept of "creative destruction," that is, that poorly run firms must be allowed to go extinct and die so that new dynamic ones can take their place. Nowhere in classical economics does one find the phrase "too big to fail." This also raises the argument that there are two types of capitalism in the US: one for well-connected and powerful banks who get saved no matter what the cost, another for the small business owner.

In an attempt to limit the chances of another financial meltdown, in 2010 the Dodd-Frank Act was passed. This law tries, once again, to restrict the speculative activities that banks can take part in. Disturbingly, a provision to the law was passed in December 2014 that lets banks use federally insured deposits to take part in speculation in the derivatives markets, the exact kind of behavior that led to the 2008 crisis. The main proponent for changing the Dodd-Frank Act? Citigroup.

NOTES

1   Testimony of Chairman Alan Greenspan, Monetary policy and the economic outlook, Before the Joint Economic Committee, US Congress, April 17, 2002, online.

2   Pam Martens and Russ Martens, "Warren: Citigroup, Morgan Stanley, Merrill Lynch Received $6 Trillion Backdoor Bailout from Fed," Wall Street on Parade (March 4, 2015), online.

DISCUSSION QUESTIONS

(1) The Great Crisis of 2008 was caused by poor government oversight, a poor understanding by financial institutions of the products they were selling, and a poor understanding by investors of the products they were buying. Which party was most responsible for the crisis? Which party was least responsible? Why?

(2) In the aftermath of the crisis, what do you believe the government did right? What do you believe the government did wrong? Explain.

(3) What part (if any) did the effective undoing of the Glass-Steagall Act of 1933 play in causing the Great Crisis of 2008?

(4) Do you believe that financial institutions like Citigroup were held fully accountable for their complicity in causing the Great Crisis of 2008? Why?

(5) Knowing what we know now about the crisis, how would you explain the dearth of criminal prosecution by the Department of Justice in the years immediately following 2008?

(6) Do you believe that there was a conflict of interest in former Secretary of the Treasury Robert Rubin taking a position at Citigroup so soon after he left public service?

FURTHER READINGS

Jake Bernstein and Jesse Eisinger, "Banks' Self-Dealing Super-Charged Financial Crisis," *ProPublica* (August 26, 2010).

Eric Dash and Julie Creswell, "Citigroup Saw No Red Flags Even as It Made Bolder Bets," *New York Times* (November 22, 2008).

Paul Krugman, "How Did Economists Get It so Wrong?" *New York Times* (September 2, 2009).

B. McLean and J. Nocera, *All the Devils Are Here: The Hidden History of the Financial Crisis* (New York: Penguin, 2011).

"The Origins of the Financial Crisis: Crash Course," *The Economist* (September 7, 2013).

W. Poole, "Causes and Consequences of the Financial Crisis of 2007–2009," *Harvard Journal of Law and Public Policy* 33 (2010): 421.

Robert Reich, "America's Biggest Banks Are Felons—Here's How to Make Them Pay," *Salon* (June 24, 2015).

Robert Weissman, "Reflections on Glass-Steagall and Maniacal Deregulation," *Common Dreams* (November 12, 2009).

A.E. Wilmarth, "Citigroup: A Case Study in Managerial and Regulatory Failures," *Indiana Law Review* 47 (2014): 69–137.

27.
MISPLACED INCENTIVES: LARGE-SCALE FRAUD AT WELLS FARGO

IRENA DESCUBES, TOM MCNAMARA,
AND CYRLENE CLAASEN

BACKGROUND

WELLS FARGO, A FINANCIAL JUGGERNAUT, IS HOME TO 40 MILLION individual bank accounts and provides one in five loans in the United States. The third largest bank in America, Wells Fargo has long been considered a reliable and trustworthy institution, with one of its core stated values being "We value what's right for our customers in everything we do." That statement has recently been put to the test.

In September 2016, Wells Fargo's reputation was severely tarnished when it came to light that the company had created 2.1 million fictitious credit card and bank accounts between May 2011 and July 2015. In a practice known as "pinning," a Wells Fargo banker obtained a debit card number, and personally set the PIN without customer authorization. They then inputted false generic email addresses such as 1234@wellsfargo.com, noname@wellsfargo.com, or none@wellsfargo.com to ensure that the transaction was completed, and that the customer remained unaware of the unauthorized activity. "Pinning" allowed bankers to enroll a customer in online banking services, for which they would receive a sales credit, thus helping them to meet pre-established sales quotas. In August 2017, Wells Fargo admitted that they found an additional 1.4 million bogus accounts, bringing the grand total to 3.5 million.

Once the scandal was revealed, employees at the bank spoke out and denounced a business culture that they saw as flawed, corrupted by a permanent pressure to achieve ever-higher sales goals set by management. The problems centered on the Community Bank division at Wells Fargo, which was completely decentralized. Department heads were told to manage regional offices and local branches "as if they owned them," leading to a distorted sales model and performance management system that generated inappropriate and unethical behavior. Even when challenged by their regional offices' managers, the Community Bank division failed to appreciate or accept that its sales targets were too high and increasingly untenable.

In the senate hearings that followed the scandal, Sen. Elizabeth Warren (D, Massachusetts) publicly shamed Wells Fargo Chairman and CEO John Stumpf with the following statement: "You haven't resigned, you haven't returned a single nickel of your personal earnings, you haven't fired a single senior executive," she said. "Instead, evidently, your definition of accountable is push the blame to low-level employees who don't have the money for a fancy PR firm to defend themselves. It's gutless leadership."

After the discovery of the illegal actions in September 2016, 5,300 employees were fired and Wells Fargo was fined $185 million by the Consumer Financial Protection Bureau (CFPB), the Office of the Comptroller of the Currency, and the City of Los Angeles for opening two million bank accounts and 500,000 credit card accounts without their clients' knowledge and then charging fees.

In October 2016 John Stumpf was forced to resign and had to give up $41 million in stock options. Shortly thereafter, the CFPB opened an investigation in order to determine whether or not customers had been affected by the closure or freezing of their savings accounts after suspicious activity had been detected as a result of the pinning scandal. If proven, this may result in more lawsuits and fines being paid by the bank. Wells Fargo has already been obliged to increase refunds to injured customers from an originally planned $3.3 million to $6.1 million. Adding insult to injury, a survey conducted by the independent consulting firm Oliver Wyman has uncovered what are believed to be 528,000 potentially illegal entries to the online bill payment service of the bank, which would have resulted in undue charges and levies to customers.

But the bad news doesn't stop there. In late July 2017 Franklin R. Codel, the bank's head of consumer lending, had to admit that Wells Fargo forced more than half a million customers to pay unwarranted insurance premiums on their auto loans between 2012 and 2017. The bank obliged customers to subscribe to collateral protection insurance (CPI) when they took out a car loan. CPI is an additional layer of insurance that provides protection to banks making loans in case the vehicle is damaged. However, it is often not included when customers takes out a loan because they are usually already protected by their car insurance. Wells Fargo admitted that about 570,000 customers were deceptively charged additional CPI payments. Approximately 20,000 vehicles were repossessed from their owners because they could not pay these abusive insurance fees. These customers have now been reimbursed and received additional payments as compensation. The total amount of these indemnifications, according to the latest estimates, is approximately $80 million, of which $64 million will be paid directly as cash to injured clients, with the remaining $16 million granted to them in the form of an adjustment to their bank account. Wells Fargo began issuing refunds in September 2017 to customers hurt by the forced insurance. It is expected that all impacted borrowers will be reimbursed by mid-2018.

Aside from the traditional activities of universal banking (i.e., loans, investments, savings for households and small businesses), the investigations into the commercial practices inside Wells Fargo have recently been extended to investment banking (i.e., business advising and speculative activities). On October 20, 2017, the bank announced that four traders specializing in currency brokerage, including the manager of this trading room, were asked to leave the company. This new case in Wells Fargo's investment-banking arm adds to the difficulties already facing Wells Fargo due to the previous scandals surrounding the opening of 3.5 million fictitious accounts and superfluous insurance premiums sold to customers who took out car loans with the bank.

More misconduct has been revealed in yet another section of the scandal-ridden bank. The CFPB has started investigating $98 million that Wells Fargo charged in questionable fees to customers to "lock-in" mortgage rates. It is suspected that approximately 110,000 customers, between September 2013 and February 2017, were charged fees that they did not deserve. During that period when a person applied for a mortgage,

Wells Fargo proposed an interest rate, but that rate carried an expiration date. Sometimes the rate expired before the customer officially signed for the home loan due to delays. If the delay was the customer's fault, they were required to pay a fee to extend or "lock in" the interest rate. However, there is evidence showing that in many cases it was Wells Fargo's fault that a loan was not processed on time. In mid-November 2017, Franklin Codel, Head of Wells Fargo's consumer lending division handling mortgages and auto loans, was fired because he allegedly "violated company policy during a communication he had with a former team member regarding that team member's earlier termination," according to the bank's spokesperson Josh Dunn.

ANALYSIS

GOLD! GOLD! IN THE SPRING OF 1848, GOLD WAS DISCOVERED IN the territory of California. Within only a few of months, tens of thousands of prospectors from America, but also Europe, Mexico, Chile, Australia, and even China, rushed to San Francisco. In New York, two enterprising business men, Henry Wells and William Fargo, understood very quickly that this gold rush was an immense opportunity to extend their courier service from the civilized East to the "Wild West." Hundreds of mining towns, comprised mostly of tent villages, had sprung up near the gold mines. Wells and Fargo created their first outposts not as simple courier relays but as real bank branches which were difficult to rob and were equipped with secure strong boxes. The firm transported gold from isolated mining camps to larger towns and provided prospectors with cash transfer services. Wells Fargo also guaranteed the security of goods transported, providing reimbursement up to a certain percentage of their value if lost or stolen.

Wells Fargo was not the only company to see an opportunity in California. They were soon joined by another East Coast courier company called Adams & Company, who immediately challenged them with a fierce price war for control of banking activities and recruited the fastest messengers for mail delivery. In what would later become an ironic twist, Wells Fargo rid itself of Adams & Company in 1855 when the latter was convicted of speculating with the deposits of their customers and went bankrupt.

No less a captain of industry than Henry Ford II once wrote that "a company's main two assets are its [employees] and its reputation." In the blink of an eye, Wells Fargo demoralized the former and lost the latter through scandal. The cost of all this? Wells Fargo's stock lost $70 billion in market value in the single month of October 2016, and the number of new accounts being opened in the fourth quarter of 2016 fell by 40 per cent. For years the company was in the top tier of Fortune magazine's "Most Admired Companies." In 2017's ranking, Wells Fargo was nowhere to be found.

So what went wrong at Wells Fargo? What would cause a company, long admired for its reputation for conservativism and careful money management, to become as reckless as its competitor Adams & Company was 160 years ago? The cause of the wrongdoing was primarily blamed on the bank's marketing incentive called the "Gr-eight initiative," a play on the word "great" and the number "eight." This plan, initiated by Wells Fargo back in 2006, required front-office employees to meet outrageously high sales goals, i.e., sell at least eight financial products per customer. In the 11th edition of the bank's Vision and Values booklet published in 2006, one can read the following: "We've Over Five! Shooting for Six! Going for Gr-eight! We have the highest cross-sell levels in our industry. It now takes two hands to count our cross-sell ratio. In retail banking, our cross-sell ratio is over five products per household, almost six for customers who've been with us for three years or more. This is about double the industry average." When employees met their very aggressive targets, they got a bonus and were seen as being good performers by upper management, who even turned a blind eye when ethical and legal lines were crossed. These fraudulent marketing incentives were clearly in conflict with the Vision and Values standard that placed Wells Fargo "among the world's great companies for integrity and principled performance."

From a corporate social responsibility perspective, the Wells Fargo scandal is a stark example of multi-level failures on the part of regulators and senior management and the board of directors, the latter of which one would expect to be accountable vis-à-vis the bank's primary stakeholders: shareholders, customers, and employees. It raises disturbing questions about Wells Fargo policies that efficiently stifled any attempts at whistleblowing, especially from those employees who could not tolerate the conflict between their personal ethical standards and the (unreasonable) professional targets that they were supposed to meet.

Beyond the responsibility that the top management and the board should take for having, at a minimum tolerated, at worst, created, a rotten corporate culture at Wells Fargo, one can question the efficacity and integrity of America's banking system in general. The behavior of some of the largest financial institutions on the planet in the run up to the financial crisis of 2008, and its immediate aftermath, was in many respects morally questionable. Was Wells Fargo's questionable interpretation of free market capitalism, i.e., an aggressive pursuit of profit to satisfy shareholder interests, with limited if no attention being paid to business ethics, an aberration or business as usual?

A standard bearer of good financial ethical practice in the United States is the Institute of Management Accountants (IMA), of which Wells Fargo is a member. The IMA's Statement of Ethical Professional Practice requires that all IMA members "communicate information fairly and objectively" and "provide all relevant information that could reasonably be expected to influence an intended user's understanding." By knowing about ethical lapses and not making changes to their marketing incentive program, Wells Fargo's senior managers violated the first two credibility standards of the IMA practice.

John Stumpf sadly confirmed the bank's lack of attention to ethics during a 2016 public hearing in front of a US Senate panel. He was forced to admit that senior management at Wells Fargo knew about potentially unethical activities in the bank's retail banking sector since 2013. And this was not just several "bad-apple" kind of crooked employees abusing the system in their zeal to collect bonuses, as initially suggested by Wells Fargo top management. A *State of California v. Wells Fargo* lawsuit alleges that those employees who failed to meet their daily goals were "reprimanded and told to do whatever it takes to meet individual sales quotas." They were even encouraged to "achieve 'solutions' through family members." One low-ranked employee reported, "There would be days where I would open five checking accounts for friends and family just to be able to go home."

An internal investigation carried out by a committee of independent directors of Wells Fargo, published in April 2017, revealed the defective practices of the Director of Retail Activities, Carine Tolstedt, who pushed her subordinates to meet the aggressively set targets of the "Gr-eight initiative." Wells Fargo decided in September 2016 to terminate Tolstedt's contract in a public and vocal manner, which is rather unusual in the banking industry. Some people raised the issue of apparent uneven gender treatment in regard to shamed executives in the fake-account scandal. In addition to Carine Tolstedt, four other executives were terminated.

Interestingly enough, out of the four, three were women (Pam Conboy, Shelley Freeman, and Claudia Russ Anderson).

Disturbingly, questions regarding ethical behavior have now spread to the US government. In September 2016 the US Department of Labor (DOL) created a website that it used to collect complaints from internal "whistleblowers" at Wells Fargo who had been sanctioned for refusing to engage in fraudulent practices. Oddly, since January 24, 2017, people trying to access the site receive the error message "page not found." The previously mentioned Senator Warren wrote at the end of January 2017, "I am concerned that the Department of Labor has removed the web-site where Wells Fargo's employees who were victims of the company's fraudulent actions could file labor complaints or report illegal activity.... Taking down this website enables Wells Fargo to escape full responsibility for its fraudulent actions and the Department to shirk its outstanding obligations to American workers."

Julie Ragatz, director of the Center for Ethics in Financial Services at the American College of Financial Services, believes that "The culprit in this case is not just the individuals involved, but the corporate culture itself." The CEO and top management should have been alerted by the fact that customers were putting little or no money into their newly created bank accounts. "Wells Fargo knew, or in the exercise of reasonable care should have known, that its employees open unauthorized accounts," according to a statement from the Los Angeles City Attorney's office. In defense of the bank's senior management, it is hard to believe that they all deliberately wanted to engage in fraud. Instead, most probably thought that thanks to the bonus system that they put in place, employees would be encouraged to get real clients to open new accounts. But the reality is that the bonus system was poorly designed and encouraged fraud. After reviewing several customer complaints received in 2016 related to this issue, Wells Fargo's top management said that it had come to the conclusion that its internal controls were "unsuitable."

Warren Buffet, Wells Fargo's largest shareholder, told CNN's Poppy Harlow in November 2016 that "It was a dumb incentive system, which when they found out it was dumb, they didn't do anything about it."

Wells Fargo's current CEO Timothy J. Sloan stated, "As the new CEO, my immediate priority is to restore trust and confidence in Wells Fargo. We are fully aware of the fact that it will take time and a lot of energy to rebuild our reputation. We have made mistakes and we apologize." Those changes include enhanced training that values ethics and how to report concerns, increased risk management professionals at branches and additional mystery shoppers. Sloan is, however, blamed for being a "pure product" of the same culture as John Stumpf. In his previous position, he was heading different divisions that included the troubled retail banking one. This raises concerns about whether Wells Fargo will genuinely transform its culture or merely engage in damage control.

DISCUSSION QUESTIONS

(1) Caveat emptor, or "let the buyer beware," is a basic tenet of commercial law. Yes, Wells Fargo has a legal and ethical responsibility to treat its customers fairly, but shouldn't the people who were affected by the various scandals have been a bit more prudent and involved in how their accounts and loans were managed? Discuss.

(2) What steps did Wells Fargo take to remedy the problems that arose as a result of the various scandals involving its retail banking customers? Do you believe that they were satisfactory? Please explain.

(3) How could the sales initiatives and associated goals that Wells Fargo's employees were required to meet have been better designed? If you wished to motivate employees in an ethical and responsible fashion, in order to increase sales, what would be some of the key elements of your sales initiative?

(4) In the aftermath of the financial crisis of 2008, Wells Fargo received an estimated $36 billion taxpayer-backed bailout. Since it is essentially the "lender of last resort," doesn't the government have a bigger role to play in the day-to-day management of large financial institutions in order to prevent scandals and another possible financial crisis? Explain and justify your position.

(5) There is a joke on Wall Street that "Too big to fail means too big to jail," in that whenever a large bank is found to have broken the law, it simply pays a fine, with senior management having no fear of prosecution and jail time. Should prosecutors insist that in cases of large-scale and premeditated fraud, criminal charges be brought against bank presidents and CEOs? Be sure to justify your answer.

FURTHER READINGS

S. Barlyn, "Mandatory Arbitration Clause Could Thwart Wells Fargo Customers' Lawsuits," *Insurance Journal* (September 22, 2016).

F. Cavico and B. Mujtaba, "Wells Fargo's Fake Accounts Scandal and Its Legal and Ethical Implications for Management," *SAM Advanced Management* 82.2 (2017): 4–19.

A. Davidson, "How Regulation Failed with Wells Fargo," *New Yorker Magazine* (September 12, 2016).

IMA Statement of Ethical Professional Practice, online.

B. McClean, "How Wells Fargo's Cutthroat Corporate Culture Allegedly Drove Bankers to Fraud," *Vanity Fair* (May 31, 2017).

C. Verschoor, "Lessons from the Wells Fargo Scandal," *Strategic Finance* 98.5 (2016): 19–20.

C. Verschoor, "Wells Fargo Scandal Continues," *Strategic Finance* 99.5 (2017): 18–20.

"Wells Fargo: What It Will Take to Clean Up the Mess," Knowledge @ Wharton, The Wharton School of Business (August 8, 2017).

A.A. Zoltners, PK Sinha, and S.E. Lorimer, "Wells Fargo and the Slippery Slope of Sales Incentives," *The Harvard Business Review* (September 20, 2016).

28.
NESTLÉ AND ADVERTISING:
AN ETHICAL ANALYSIS

CHRIS RAGG

BACKGROUND

SINCE THE 1970S, THE NESTLÉ CORPORATION HAS BEEN THE SUBJECT
of an international boycott. The set of products that have been the
source of public outcry are newer versions of a product that Nestlé has
been making since its inception in 1866: baby formula. Boycotters argue
that the advertising campaigns promoting the formula in impoverished
countries have been unethical, and have contributed to the deaths of
millions of infants.

According to UNICEF and the World Health Organization, approximately 1.5 million infants die each year from complications related to
bottle feeding, many from what has been called "baby-bottle disease."
This refers to the combination of diarrhea, dehydration, and malnutrition which result from unsafe bottle feeding. A typical case of baby-
bottle disease might arise as follows: low-income parents purchase baby
formula for their infant. Since the local water supply is contaminated
and unsafe, however, the baby's ingestion of the diluted formula can

soon lead to diarrhea, a common indicator of gastrointestinal distress and a cause of dehydration. Furthermore, due to the cost of the baby formula, parents will often over-dilute it or spend less on additional food supplies—behaviors that can lead to malnutrition for the infant.

When growing up in an area with contaminated water, a bottle-fed child is 25 times more likely to die from diarrhea than a breastfed child. Even in areas with cleaner water, such as the United Kingdom, a bottle-fed child is 10 times more likely to suffer from the same condition. In most cases, in fact, doctors recommend strongly that mothers breastfeed their children. Breastfed babies need no other food or drink for about the first six months of life, and have reduced risk of diabetes, pneumonia, ear infections, and some cancers. Further studies have shown that women who breastfeed may have a lower risk of breast and ovarian cancers. This does not, to be sure, imply that bottle-feeding is *never* the best option. There are some cases where baby formula can be beneficial; with the right information, mothers can decide for themselves whether or not theirs is such a case.

This requisite information, however, is not made available to many women in poorer nations. In the 1960s and 1970s, Nestlé developed extensive advertisement campaigns for its baby formula worldwide. The pamphlets they distributed highlighted the potential benefits of baby formula while ignoring the drawbacks. Free samples were also dispersed among the public. Nestlé's profit-driven actions began to outrage the public. Although these actions were not illegal, the boycotters claimed that Nestlé's actions were immoral and socially irresponsible. While corporations are free to use various means to pursue the largest profit available, the Nestlé boycotters claim that an ethical corporation must avoid deliberate harm in its pursuit of success.

ANALYSIS

ADVERTISEMENTS ARE ALL AROUND US; IT WOULD BE DIFFICULT to go even a single day without coming into contact with at least one. In our capitalist society, a good marketing strategy can be the difference between a successful and a failed business venture. In light of this, it is not all that surprising that in some countries Nestlé reportedly spends more money promoting their product than the respective country's government spends on health education. The information available to young mothers, then, can be highly biased. In the United States there are laws against false advertising, but these laws only protect consumers from lies and unsubstantiated claims.

Of course, companies can fool the public without resorting to outright lies. Many companies choose to tell the truth, but not quite the whole truth. This was the case with Nestlé's pamphlets 35 years ago; their advertisements would explain all the potential benefits of the product while neglecting to mention its potential drawbacks.

In 1981, the policy-setting body of the World Health Organization adopted the International Code of Marketing of Breast-milk Substitutes. Those who agreed to accept the code swore that they would not provide free samples to hospitals or mothers, promote their product for use with children under six months of age, or promote it to health workers. Nestlé has publicly agreed to abide by these standards. Nevertheless, it is claimed by IBFAN (the International Baby Foods Action Network) that Nestlé has repeatedly violated the code. In particular, there is evidence that Nestlé has aspired to win the approval of health care and hospital workers by giving them gifts, so that they will personally recommend Nestlé products to young mothers. This is often cheaper and more effective than trying to influence mothers one-by-one. Another strategy used by Nestlé has been to provide free samples to hospitals and maternity wards. A mother will then begin using the formula at the hospital, and by the time she leaves it will have interfered with her lactation process. Once home, the formula is no longer free and the mother is left without much choice but to purchase the product.

It does seem, however, that setting too many restrictions on advertising may lead us down a slippery slope. Nestlé's chocolate products, for instance, can contribute to obesity, which leads to a host of health issues. It might be argued that, if all these restrictions apply to the advertisement of baby formula, then similar restrictions should apply to other unhealthy products. But then where will this proliferation of warnings and restrictions end? To what extent (if at all) should manufacturers be held accountable for misuses of their products?

DISCUSSION QUESTIONS

(1) Should definitions of "false advertising" be extended to include cases in which a company is not forthright about all potential negative side effects

of its products? Or only some of them? If a company can't be expected to be forthright about all such negative side effects, is it possible to develop useful criteria as to which types of negatives must be mentioned?

(2) Although it is not clear that Nestlé has done anything illegal, have they done something unethical? Should we expect corporations like Nestlé to abide by certain standards of ethics, or are their only responsibilities to obey the law and maximize profit?

(3) To what extent, if any, should a company be held responsible for the safe use of its products? If this responsibility does not fall to the corporation, to whom does it? To a separate legal body? To the distributors—for instance, the healthcare practitioners whom Nestlé convinced to promote the product? Or just to the consumers themselves?

(4) Are there any differences between the case of Nestlé's baby formula and the case of unhealthy chocolate products? If so, what are they?

FURTHER READINGS

James E. Britain, "Product Honesty Is the Best Policy: A Comparison of Doctors' and Manufacturers' Duty to Disclose Drug Risks and the Importance of Consumer Expectations in Determining Product Defect," *Northwestern University Law Review* 79 (1984).

Patrick Hannon, "The Ethics of Advertising," *The Furrow* (1989): 393–403.

James E. Post, "Assessing the Nestlé Boycott: Corporate Accountability and Human Rights," *California Management Review* 27 (1985).

S. Prakash Sethi, *Multinational Corporations and the Impact of Public Advocacy on Corporate Strategy: Nestlé and the Infant Formula Controversy*, Science & Business Media, vol. 6 (New York: Springer, 2012).

29.
PHARMACEUTICAL PAYMENTS AND OPIOID PRESCRIPTIONS

FRITZ ALLHOFF

BACKGROUND

OPIOIDS KILL MORE THAN 100 AMERICANS EACH DAY.[1] WHILE ILLEGAL heroin and fentanyl—and, increasingly, fentanyl-laced heroin—are substantial culprits in this epidemic, more than 40 per cent of opioid-related deaths are from legally prescribed opioids. The most common of these include methadone, oxycodone (e.g., OxyContin), and hydrocodone (e.g., Vicodin). Prescription overdose deaths most often afflict people aged 25–54 years and are highest among non-Hispanic whites, American Indians, and Inuit in Alaska. The rates are approximately 6.2 deaths per 100,000 men and 4.3 deaths per 100,000 women. Within the United States, there are geographical variations in prescription opioid deaths, with rates being the highest in West Virginia, Maryland, Maine, and Utah. While the prescription opioids can be lethal themselves, they also can lead to the use of more lethal (and illegal) opioids, such as the aforementioned heroin and fentanyl. Prescription rates have generally declined nationally, but are still as much as three times those of 15 years ago.[2]

Pharmaceutical companies are, of course, invested in the sale of their drugs, and so they market those drugs to physicians.[3] For present purposes, let us consider "non-research opioid-related payments," which include speaking fees and/or honoraria, meals, travel, consulting fees, and education. In 2014, over 25,000 physicians—approximately 7 per cent of the national total—received such payments from pharmaceutical companies, which totaled over $9,000,000.[4] Speaking fees and/or honoraria were the largest categories, accounting for over $6,000,000. The payments were generally small, with only a couple hundred physicians receiving more than $1,000 each; the median meal payment, for example, was only $13.[5]

A recent study investigated the extent to which these non-research payments correlated to the prescription rates of their beneficiaries. The key finding of this study was that physicians who did not receive opioid-related payments prescribed fewer opioids in 2015 than in 2014. However, physicians who did receive opioid-related payments prescribed more opioids in 2015 than in 2014, by 9.3 per cent. And so the upshot is that physicians who receive payments from pharmaceutical companies are more likely to prescribe opioids than physicians who receive no such payments.

While the nation continues to wrestle with prescription practices, the Centers for Disease Control (CDC) has undertaken a range of steps. In 2016, it released prescription guidelines, the aim being to "ensure that patients have access to safer, more effective chronic pain treatment, while reducing the number of people who misuse opioids, develop opioid use disorder, or overdose."[6] This initiative was specifically aimed to target "the prescribing of opioid pain medication to patients 18 years and older in primary care settings outside of active cancer treatment, palliative care[,] and end of life care."[7] In other words, the target demographic is the one least in need of indefinite access to opioids, and the one with the highest propensity for long-term abuse and dependency.

As of 2018, 46 states are implementing prescribing practices in accordance with the new CDC guidelines. Providers have undertaken thousands of hours of continuing education with regards to these guidelines and the majority of states' Medicaid programs have also prioritized compliance with the guidelines; even the associated mobile app has been downloaded over 30,000 times.[8] The effectiveness of these educational initiatives will be evaluated as more data become available, but they certainly come at a critical time, with myriad public health considerations hanging in the balance.

ANALYSIS

FOR THE PURPOSES OF THIS CASE STUDY, LET US SET ASIDE THE opioid epidemic more generally and focus on the potential conflict-of-interest issues that attach to pharmaceutical companies' payments to physicians, and the propensity of those payments to increase opioid prescriptions. At first pass, this might look like an egregious dereliction of professional responsibility. A physician's primary obligation is to his patients, as is underwritten by medical ethics' four core values: beneficence, non-malfeasance, autonomy, and justice. Over-prescribing opioids runs afoul of all these, most obviously non-malfeasance insofar as the propensity for opioid addiction is deeply harmful. But addiction also undermines autonomy, by subjugating the patients' autonomous will to the neurochemical correlates of dependence. And over-prescribing hardly *helps* anything, either (cf. beneficence); aside from the propensity of harm, *over*-prescription is, ex hypothesi, not in the patients' best interests. Justice is always a bit trickier to analyze, but suffice it to say that over-prescribing potentially lethal drugs is not a just practice—more directly, some of the geographic variations we see in opioid overdoses cut against principles like equality if some populations are at greater risk than others.

And so we can see that over-prescribing opioids violates physicians' obligations to patients. But that alone does not make it a conflict of interest: those derelictions could simply be the result of ill will, incompetence, or a host of other factors. What makes it a conflict of interest is that they are getting paid—by the pharmaceutical companies no less—to over-prescribe. This is actually worse than other sorts of reasons that might undergird over-prescription. Incompetence, for example, can be remedied by further education or training. But the ongoing availability of money does not go away, the temptation does not go away, and the "incentives" always push against professional obligation.

This analysis, though, presupposes that physicians prescribe more opioids *because* of the availability of non-research payments. However, the Hadland et al. study cited above does not bear this out; that study is completely silent as to *why* physicians who receive the payments are more likely to prescribe the opioids. Maybe it is because of the payments, but maybe it is for some other reason altogether. More technically, the correlation between the payments and the prescription rates does not establish that those increased prescription rates are caused by the payments.

For example, the time spent with pharmaceutical representatives over a meal might well serve an educational function, alerting physicians to risks and benefits, best practices, and so on. Perhaps the physicians who did not have those meals were simply being conservative—lacking full information or resources and choosing to err their prescriptive practices on the side of caution. Or perhaps the interactions with the pharmaceutical representatives led to implicit bias: the physicians might simply be—and probably are—susceptible to marketing, like any of the rest of us. And so maybe they did not consciously increase their opioid prescriptions at all, but rather were affected in other ways.

In other words, the strengths or merits of this study need not presuppose any untoward motivations on the part of the physicians. They could be bad professionals, chasing the money. Or they could be good professionals, critically engaging the pharmaceutical representatives. Or they could just be normal people, subject to all sorts of subconscious processes, none of which cuts against their professional integrity. I would certainly think that *at least some of* the correlation could be explained away by these less nefarious explanations, just as I would equally think that at least some of it could be explained by exactly these more nefarious motivations. But we cannot simply read the intentions or motivations off of the existing data.

It is also important to note what this argument is not: specifically, there is no argument here that we should not have greater oversight and regulation of prescriptive practices. Nor is there any argument that pharmaceutical representatives should have continued unfettered access to physicians, or even that non-research payments should be allowed at all (i.e., maybe they should be banned, or at least heavily restricted). Rather, the observation is far narrower, which is simply that there is a range of reasons that prescriptive practices could correlate to non-research payments, and that the professional integrity of physicians should probably be assessed on a case-by-case basis, rather than as a blanket indictment of any who receive payments from pharmaceutical representatives. There might be other reasons that no physician should accept these payments—like optics—but those reasons would be separate from ways in which professional responsibility intersects with putative conflicts of interest.

NOTES

1   Ayesha Rascoe and Scott Horsley, "Signing Opioid Law, Trump Pledges to End 'Scourge' of Drug Addiction," *NPR* (October 24, 2018).

2   Centers for Disease Control and Prevention, "Prescription Opioid Data" (2017), online.

3   Professional ethics has, in my view, generally overemphasized the focus on physicians, as against other health care providers (e.g., nurses, physician assistants, etc.). However, with regards to opioid prescriptions, the focus is more appropriate, since many other providers are not able to prescribe narcotics or other controlled substances.

4   Almost half of this was paid out by a single pharmaceutical company, INSYS Therapeutics, which manufactures a fentanyl-based sublingual spray, Subsys, which is primarily used for pain relief in cancer patients.

5   Scott E. Hadland, Magdalena Cerdá, Yu Li, Maxwell S. Krieger, and Brandon D.L. Marshall, "Association of Pharmaceutical Industry Marketing of Opioid Products to Physicians with Subsequent Opioid Prescribing," *JAMA Internal Medicine* 178.6 (2018): 861–63.

6   CDC (2017).

7   Ibid.

8   Ibid.

DISCUSSION QUESTIONS

(1) What should be the relationship between doctors and pharmaceutical companies? How might we formulate this relationship in order to mitigate conflicts of interest?

(2) Do doctors have an obligation to inform their patients when they are receiving non-research funding from pharmaceutical companies?

(3) If it was found that non-research funding did not directly cause doctors to overprescribe patients certain opioids, would other factors, such as representatives meeting with physicians or marketing exposure, still warrant cause for concern? If yes, then what limits should be imposed on pharmaceutical companies in order to avoid these scenarios?

(4) Should pharmaceutical companies advertise addictive opioids to physicians or offer non-research funding at all?

FURTHER READINGS

David Blumenthal, "Doctors and Drug Companies," *The New England Journal of Medicine* 351.18 (2004): 1885–90.

Kirk L. Cumpston, "Regurgitation of My Free Lunch: The Clinical Toxicology and Pharmaceutical Company Relationship," *Journal of Medical Toxicology* 5.4 (2009): 257–58.

Joel Lexchin, "Interactions between Physicians and the Pharmaceutical Industry: What Does the Literature Say?" *Canadian Medical Association Journal* 149.10 (1993): 1401–07.

Ray Moynihan, "Who Pays for the Pizza? Redefining the Relationship between Doctors and Drug Companies," *British Medical Journal* 326.7400 (2003): 1189.

Rosie Taylor and Jim Giles, "Cash Interest Taint Drug Advice," *Nature* 437 (2005): 1070–71.

30.
CONFLICT MINERALS AND SUPPLY CHAIN MANAGEMENT: THE CASE OF THE DRC

SCOTT WISOR

BACKGROUND

THE DEMOCRATIC REPUBLIC OF CONGO IS HOME TO ARGUABLY THE deadliest conflict since World War II. Several million people have died in warfare and from war-related causes such as disease and malnutrition since 1998. The United Nations High Commissioner for Refugees reported in 2015 that 430,000 refugees remain in neighboring countries, and that 2.7 million internally displaced people within the country are unable to return to their homes. Though the civil war officially ended in 2003, multiple conflicts have continued to add to the causalities and to sexual violence against women, men, and children.

For many years the war in the DRC remained low on the agenda of international human rights organizations, despite the mounting death toll. But beginning in the late 2000s, advocacy organizations began to direct their attention to it. In particular, they focused on the role of the natural resource trade in fueling civil war. These organizations argued that armed militias were funded through the illicit trade in tungsten, tin, tantalum, gold, and other valuable minerals mined largely in the eastern provinces. Advocates claimed that these valuable minerals both financed armed militias and provided incentives for warring parties to continue fighting for territory in which these resources could be found.

To target the finances of armed groups in the DRC, advocacy organizations, led by the ENOUGH Project (an NGO working on atrocity prevention), launched a campaign focusing on the role of major electronics companies in sourcing minerals from the DRC. Drawing on campaigns targeting the "blood diamonds" that fueled the wars in Liberia and Sierra Leone, they targeted major brands including Apple, Intel, and Motorola, arguing that the companies were using "conflict minerals."

In addition to exerting direct pressure on major electronics companies through savvy campaigns using well edited viral videos disseminated through social media, advocates also worked to change the laws regulating supply chain management. In the Dodd-Frank Wall Street Reform and Consumer Protection Act (2010), a small provision was added governing so-called conflict minerals. Section 1502 required companies listed on the SEC to report on whether they sourced minerals from provinces in conflict in the DRC, and if so, what steps they were taking to ensure that they were not complicit in funding armed groups.

A certification scheme was to be put in place to name mines that were "conflict free." These mines needed third-party verification to be deemed responsibly trading in conflict minerals. Similar legislation was considered in Europe and Canada, as the movement to halt the civil war in the DRC focused on the natural resource sector spread internationally.

Feeling the pressure of both reputational risk and regulatory pressure, major brands revised their supply chain policies to avoid alleged complicity involved in trading in minerals sourced from the Democratic Republic of Congo. Many companies simply went Congo-free, ensuring that they did not source materials from the country, avoiding the risk that they would be inadvertently funding conflict in the region.

The passage of Dodd-Frank and the suspension of some commercial ties to the DRC were initially hailed as major achievements by some human rights organizations. But a growing chorus of critics argued that the campaign had been ill-conceived and was not only failing to end the conflict, but was actively harming workers in conflict-affected provinces and potentially exacerbating the deleterious role of mining in driving armed conflict in the DRC. A scathing open letter written by academic researchers and civil society representatives argued that four years after the passage of Dodd-Frank, external advocacy organizations had failed to listen to the relevant stakeholders among Congolese civil society and their employers, and to take into account ongoing efforts to reform the resource trade; and as a result they had caused great economic harm to communities dependent upon mining for their livelihoods.

> Nearly four years after the passing of the Dodd-Frank Act, only a small fraction of the hundreds of mining sites in the eastern DRC have been reached by traceability or certification efforts. The rest remain beyond the pale, forced into either illegality or collapse as certain international buyers have responded to the legislation by going "Congo-free."
>
> This in turn has driven many miners into the margins of legality (for instance, feeding into smuggling rackets), where armed actors return through the loopholes of transnational regulation. Others have simply lost their jobs, and in areas where mining has ceased, local economies have suffered.[1]

CONGRESSIONAL HEARINGS RECEIVED TESTIMONY NOTING THE unintended and harmful consequences of 1502, and many media organizations began to cover "Obama's law," as it was known in the DRC, criticizing the alleged harmful impact it was having on local economies and artisanal miners.

Efforts to address the problem of mining in the DRC are an example of the more general trend toward institutional reform that attempts to mitigate the resource curse. The "resource curse" is a phenomenon that economists and political scientists argue affects national development. The idea here is that countries that have not yet developed high-quality institutions (such as democratic, accountable government, the rule of law, a free and open media, etc.) and gain access to large reserves of oil or minerals, will be disproportionately likely to suffer from civil war, authoritarianism, gender inequality, and underperforming economic growth. In other words, if you don't have good institutions, and valuable natural resources come into production, your chances of institutional improvement decrease significantly.

There are several mechanisms that are thought to cause the resource curse. In conflict, valuable commodities may provide the capacity (by funding armed groups) and motivation (to gain control of valuable resources) for armed conflict where it would otherwise not exist, or not be as strong. Authoritarian governments get extra motivation in maintaining power when they are capturing the rents involved in mining; and this finances the armed forces that repress dissent and purchase allegiance. Gender inequality is perpetuated due to the absence of stable democratic governments, under which effective women's rights movements might emerge, and due to the difficulty in establishing export-led economic growth, weakening economic opportunities for women outside the home. And when domestic currencies are buoyed by high resource prices, it is difficult to build a successful non-resource based exports sector, and poor economic performance results.

Efforts or proposals to address the resource curse include: transparency requirements specifying that extractives companies publish what initial and ongoing payments they make to governments to secure mineral rights; improvements in the process of bidding for and contracting the sale of mineral rights; targeted and general sanctions against resource-reliant regimes that abuse human rights; the establishment of trust funds to shield national budgets and domestic currencies from the boom-bust cycle of resource prices; and corporate social responsibility programs that include local communities in decision-making about resource exploitation and in the benefits arising from resource extraction.

ANALYSIS

IN ATTEMPTS TO ADDRESS THE ROLE OF BUSINESS IN RESPONDING to the resource curse in the DRC and in other states, there are a number of ethical themes which emerge from the controversy over efforts to manage from afar the trade in natural resources.

The case of conflict minerals acutely raises the question of consumers', companies', and governments' moral responsibility for their consumption of products sourced from countries that are embroiled in violent conflict, plagued by human rights abuses, or governed by autocrats. Do such moral responsibilities exist, and if they do, how strong are they? How far down the supply chain do these responsibilities reach? When has a consumer or company done enough to address the problems facing innocent civilians and low-wage miners in the DRC?

Responses to these questions track a more general issue that has animated contemporary moral and political philosophers. To what extent do moral and political obligations extend beyond one's own community?

Are there duties of global ethics and justice, and if so, what do they require of individuals and corporations? According to one line of thinking, moral duties arise when certain structural relations hold between rights bearers and duty bearers. For example, consumers of products made in "sweatshops" or low-wage conditions may have some duties to attempt to protect and promote the labor rights of workers in these industries. It is because enduring structural interactions are maintained between people vulnerable to low wages and exploitative work arrangements that such responsibilities are held by consumers and companies.

A closely related line of thought is that such duties arise when individuals are responsible for harming others, either directly or through the design of institutional arrangements. Institutional arrangements are thought to be harmful to others when they produce foreseeable human rights deficits and when feasible alternative institutional arrangements are available. For the theorists concerned with institutional harm, the argument is that consumers, companies, and governments have harmed innocent civilians in the DRC by permitting the natural resource trade to take place under rules and practices which incentivize warfare, whereas alternative methods of engaging in this trade would not provide such incentives and would therefore be less harmful.

An important question arises in light of the failure of 1502: how much evidence is needed to justify selecting feasible alternatives, especially under the conditions of complexity and uncertainty that are typical in these sorts of situations? The Congolese themselves do not appear to prefer the situation produced by that law to the previous anarchic trade.

A third line of thinking holds that ethical duties are established only in so far as some individuals are suffering and other individuals or institutions are in a position to provide assistance. These duties of beneficence are not specifically grounded in the relationships between companies and their supply chains. But it may be that companies sourcing materials from the DRC are better positioned to assist people who are suffering there, and so they have stronger humanitarian duties than other corporations who do not operate there.

Critics who reject such duties, especially with reference to the DRC, make several points. First, they argue that the alleged role of the resource trade in fueling warfare is overstated. There is a general war economy in the DRC, and all goods and services can be subject to the exploitative aims of armed groups; and it is far from clear that companies either have the knowledge or capacity to contribute to peace-building in the region.

Second, it is not the primary task of corporations to secure basic human rights. This is the task of governance, and bad governance is the source of conflict in the DRC, not the minerals trade. Echoing classic opposition to corporate social responsibility from Milton Friedman, the business of business is to make profit, and the business of government is to secure rights.

Third, those corporations that have been targeted by advocacy campaigns have no direct presence in the DRC, and thus little standing to advocate for reform. They simply are the end users of natural resources that may have passed through several different businesses before arriving in the finished product of a smartphone or laptop computer. To extend moral responsibility from these companies to their distant suppliers, many of whom may be unknown given their distance in the supply chain, is to exceed the plausible bounds of corporate responsibility. It is only the direct activities and relationships of a company that are properly subject to moral critique and legal regulation.

The Dodd-Frank legislation, which places obligations on companies to report on their supply chains, and which to some extent displaced or superseded other efforts to improve mining in the DRC, highlights the tension between legally binding regulatory efforts to improve corporate responsibility and voluntary initiatives that corporations choose to undertake to improve outcomes for relevant stakeholders. At the time that Dodd-Frank was passed, a number of other voluntary initiatives were under way to improve the conflict sensitivity of business practices affecting local communities in the DRC. These efforts often involved local civil society groups and companies who were at least somewhat interested in improving outcomes for relevant stakeholders.

Proponents of voluntary initiatives argue that they are likely to be better designed than formal regulation, to be more adaptable to changing circumstances, and to properly reflect the primary role of the business organization, which is responsibility for market activities, not for securing justice and human rights. Opponents of voluntary initiatives favor legally binding regulation. They argue that voluntary efforts often fall short of what is required to protect the rights of stakeholders, and that companies will undertake costly efforts to secure the rights of stakeholders only when legally compelled to do so.

A more general issue that arises from the attempts to regulate the resource trade in the DRC applies not only to the ethics of for-profit business enterprises but to the ethics of not-for-profit organizations. Innocent civilians harmed by either commercial activity or general conflict in the DRC are often neither able nor capable of being heard by major multi-national corporations who may have links to the area of conflict. Non-governmental organizations often take it as their responsibility to speak on behalf of the victims of abuse, given that these victims might have no other outlet to exercise their voices. But with the power to speak for others comes the opportunity to misrepresent their views, to ignore internal disagreements among community members, to deny the agency of individuals and groups who were otherwise working to secure just outcomes, and to misdiagnose social and political problems.

Critics of the ENOUGH Project and their campaign to regulate the DRCs resource trade argue that their campaign was insensitive and unresponsive to the stated aims and goals of at least some members of civil society in the DRC, not to mention the commercial actors who were already undertaking efforts to improve supply chains in the DRC. While the problem of speaking for others is most apparent for non-governmental organizations that aim to speak on behalf of victims, it may also arise for business enterprises who may come to indirectly represent the interests of their customers or stakeholders' interests in various regulatory fora.

Operating in frontier markets plagued with authoritarian governance, human rights abuse, and civil conflict presents unique ethical challenges to companies and consumers. One option is of course simply not to operate there. But if companies halt operations in ethically risky areas, this may make populations in those areas worse off. Moral purity, in the form of non-participation, may be far worse than remaining in the country and attempting to negotiate the difficult ethical and policy terrain. There are two reasons for this. First, if a business departs and it is not replaced, this may mean fewer livelihood opportunities for people already facing significant material deprivation. Second, when a morally concerned business departs and is replaced by a less responsible corporate actor, there are fewer possibilities for civilians to work with this new actor, or to establish good community relations, or to have in place a meaningful grievance procedure. The moral problem of worse actors suggests that in at least some cases, it is better for companies to continue operating with "dirty hands" than to leave with "clean hands." This is not to deny that additional moral responsibilities are incurred by companies who do continue operations in conflict zones. These derivative duties to stakeholders will arise from the unique relations they have with them in highly non-ideal circumstances.

NOTE

1   Christoph Vogel, "An Open Letter," online.

DISCUSSION QUESTIONS

(1) If someone approaches you on the street, and offers to sell you stolen
     goods, is it wrong to purchase them? If a government plunders its natural
     resources to the detriment of its citizens, is it wrong for companies to buy
     these natural resources?
(2) You likely own electronics that source materials from the DRC. Do you,
     as a consumer, bear responsibility for improving the situation in the
     country?
(3) To what extent should companies make moral demands of the companies
     they do business with, including companies that supply them with raw
     materials?
(4) To what extent should corporations be held responsible for the conduct of
     third-party businesses from whom they purchase goods or materials?
(5) If refraining from doing business in a particular country may harm
     workers in that country, do businesses have a responsibility to continue to
     work in countries that may present environmental and social risks?

FURTHER READINGS

Virginia Haufler, "Governing Corporations in Zones of Conflict: Issues,
     Actors, and Institutions," in *Who Governs the Globe?*, ed. Deborah Avant,
     Martha Finnemore, and Susan Sell (New York: Cambridge University
     Press, 2010).
Virginia Haufler, "The Kimberley Process, Club Goods, and Public
     Enforcement of a Private Regime," in *Voluntary Programs: A Club Theory
     Approach*, ed. Aseem Prakash and Matthew Potoski (Cambridge, MA:
     MIT Press, 2009).
Jennifer Rubenstein, "Why It Is Beside the Point That No One Elected Oxfam,"
     The Journal of Political Philosophy 22 (2014): 204–30.
John Ruggie, *Just Business: Human Rights and Multinational Corporations*
     (New York: W.W. Norton, 2013).
Laura Seay, "What's Wrong with Dodd-Frank 1502? Conflict Minerals,
     Civilian Livelihoods, and the Unintended Consequences of Western
     Advocacy," Center for Global Development Working Paper 248.

Leaf Wenar, "Property Rights and the Resource Curse," *Philosophy and Public Affairs* 36 (2008): 2–32.

Scott Wisor, "The Moral Problem of Worse Actors," *Ethics and Global Politics* 7 (2014): 47–64.

31.

DEMOCRACY IN BUSINESS: THE MONDRAGON WORKERS COOPERATIVE

TOM MCNAMARA, CYRLENE CLAASEN,
AND IRENA DESCUBES

BACKGROUND

THE BLACK STAR PUB & BREWERY, LOCATED IN AUSTIN, TEXAS, IS a great place to meet, eat, and drink (according to many of the reviews on Yelp). You'll see a lot of interesting people having a good time. What you won't see is the staff wearing uniforms. That is because one employee, Dana Curtis, didn't want to wear one. What kind of business would let employees make day to day decisions about how things are run? One that is actually owned and operated by the employees. The Black Star, which opened in 2010, is a worker-owned cooperative. This means that the people who work there also have a stake in the business. Decisions are usually taken collectively, with an emphasis on finding a consensus through democratic means wherever possible.

While often overlooked, the United States has a rich history of worker cooperatives dating back to at least the early nineteenth century. And the phenomenon appears to be growing. The US Federation of Worker

Cooperatives estimates that there are around 300 businesses that can be deemed "democratic workplaces," providing jobs to over 3,500 people. A majority of the cooperatives currently in operation in the US were created sometime after the year 2000.

One of the largest, and most famous, cooperatives in the world is Mondragon. It is a manufacturing and service cooperative, an enterprise that is fully owned by the people who work for it. The group was founded in the Basque region of Spain in 1956 and originally had about two dozen workers. Today, that number is over 73,000 and almost 80 per cent of the employees are cooperative members. To become a member/owner, an employee is required to make an investment in the business, usually around €14,000 (about $16,500 USD). The money is deducted from their salary over the course of three or five years.

The organization was originally made up of mostly manufacturing cooperatives, but the company soon diversified. Today Mondragon is focused primarily on four activities: industry, finance, retail, and high-tech (or what the company calls "knowledge"). With a revenue in 2016 of over €12 billion, it is the tenth largest business in Spain. Mondragon says that it is committed to democratic principles and their application in the way it organizes and runs its businesses. It is also dedicated to creating jobs, training and developing its workforce, and promoting various social initiatives. While many classical corporations would profess to having the same values, Mondragon is unusual in its commitment to putting them into practice (in their 2016 annual report there is a section titled "Solidarity"). Proof of this commitment to worker solidarity is the fact that managers are prohibited from making more than six times what the average worker makes. This is in stark contrast to the average pay for a CEO at a top US firm who is paid about 300 times what a normal worker makes (in 1965 this ratio was 20 to 1).

Despite its size, Mondragon is a minnow in a sea of sharks. Direct competitors include such world-class companies as Mitsubishi, General Electric, Hitachi, and LG. Moreover, the top 100 corporations on the planet have a combined market capitalization of almost $16 trillion. Their power to control, shape, and dominate global markets is astounding and appears to be only growing. How can a workers' cooperative ever hope to challenge a behemoth like Walmart, whose annual revenue is larger than the GDP of Belgium?

ANALYSIS

MONDRAGON IS A "CO-OPERATIVE BUSINESS ORGANIZATION", comprising "autonomous and independent cooperatives" that compete internationally. Its current President, Mr. Iñigo Ucín, is well aware of the challenges that Mondragon is facing. He believes that "competitiveness, the ability to innovate in business, and intelligent intercooperation" between the group's different divisions and subsidiaries will be key factors to successfully achieving growth in the future. Ultimately, what makes Mondragon different from a classical corporation is its unconventional origins. At heart, it is a socio-economic organization, not a purely profit-generating one. But at the same time, it would have many characteristics of a multinational conglomerate (Mondragon comprises 261 different companies and co-operatives), something that was in vogue in the 1970s.

Conventional economic thought would suggest that it is impossible to manage such an unwieldy enterprise, let alone for it to thrive or even survive. Starting around the 1980s, the trend was for corporations to shed their different divisions, focus on "core competencies," and unlock shareholder value. General Electric is usually considered the last company that would come close to representing what could be considered as a successful conglomerate. Is Mondragon an exotic species soon headed for extinction?

Proponents of a classic corporate structure, with a president, CEO, board of directors, and possibly millions of anonymous shareholders, would point to the massive efficiencies and economies of scale that are derived from having a clear hierarchy in conjunction with a command and control structure. Another advantage of large corporations is their ability to raise vast sums of money through new share offerings or the issuance of corporate debt, something that might not be immediately available to a worker-run cooperative. And contrary to popular opinion, large corporations are not exactly the slow-moving dinosaurs they are often portrayed as. One need only look at the myriad multi-billion dollar companies based in Silicon Valley to invalidate that stereotype.

But is giving a voice to workers and encouraging democratic participation in corporate decisions necessarily at odds with the concepts of modern management and profits? It can be argued that the basic notion of free market capitalism was built upon the concept of "egalitarianism" and challenging the power of monopolies or well established special interests, with their associated rigid hierarchies. One of the key elements of early capitalist theory (and practice) was this notion of "distributive justice," something that would clearly be in the spirit of such liberal and democratic thinkers as Adam Smith, John Locke, and Thomas Paine. From a managerial perspective, it appears that workplace democracy simply makes good business sense. With US unemployment rates at lows not seen for decades, and with millennials demanding a greater say in how their work is managed, it appears that calls for democracy in the workplace will only grow louder in the near future.

Increasingly consumers, as well as employees, are demanding that modern companies act like the responsible corporate citizens they say they are, taking into account the needs of their many stakeholders. For their part, many corporations have adopted a discourse that reflects the changing desires of many consumers, but therein lies the problem. Socially aware critics believe that efforts in terms of corporate social responsibility (CSR) and respect for workers on the part of the companies that would make up the S&P 500 have fallen short. Large institutional investors, however, would complain about a lack of focus on the bottom line, and that CEOs are more concerned about the interests of stakeholders than they are about those of shareholders. Does a workers' cooperative like Mondragon offer a way to resolve this conflict, merging concerns about sustainability with activities that make a profit?

As a result of the 2008 financial crisis, companies have relentlessly focused on driving down costs, increasing margins, and gaining a market share at the expense of less powerful rivals. What hope does a workers' cooperative based in the Basque region of Spain have against some of the largest and most focused corporations on the planet? Luckily for Mr. Ucín, evidence indicates that the cooperative model of organizational management can be an effective tool in meeting the challenge of successfully competing in dynamic environments.[1,2] The main reason is that democratic principles, when applied to corporate governance, can lead to increased levels of innovation and productivity. For this to be achieved, however, employees must be able to directly take part in any critical decisions regarding strategic issues. A complementary factor would be that collective ownership of the enterprise tends to result in higher levels of loyalty and dedication. The mechanism through which Mondragon realizes its commitment to democratic principles and employee participation is through a Cooperative Congress comprising 650 delegates who represent all of the firms that make up Mondragon.

The Congress allows employees to discuss important issues and develop a strategic vision for Mondragon. The 2016 Congress resulted in the company's Socio-Corporate Policy for 2017–20, with a focus on developing ways for the company to remain both competitive and sustainable.

Another element that helps Mondragon is its reliance on the concept of Total Quality Management (TQM). This is a management approach in which the focus is on achieving 100 per cent total customer satisfaction. This goal is realized through the active participation by all employees in "processes, products, services, and the culture in which they work." Something which one would imagine could be readily achieved in a worker cooperative.

In spite of all of the competitive advantages that come with being a cooperative, Mondragon is no stranger to failure. In 2013 its household and commercial appliance manufacturing unit, Fagor Electrodomésticos, went out of business, another casualty of the economic fallout from the 2008 crisis. About 2,000 workers were facing unemployment, but thanks to Mondragon's commitment to social values, an effort was made to find them other jobs. "If a co-op within the group has an excess of members, then we relocate them to other co-ops within the group," explained an executive. A year after Fagor's collapse, 1,700 people had either found employment in other cooperatives or were allowed to retire.

In a never ending search for new markets (and increased profits), global expansion is seen as a solution for more and more companies. Starting in the early 1990s, Mondragon realized that in order to be competitive and protect the jobs of its workers/members it needed to grow internationally. As one manager puts it, "The decision is simple in our sector: it is to eat or to be eaten. If we want to survive and keep our jobs, we must be present abroad. We are aware that growth and internationalisation pose great challenges for our cooperative values and practices in many ways but, otherwise, we would disappear."[3]

Internationalization at Mondragon does not have the same immediate implications that it does with a conventional corporation. For the most part, when Mondragon sets up a foreign enterprise the goal is to support jobs back in the home region of Basque, not close down a Spanish facility or relocate jobs to a low cost/low wage country. However, these new entities are usually closely controlled by the parent cooperative that created them. Also, these foreign subsidiaries are classical firms in which the local employees don't have the same membership rights as those working for Mondragon proper. Furthermore, a dedicated effort is made to keep the high value-adding activities and R&D in the home country of Spain, something which, to be fair, would be a practice of many large corporations as well. But for cooperative "purists," this two-tier system of worker involvement is troubling. To its credit, Mondragon has, where possible, implemented progressive Human Resources Management (HRM) practices. Emphasis on training, teamwork, job stability, equality, and fair wages would be just some of the examples of Mondragon's efforts to treat its foreign subsidiaries fairly. Missing, however, would be increased levels of communication with regard to such sensitive matters as strategy and financial performance.

More awkwardly for a subsidiary of a workers' cooperative, there is a lack of profit-sharing schemes and employee ownership programs. Proponents of classical capitalism might feel vindicated by the fact that once Mondragon reached a critical size it had to be more judicious with its efforts towards worker solidarity and empowerment, and adopt a more traditional command and control posture for some of its operations.

As a result, tensions are already starting to show. As one worker/member with over 20 years of experience at Mondragon said, "The level of participation in general assemblies and other spaces of decision making has been gradually falling in recent years."[4] They believed that this decrease in democracy was a direct result of globalization and the increase in size and complexity of Mondragon's operations.

There is the idea that to meet the challenges of having now become a multinational entity, Mondragon has come to rely more and more on classical management techniques, somewhat making the emphasis on self-directed work groups and participatory management a secondary concern. As one Human Resources manager put it, "As the company has grown in recent years and has had to meet the complex demands of our international clients and the rigorous standards of the sector, we have been incorporating external professionals within the management and direction of the firm with talent and experience, which has been essential to getting where we are today."[5]

Perhaps most troubling for Mondragon is the fact that with greater size often comes the temptation to adopt a classical multinational corporate structure. This phenomenon is known as the "degeneration thesis" and argues that worker-owned enterprises are either ultimately doomed to failure or to "degenerate" into more traditional forms of capitalist businesses. The challenge facing Mondragon today is for it to adhere to its principles of worker solidarity and democracy, while at the same time find a way to adapt them into a strategy that will rise to meet the economic pressure just to survive.

Some fear that creeping "managerialism" at Mondragon will cause the company to lose its "special sauce" and become just like every other corporation competing in the market today. And there are signs that worker dissatisfaction has already begun. As another Mondragon worker says, "We carry out our activities in self-managed teams. However, there is a general feeling that we do not have a voice in some important decisions that affect the management of the company. They are arranged previously, at the top."[6] Worrying criticism for a company that prides itself on worker empowerment and inclusion.

NOTES

1   M. Moye, "Mondragon: Adapting Co-operative Structures to Meet the Demands of a Changing Environment," *Economic and Industrial Democracy* 14.2 (1993): 251–76.

2   M. Nunez and J. Moyano, "Ownership Structure of Cooperatives as an Environmental Buffer," *Journal of Management Studies* 41.7 (2004): 31–52.

3   Ignacio Bretos, Anjel Errasti, and Carmen Marcuello, "Ownership, Governance, and the Diffusion of HRM Practices in Multinational Worker Cooperatives: Case-Study Evidence from the Mondragon Group," *Human Resource Management Journal* 28.1 (2018): 76–91.

4   Ibid.

5   Ibid.

6   Ibid.

DISCUSSION QUESTIONS

(1)   What can Mondragon do to promote the implementation of its worker/owner model in countries where it has foreign subsidiaries? Provide a detailed explanation.

(2)   List and explain, from a managerial perspective, the advantages, if any, that the worker-owned cooperative model of a business would have as compared to the classical shareholder one.

(3)   Imagine that you are a consultant. Provide a detailed list of action steps that the management of Mondragon can take in order to avoid the phenomenon of "degeneration thesis." Be ready to defend your suggestions.

(4) Are worker cooperatives a two-way street? That is to say, is there any way for a Fortune 500© company to duplicate some of the best practices, in terms of human resources management, found at Mondragon? Justify your answer.

(5) From a strategic point of view, do you believe that there are certain sectors or markets that readily lend themselves to the worker cooperative model? Why? Conversely, do you believe that there are certain industries where it would be extremely difficult to implement the worker cooperative model? Be sure to justify your answer.

FURTHER READINGS

I. Bretos, A. Errasti, and C. Marcuello, "Ownership, Governance, and the Diffusion of HRM Practices in Multinational Worker Cooperatives: Case-Study Evidence from the Mondragon Group," *Human Resource Management Journal* (2017).

P. Moskowitz, "Meet the Radical Workers' Cooperative Growing in the Heart of the Deep South," *The Nation* (April 24, 2017).

A. Semuels, "Worker-Owned Cooperatives: What Are They?" *The Atlantic* (July 8, 2015).

G. Tremlett, "Mondragon: Spain's Giant Co-operative Where Times Are Hard but Few Go Bust," *The Guardian* (March 7, 2013).

32

THE EQUIFAX HACK

LEONARD KAHN

BACKGROUND

IN 2017 HACKERS SUCCESSFULLY TARGETED EQUIFAX, A DATA BRO-kerage firm. In the process these hackers obtained sensitive—and potentially damaging—information concerning about half of the population of the United States. The hackers were able to gather highly sensitive data—including social security numbers, home addresses, and birth dates—on nearly 150 million Americans. The hackers were also able to access the driver's license numbers of about 10 million Americans,[1] as well as tens or even hundreds of thousands of credit card numbers and credit dispute reports.[2] The initial estimate was that another 400,000 British customers were also affected by this cyber attack; however, this number was later raised to over 15 million.[3] In order to understand this significant case, we need to begin with a little background information about the nature of big data and big-data brokerage.

Big data can be big in three distinct but mutually compatible ways. First, data can be big in terms of their volume. The number of elements in data sets can be so great that the sets are hard or even impossible for non-specialists to store and to understand fully. Second, data can be big in terms of their velocity. New data can accumulate so quickly that we lack the computer processing power to analyze the data in real time. Lastly, data can be big in terms of their variety. Data sets that are big in this sense might contain not only conventional data such as integers, floating-point numbers, names, and dates but also such elements as sound files, unstructured text, radio-frequency identifications, remote sensory readings, encryptions, URLs, photographs, freehand drawings, real-time GPS coordinates, and biometric information like finger prints. Of course, the very same data sets are often big in more than one—or even all three—of these senses.[4]

The rise of data sets that are big in terms of their volume, velocity, and/or their variety has given rise to new kinds of business, one of which is data brokerage. Data brokers are firms that collect, analyze, and package information for resale to other firms. Data brokerage firms specialize in having enough storage to take on data that are big in terms of its volume, in having enough processing power to analyze the data in real time, and in having enough expertise to handle the wide variety of data that we generate.

A simple example will help to illustrate how big data and data brokerage have become part of our lives. Consider José, who buys a quart of milk every week at his local grocery store. Until recently, José's milk-buying behavior would be known only to himself and to those few who work at the store that José frequents. But the rise of big data has changed the landscape. Because of the massive increase in our ability to store data, it is possible to keep track of shopping data for hundreds of millions of consumers, including José, over years and even decades. And because of advances in both software and hardware, it is possible to process much of this data in real time. Data brokers such as Acxiom, Datalogix, Equifax, and Experian purchase this kind of data. They then combine disparate data sets and assemble portfolios on individuals such as José. Data brokers can combine, for example, information about José's shopping history at his local grocery store with information about his use of gas and electricity, his monthly purchases at a pharmacy, queries to search engines such as Google, how likely a given political party is to target him before an election, his followers and his likes on a social media platform such as Facebook, Twitter, or Snapchat, and even his browser history. Of course, this data often includes highly personal information, and much of it is collected and sold without the explicit awareness or consent of those who are being monitored.[5]

Though there are many ways in which data brokerage can be morally challenging, an especially salient one concerns the manner in which it makes our personal information vulnerable to hackers. For example, Equifax is today one of the world's largest data brokers, even though it began life in the nineteenth century as a retail credit company. Today it assembles and amasses data on nearly one billion people worldwide. In May 2017 hackers initiated a successful cyber attack on Equifax and gained access to much of the firm's data. The hackers continued to access this data without Equifax's knowledge until July 29 of the same year. Though Equifax, with the help of the independent cyber security firm Mandiant, was able to regain control of its data in the following days, the damage was already done. A theft of this kind would have been a virtual impossibility until the rise of big data. Only a few decades ago, stealing this much information would have required years of effort and several large trucks worth of paper files. Hence, it is not surprising that some sources claim that this is "very possibly the worst leak of personal data ever."[6]

The cyber attack on Equifax exploited a vulnerability in Apache Struts, an open-source application that the firm used to build its website. However, this vulnerability—and the patch needed to fix it—had been made public on March 7, 2017, a full two months *before* the hack occurred.[7] Equifax has not yet provided an explanation of why it did not remove this vulnerability and provide adequate layers of security to prevent a breach of this kind.[8]

Equifax's response to the data breach has been problematic on a number of fronts. Despite learning in July that hackers had breached their defenses, management at Equifax waited six weeks to divulge this information to the public. Nevertheless, three executives at Equifax—John W. Gamble, the Chief Financial Officer; Joseph M. Loughran III, the President of US Information Solutions; and Rodolfo O. Ploder, the President of Workforce Solutions—sold company stock worth almost $2 million immediately after management at the firm became aware that it had been hacked. Selling stock at this point certainly raises concerns, since when the news that Equifax had been hacked finally broke, the company's stock lost nearly one-third of its value. As of this writing, the US Department of Justice had opened a criminal investigation to determine whether these executives were guilty of insider trading.[9]

Nonetheless, they are still employed by Equifax, though both the firm's Chief Information Officer and Chief Security Officer have retired. Moreover, while Equifax set up a website to help answer questions about the breach and to offer free credit monitoring, this site was also vulnerable to hacking and exposure of users' personal information.[10]

It is not currently known who hacked Equifax, and perhaps we will never know. The hacking community appears to have become aware of Equifax's vulnerability as little as 72 hours after the Apache Struts flaw was discovered. There is reason to believe that the first group of hackers who penetrated Equifax's defenses handed off their operation to a second, more sophisticated group, as often happens in attacks of this sort. Some have speculated that the second group was state-sponsored, with many fingers pointed toward China because of the methods and tools used by the hackers.[11] Nevertheless, no definitive evidence supporting this speculation has been made public.

ANALYSIS

THERE IS PLENTY OF BLAME TO GO AROUND FOR THE EQUIFAX hack. It is obviously true that the hackers who attacked Equifax acted immorally and illegally. However, our main concern here is with Equifax and its management. Why? Consider a parallel situation in the banking industry. While a person who robs a bank acts immorally and illegally, the owners and managers of the bank might well be responsible for many aspects of the outcome if, for example, they failed to take the steps necessary to prevent a robbery or if they handled the aftermath of the robbery incompetently or carelessly. The bank's responsibility originates in large part from the fact that it is entrusted to protect its customers and their assets; indeed, the bank's owners and managers often profit handsomely from this trust. If the bank has failed to act appropriately with regard to this trust, it is morally—and perhaps legally—liable. Much the same can be said for data brokerage firms such as Equifax. These firms are entrusted with our personal data, and they regularly reap enormous profit by means of it. If they allow us to come to harm, then they bear at least some of the moral blame.

Could Equifax have seen this coming? In fact a hack of this nature of a data broker was not only predictable; it was widely predicted.[12] Personal data—especially the sort of personal data stolen in the Equifax hack—is valuable. As such, it is easily foreseeable that nefarious interests will attempt to pilfer it. Recent hacks of other big data, and big data-related ones, show that firms such as Yahoo, eBay, Dropbox, Facebook, MySpace, Spambot, Deep Root Analytics, Tumblr, and Evernote present a clear pattern of data vulnerability and suggest that unless management at big data firms take action, breaches like this one will continue to occur. Indeed, as big data becomes easier to store and easier to process, the vulnerability of our personal information is likely to increase. Arguably, big data brokers such as Equifax assume a high level of responsibility for the information that they possess. The fact that they earn a profit by buying and selling data makes it clear that they recognize the value of this commodity. Since data brokers recognize this value, they have a responsibility to take reasonable steps to preclude its theft and, thereby, to prevent damage to vulnerable individuals. However, Equifax clearly failed to do so. As noted above, the firm did not even take the minimal step of installing the patch to Apache Struts in a timely manner—a step that would have foiled the hack before it began.

One question we must ask ourselves is just how far data brokerage firms must go in order to protect our data. What would constitute even minimal standards of security that every firm must meet? And what would comprise the standards to which firms should aspire? Given the degree to which ordinary citizens are vulnerable, should governments take a greater role in regulating the data brokerage industry? Such regulation might take the form of licensing firms. For instance, only firms that meet certain standards for security would receive a license, and only firms with a license could legally resell data. Likewise, firms that failed to take even minimal steps, such as installing the patch to Apache Struts, quickly could face fines or even the loss of their license to do business. Alternatively, regulation might be broader and more aggressive. Firms might be required to store data only on government-owned secure servers. However, it should be noted that regulations of this sort are far from costless, that the government itself is capable of being hacked,[13] and that there are legitimate concerns about governments having access to and control over personal data.[14]

Of course, the mere existence of data brokerage firms creates some ineliminable risk. What are the responsibilities of the owners and managers of data brokerage firms if a breach does in fact occur? It is difficult to see what counts against a prompt and frank admission of the situation, as painful as that might be. As we have already seen, Equifax waited a month-and-a-half before telling the public what had occurred. During that time millions of people were vulnerable without knowing it. While members of the firm might have gained a little breathing room by putting off the inevitable, the only winners in the long term were the hackers who breached Equifax's security.

Must every firm immediately make public every case in which data is stolen from it? An industry-wide policy of complete transparency would have prevented at least some of the damage that occurred as a result of the Equifax hack. There are, however, some downsides to this approach. First, the regular release of information of this kind might leave many of us indifferent to the problem. If we knew that it was as common as it is, we might think of it as inevitable and, in a sense, not worthy of our attention. That impression would serve us poorly when massive hacks like the one on Equifax occur. Second, the release of information might be useful to hackers. If a group knew that, for example, Facebook had been hacked, they might be quick to join in the attack.

Yet even if complete and immediate transparency is not optimal, it seems clear that far less opacity would be preferable to the status quo. One possibility would be to allow data brokerage firms to be sued for withholding information about breaches. The threat of financial loss might be enough to motivate the ownership and management of firms to be forthcoming. However, in the United States this might be impossible. Recently the US Senate voted to remove a rule in the Federal Register that would have allowed those affected by the Equifax hack to sue the company.[15] Another possibility would be closer regulation of the industry. If the firms in question cannot notify citizens of the harm being done to them, then their government is the natural authority to which to appeal.

NOTES

1   Laura Hautala, "Equifax Hackers Took Driver's License Info on 10 Million Americans," *CNET* (October 10, 2017).

2   Craig Timburg, Elizabeth Dworkin, and Brian Fung, "Data of 143 Million Americans Exposed in Hacking of Credit Reporting Agency Equifax," *Washington Post* (September 7, 2017).

3   John McCrank, "Equifax Says That 15.2 Million UK Records Exposed in Cyber Breach," *Reuters* (October 10, 2017).

4   Edd Dumbill, "Volume, Velocity, Variety: What You Need to Know about Big Data," *Forbes* (January 19, 2012).

5   Steve Croft, "The Data Brokers: Selling Your Personal Information," *CBS: Sixty Minutes* (March 9, 2014).

6   Dan Gooding, "Why the Equifax Breach Is Very Possibly the Worst Leak of Personal Data Ever," *Ars Technica* (September 8, 2017).

7   Lily Hay Newman, "Equifax Officially Has No Excuse," *Wired* (September 14, 2017).

8   Nicole Perlroth and Cade Metz, "Equifax Breach: Two Executives Step Down as Investigation Continues," *New York Times* (September 14, 2017).

9   Tom Schoenberg, Anders Melin, and Matt Robinson, "Equifax Stock Sales Are the Focus of US Criminal Probe," *Bloomberg* (September 18, 2017).

10 Zack Wittacker, "Equifax's Credit Monitoring Site Is Also Vulnerable to Hacking," *Ziff Davis Net* (September 12, 2017).

11 Michael Riley, Jordan Robertson, and Anita Sharpe, "The Equifax Hack Has the Hallmarks of State-Sponsored Pros," *Bloomsburg Businessweek* (September 29, 2017).

12 For example, Christopher Mims, "The Hacked Data Broker? Be Very Afraid," *Wall Street Journal* (September 8, 2015).

13 For example, Evan Perez and Shimon Prokupecz, "First on CNN: US Data Hack May Be 4 Times Larger Than the Government Originally Said," *CNN Politics* (June 23, 2015).

14 Bruce Schneier, "What's Next in Government Surveillance," *The Atlantic* (March 2, 2015).

15 Devin Coldewey, "Congress Votes to Disallow Consumers from Suing Equifax and Other Companies with Arbitration Agreements," *TechCrunch* (October 24, 2017).

DISCUSSION QUESTIONS

(1) What, if anything, could Equifax have done prior to the hack to prevent themselves from being morally responsible for it? What, if anything, could they have done after the hack to lessen their responsibility?

(2) Are there any non-governmental institutions that should have a greater role in the management of data brokerage firms? If so, what are they, and what obligations do they have?

(3) Do customers who provide the data that firms like Equifax collect have any blame for making the hack possible? If so, why? If not, why not?

(4) Should the management and owners of data brokerage firms be personally liable for preventable hacks and/or for failing to be forthcoming about hacks?

(5) Is it possible that we need fundamentally to rethink our relationship with the data that we produce? What would an alternative to the current situation look like and why might it be worth pursuing?

FURTHER READINGS

Jeff Collman and Sorin Adam Matei, eds., *Ethical Reasoning in Big Data: An Exploratory Analysis* (Switzerland: Springer, 2016).

Kord Davis with Doug Patterson, *Ethics of Big Data: Balancing Risk and Innovation* (Sebastopol, CA: O'Reilly Media, 2012).

Dave Eggers, *The Circle* (New York: Vintage, 2014).

Viktor Mayer-Schönberger and Kenneth Cukier, *Big Data: The Essential Guide to Work, Life, and Learning in the Age of Insight* (London: John Murray, 2013).

Cathy O'Neil, *Weapons of Math Destruction: How Big Data Increases Inequality and Threatens Democracy* (New York: Broadway Books, 2016).

Seth Stephens-Davidowitz, *Everybody Lies: Big Data, New Data, and What the Internet Can Tell Us about Who We Really Are* (New York: HarperCollins, 2017).

33.

THE CASE OF SCI-HUB AND THE "ROBIN HOOD OF SCIENCE"

GEORGIANA TURCULET[1]

BACKGROUND

WITHIN A FEW YEARS OF LAUNCHING THE SCI-HUB WEBSITE, information technology student Alexandra Elbakyan had become a famous fugitive, compared by some to Edward Snowden.[2] The 22-year-old Kazakhstani graduate student created the site in partnership with Library Genesis, or LibGen, in 2011, thereby creating a de facto global and free access online scientific library. By making much of the global scientific literature available through a few "clicks" on either one of the platforms, Elbakyan radically changed the ability of researchers and the general public to access scientific knowledge. Her work was done largely in response to a growing concern that access to scientific research had become prohibitively expensive for many in the global scientific community; Sci-Hub took this research and made it freely accessible to anyone interested in consulting it from anywhere in the world, independently of one's affiliation with a specific higher education institution. In 2016, prestigious international journal *Nature* listed Elbakyan as one of the

278

top 10 scientists who mattered in science. However, her emerging recognition in the international scientific community as a contributor to science comes with condemnation as well as acclaim, with different stakeholders in the scientific community in disagreement as to the ethical validity of her actions.[3]

The corporate publishing business considers Elbakyan's online library to be illegal piracy that infringes on publishers' copyrights. During the heated public debate over Sci-Hub, Alicia Wise, director of universal access at one of the most prominent publishing companies on the market, Elsevier, tweeted: "I'm all for universal access, but not theft!" She advised that "there are lots of legal ways to get access."[4] Wise's comment alluded to the various initiatives that companies like Elsevier have taken part in as an attempt to make access more affordable. Such initiatives include Research4Life, a partnership of several organizations and well over 100 international publishers that aims to make research more affordable for global scientific and academic communities. Wise's claim would seem to imply that Elsevier and Sci-Hub in fact share a common goal of providing free access to scientific knowledge. What publishers condemn, then, is not Sci-Hub's end goal but its means of getting there through illegally pirating published content.

Some, however, argue that Wise's statement about Elsevier's commitment to universal access is hard to sustain, pointing out that, in the experiences of many researchers, these initiatives have done relatively little to actually help them access research. After all, Elbakyan created Sci-Hub precisely because of the obstacles she and her colleagues faced when trying to access publications. Elbakyan began the project in 2009 while completing her final-year research project in Almaty, Kazakhstan, having found the cost of journal access to be prohibitively expensive. She developed a means of circumventing publishers' paywalls, a means then expanded to create an online library available to other researchers. Unsurprisingly, many other students, researchers, and professors found that Sci-Hub was a significant aid to advancing their academic work. By 2016, Sci-Hub hosted 60 million papers and registered 75 million user downloads. Since then, the number of yearly downloads has increased steadily.

Accessing scientific articles through Sci-Hub is completely free of charge. Subscription to the website as a user is not required. Nor do users pay a registration, a per-item, or a per-journal fee. The websites do accept and receive donations, which are used to manage and maintain the functioning of the library.

Prior to Sci-Hub, access to scientific publications was fully regulated by paywalls. Publishers such as Elsevier charge around $30 per article. As the average PhD researcher must access and read many articles for each project he or she undertakes, publisher fees can accumulate quickly. Most students and faculty members cannot afford such costs on their own.

A researcher may receive access to scientific publications via his or her institution's library. Many universities have also built VPN (virtual private network) systems, to allow remote access to library resources when a researcher is not physically on campus. Universities purchase access to journals from publishers—who are mainly located in the US and the EU—in two main ways. In countries where public education is subsidized by tax payers, public money is spent to pay publishers for their services. Some higher-education institutions are private and manage their own budgets to purchase access to scientific articles from publishers. However, a given institution's access to published research is always determined by its budget; the lower the budget of one's institution, the less access one will likely have to published materials. Researchers unaffiliated with institutions will possibly not have any access to published scientific materials unless they live near a well-resourced public library, such as the New York Public Library or the Library of Congress in Washington, DC.

Many have pointed out that access to knowledge in the modern world takes place in the context of a Global North and Global South "divide," where the latter suffers from shortages of or restrictions to access, in many cases because Global South institutions lack the resources to pay for expensive journal subscriptions. Again, publishers such as Elsevier have worked to establish access and outreach initiatives aimed at such institutions in poor countries; but many have pointed out that these systems are highly inefficient and limited in the range of journals they provide access to.[5]

Perhaps surprisingly, data from Sci-Hub suggests that a significant proportion of activity on the site is from users in the US and the EU. This might suggest that part of Sci-Hub's extraordinary popularity is more about convenience than necessity; the Sci-Hub platform is extremely quick and easy to use. But while the "principle of least effort" may be the driving factor for many users in the Global North, it is worth noting that, even there, accessibility to scientific publication varies significantly from institution to institution. Notably, Harvard University, one of the world's wealthiest and most prestigious institutions, declared in 2012 that it could no longer afford paying the price—currently around $3.5 million per year—of accessing academic research.[6] In view of the rising prices of subscriptions, the university encourages its faculty members to make their research available through open access journals and to resign from publications that keep articles "locked" behind paywalls.

In 2016, a New York judge ruled against Sci-Hub for infringing on Elsevier's legal rights as a copyright holder and ordered the website closed. In defiance, Elbakyan claimed that she would not cease operating Sci-Hub. She declared in a number of public statements that she considers it her moral responsibility to keep the website open, given the vast number of researchers globally for whom it is an essential tool for completing their degrees and advancing their academic careers. Shortly after the original sci-hub.org domain was rendered illegal and terminated, the same website popped up on the Internet under a variety of other domains based in Russia, which is beyond the jurisdiction of the US legal system. Furthermore, Elbakyan has publicly declared that she will keep the free online library running even if she is imprisoned, as she has arranged for others to manage the website. She is currently reported to be in hiding, yet continues to take responsibility in public statements and at academic conferences.

What lies at the heart of the dispute between Sci-Hub and Elsevier? Do Elbakyan's claims challenge the very notion of intellectual property? How should knowledge under the form of article-based scientific results be managed? Should solutions be found for individual countries, or at a global level? Should research be published in journals in the first place, and if so, how should journals manage their business with regards to the access they allow to scholars? Should the dissemination of knowledge be controlled by for-profit businesses, or through not-for-profit means? Do researchers have an inherent right to access the published work of other researchers? Should published research be provided to everyone, free of charge, as Elbakyan is advocating? How are we to decide among these positions?

ANALYSIS

IS KNOWLEDGE BEST PRESERVED, DISSEMINATED, AND PUT TO social use if it is privately owned, or if it is treated as a public, non-owned good? The Elsevier versus Sci-Hub debate appears to be primarily about whether we think that publishing companies should be allowed to sell knowledge using whatever business model they see fit (or find most prof-itable), or whether research should be freed from the realm of business and opened for universal access.

Elbakyan's main defense for the necessity of Sci-Hub is that research-ers need the website open in order to carry out their scientific work. More broadly, however, she considered scientific knowledge to be a public good,[7] and maintains that the ability to access knowledge in order to produce knowledge is a fundamental right. Elbakyan holds the position that the mission and progress of scientific knowledge should not be limited by corporate private interests, given that advancement in all research areas, from medicine to natural and social sciences, should be expected to advance and cure societies' ills. If her analysis is correct, limiting access to researchers is antithetical to the very purpose of academia and its role in our societies. If the production of a specific medicine, for instance, is dependent on researchers' access to studies, limiting this access affects not only the careers of those researchers, but also the wellbeing of those who require the medicine. Elbakyan maintains that her endeavor is moti-vated by this moral commitment to science, while also pointing out the fact that, unlike publishers and copyright holders, she makes no profit from the website.

Many people would agree with Elbakyan on at least one level: that knowledge itself is a public good, and that it is instrumentally valuable to advancing the common good of societies—for example, by support-ing the discovery of medicine. Though generally accepted, however, this understanding does not necessarily entail that access to knowledge should be universal in all cases. Many forms of exclusion from knowledge are legally and socially accepted. Examples of such legal mechanisms of exclusion include copyrights, patents, and the pricing of knowledge-based products. An exhibition in a national museum, for instance, can be considered a public good, but it is also accepted that many museums charge for tickets to such exhibitions.

In the case of research, it may be worth noting that many scholars point out a distinction between knowledge itself and the text or other medium through which that knowledge is expressed. In this formula-tion, while the ideas contained within an article may in themselves be deemed public goods, that fact does not necessitate the conclusion that the media through which those ideas are expressed—i.e., articles in jour-nals—should therefore be public goods.

One way to think about this is to compare knowledge to other material goods in our world, and consider how those are distributed. Is knowledge comparable to a substance like water, an indispensable human need that we agree should be priced accessibly—if priced at all? Or should knowledge be treated as a luxury item, priced according to its quality, prestige, and the human effort that goes into creating it—and if only a few in the world can afford it, so be it? Perhaps knowledge sits somewhere between these two extremes, or perhaps it is in a different category altogether.

We can begin by considering the interest of each contending party. As shown by the data provided by Elbakyan to a number of media outlets, researchers at every level of their careers, from studentship to professorship, are making substantial use of Sci-Hub; the motives for their research—not only academic and career development but also, in many cases, a desire to contribute to society—appear to justify the interest those researchers have in Sci-Hub's resources. In addition, the organization of the teaching of courses and entire curricula in higher education also depends in large part on accessing fresh knowledge that constitutes the current state-of-the-art in academic disciplines. Universities and higher education institutions have a responsibility to provide access to scientific publications to their faculty and students. If they cannot afford access to scientific knowledge, they fail as institutions dedicated to the pursuit of knowledge.

One response to this challenge is that of cosmopolitan egalitarianism. To put it simply, cosmopolitan egalitarians argue that access to knowledge should be universal and global, not limited by an individual's country of birth or institutional affiliation. This moral theory condemns the status quo in which knowledge remains largely "locked away" in the Global North; it thereby proposes a strong defense of Sci-Hub on the grounds that every researcher should be offered an equal chance to acquire and contribute to knowledge.

In September 2018, the EU made opening access to scientific publications a top priority of its political agenda. Unlike Elbakyan, the EU aims to open access to scientific knowledge through legal means and strategies, complying with publishers' copyright regulations. However, not everyone agrees that this is appropriate. According to Robert-Jan Smits, the EU's outgoing director-general for research, science, and innovation,

At the moment we are putting a lot of public money at the national, European and global level into science. But we don't have free access to the published results of the research we fund because this is locked behind paywalls. We have to spend an enormous amount of money each year on subscriptions to journals where scientific articles are published and on making these results immediately available in open access. Imagine if all the billions we are now putting into these expensive subscription journals could be put into research.[8]

OPENING ACCESS BY PURCHASING IT FROM PUBLISHERS MAY divert money that could otherwise be applied directly to research.

Is the model in which research is dominated by expensive subscription journals justified in the first place? If it is not, should publishers agree on a business model whereby their profits would be limited by considerations in favor of open access? Should publishers limit what they charge to the bare minimum required to operate, without amassing profit? Or should they profit, but only up to some threshold? What would this profit-making limit be and how would it be determined?

Consider again the case of Harvard, which is unable to pay the required fees for access. Other institutions have since also declared boycotts against Elsevier, with some, like University of California library director Ivy Anderson, accusing such publishers of "double dipping" when charging for content: that is, receiving the benefits of institutional funding that generates research while then charging those same institutions for access to the research they fund.[9] These institutions are taking an increasingly public position against paywalls that limit access to research, namely the position that academics should not cooperate with publishers to place research behind paywalls in the first place. While there is a legal difference between Sci-Hub, which breaks the paywall mechanism, and Harvard, which wants to avoid it, is there any ethical difference between avoiding publishers and taking away from publishers the research they placed behind paywalls? Both Sci-Hub and Harvard seem to subscribe to the principle that the financial interests of publishers should not allow for the blocking of access to research.

A libertarian approach would support the idea that profit making is legal and moral as long as it does not violate other people's rights, most notably the rights to property and ownership all people have.[10] This raises complex questions about property rights, particularly for non-rivalrous goods such as intellectual property. Do publishers violate rights by prohibitively pricing access to knowledge, and, if they do, whose rights specifically? Are the rights of researchers violated if, after producing the research, they cannot easily access it? Are the rights of citizens who cannot benefit from the advancement of research violated? Do publishers themselves have property rights resulting from their contracts with authors, and if so are these violated by the operation of Sci-Hub?

In 2017, Russian scientists gave the name *Idiogramma elbakyanae* to a newly discovered species of parasitic wasp; Elbakyan called the association an "extreme injustice," and asserted that "the real parasites are scientific publishers, and Sci-Hub, on the contrary, fights for equal access to scientific information."[11] The claim that Elbakyan makes goes against the idea that ownership of knowledge is legitimate. She further problematizes the idea of leaving ownership in the hands of a few powerful publishers. Elbakyan has taken on something of a folkloristic reputation within the scientific community, earning her titles such as the "Pirate Queen" and the "Robin Hood of science." Her supporters think of her as fighting injustice in a way comparable to the legendary Robin Hood, who stole from the rich to redistribute to the poor. In this mythology, the "real" thieves are those who use means, however legal, to appropriate large amounts of wealth through other peoples' research, and who then keep that wealth for themselves.

NOTES

1   I am indebted to Celine Cantat for her substantive feedback to the overall chapter and for editing. I am grateful to Alex Sager for his thorough editorial suggestions, which enhanced the form and substance of this case study.

2   See the *New York Times'* opinion piece by Kate Murphy, "Should All Research Papers Be Free?" (March 12, 2016).

3   Among other commendations, Elbakyan was named one of *Nature's* "Ten People Who Mattered This Year" in 2016. See Gonzalez et al., "Ten People Who Mattered This Year," *Nature* 540 (December 22/29, 2016).

4   See John Bohannon, "Who's Downloading Pirated Papers? Everyone," *Science* 352.6285 (April 29, 2016).

5   Ibid.

6   See Ian Sample, "Harvard University Says It Can't Afford Journal Publishers' Prices," *The Guardian* (April 24, 2012).

7   Generally, a public good is a commodity or service that benefits all members of a society.

8   Robert-Jan Smits, as quoted in "Open Access to Scientific Publications Must Become a Reality by 2020," *Horizon* (March 23, 2018).

9   Ivy Anderson, as quoted in Alex Fox and Jeffrey Brainard, "University of California Boycotts Publishing Giant Elsevier over Journal Costs and Open Access," *Science* 364.6446 (June 21, 2019).

10   I thank Alexander Sager for pressing the point that the libertarian perspective on intellectual property rights is unclear and disputed. More than a few libertarians see intellectual property as a government-imposed monopoly that restricts the free market. In general, however, the libertarian approach values ownership and freedom. This approach does not consider publishers' ownership of scientific copyrights as problematic.

11   Quoted in Benedicte Page, "Elbakyan Pulls Sci-Hub from Russia," *The Bookseller* (September 6, 2017).

DISCUSSION QUESTIONS

(1) Is knowledge a public good? If so, what are the implications?

(2) Who is entitled to economically profit off scientific knowledge, if anyone? Publishers who curate and edit content, provide digital platforms for its dissemination and archiving, and manage other publication processes? Or scholars who produce knowledge in the first place and largely for free, such as those who conduct the research and who author, peer review, and edit academic articles?

(3) If the development of knowledge is dependent on a global community of readers and researchers, does limiting access to knowledge and scientific debates damage the production of knowledge itself?

(4) Suppose we accept that Elbakyan's critics are right, and that Elbakyan's copyright violations are inherently unethical. Who is more to blame: Elbakyan and the other Sci-Hub managers, or the scholars, students, and researchers who continue to make use of the content they provide, thus providing an incentive for Sci-Hub to continue?

(5) Do some extra reading on the means Elbakyan has used to obtain access to Sci-Hub's library. Has this process been ethical? More generally, is it acceptable for a business to use ethically questionable means to supply a genuine social good?

(6) What justification—if any—might there be for a museum, which exhibits items of national or cultural importance, to charge visitors for tickets? Is there any relevant similarity between this case and that of academic publishers?

FURTHER READINGS

E. Archambault, D. Amyot, P. Deschamps, A. Nicol, L. Rebout, and G. Roberge, "Proportion of Open Access of Peer-Reviewed Papers at the European and World Levels, 2004–2011," Report to the European Commission (2013), Science-Metrix, online.

Benedict Atkinson and Brian Fitzgerald, "The Meaning and Future of Copyright," in *A Short History of Copyright*, ed. Atkinson and Fitzgerald (New York: Springer, 2014), 129–36.

Guillaume Calbanak, "Bibliogifts in LibGen? A Study of a Text-Sharing Platform Driven by Biblioleaks and Crowdsourcing," *Journal of the Association for Information Science and Technology* 67.4 (2016): 874–84.

Copyright & Fair Use, Chapter 1: Subject Matter and Scope of Copyright, Stanford University Library, online.

Alexandra Elbakyan, "Why Science Is Better with Communism? The Case of Sci-Hub," 7th Annual UNT Open Access Symposium, University of North Texas Libraries (2016).

In Solidarity with Library Genesis and Sci-Hub (2015), at Custodians. online.

Diana Kwon, "Publishers' Legal Action Advances against Sci-Hub. The Pirate Site Plans to Ignore the Lawsuits from Elsevier and the American Chemistry Society," *The Scientist* (2017), online.

"Sci Hub, #icanhazPDF, Alternative Access Methods, and the Lessons for Publishers and Their Customers," Society for Scholarly Publishing (2017), online.

Manuel Thomas, "How Scihub Is at the Forefront of the Quest to Frame Scientific Knowledge as Public Good," *The Wire* (2016).

Khan Abdul Waheed, "Universal Access to Knowledge as a Global Public Good," Global Economic Symposium (2009), online.

William H. Walters, "E-book in Academic Libraries: Challenges for Sharing and Use," *Journal of Librarianship and Information Science* 46.2 (2014): 85–95.

34.

SHARI'A AND THE HOSPITALITY INDUSTRY IN NIGERIA

FRANK ARAGBONFOH ABUMERE

BACKGROUND

ON MAY 29, 1999, NIGERIA ENDED THE SECOND SPELL OF ITS 29-year military dictatorship and returned to democracy. That dictatorship had committed many human rights violations, notably the infamous execution of human rights activists Ken Saro-Wiwa and his colleagues, leading to political and economic sanctions. Those sanctions, combined with the draconian laws and human rights violations of the military dictatorship, prevented many potential entrepreneurs from starting businesses.

The end of the military dictatorship was followed by the lifting of sanctions and the return to democracy. In response, the hospitality sector boomed, with hotels and restaurants appearing to serve people expected to have the means and opportunity for leisure. Many of these entrepreneurs were poor, with their nuclear and extended family members depending on them, due to the social nature of Nigeria (communitarian) and the economic condition of the country (two-thirds of the population live in poverty). With no funds of their own, they had to take out loans at high interest rates in order to launch their new ventures. These businesses were soon jeopardized by political, security, and religious developments.

Kano is the second largest city in Nigeria, the largest city in northern Nigeria and the commercial capital of northern Nigeria. On June 21, 2000, the Kano State government adopted *Shari'a*. The imposition of *Shari'a* simultaneously bankrupted many businesses. Hotels, guesthouses, restaurants, pubs, and nightclubs were seen as "sin-centers" and were targeted by Boko Haram Islamist militants.[1] Hospitality entrepreneurs risked losing money, freedom, and, ultimately, limbs and lives to terrorists. Furthermore, due to a lack of security and infrastructure, business owners had to provide their own security, pay thugs not to vandalize their businesses, bribe the police, provide their own electricity by using generators, provide their own water by sinking boreholes, and contribute money to repair the roads leading to their hotels or guesthouses.

Business owners caught breaking the rules faced heavy fines or imprisonment, or the loss or destruction of their business. Following the dictates of *Shari'a* meant hospitality entrepreneurs had to reduce the number of services they offered to customers. For instance, *Shari'a* prohibited couples not legally married from admission to hotels, the operation of nightclubs, and alcohol. This led to fewer customers and, consequently, reduced earnings, leaving some hotels and related businesses running at a loss.

The most devastating impact of *Shari'a* was the prohibition on the sale of alcohol. In Nigeria, alcohol is very important in the hospitality industry, especially for nightclubs, "beer parlors" (pubs), motels, and guesthouses. Furthermore, the consumption of alcohol is an important part of Nigerians' glamorous and ostentatious celebrations of Christmas, New Year, weddings, and birthdays. During these celebrations, hotels or guesthouses that cannot sell alcohol are not patronized. Since it is very difficult and risky for hospitality entrepreneurs to smuggle alcohol into Kano, some entrepreneurs made their own alcohol,[2] and to hide its substandard quality would attach the labels of legitimate producers to the homemade brew.

ANALYSIS

MANY POTENTIAL ENTREPRENEURS AND BUSINESS OWNERS LIVE in regions where the legal, social, and political environment creates fundamental moral obstacles to doing business. Business permits may be difficult to obtain and require political connections or substantial bribes. Doing business may involve collaborating with regimes that commit grave human rights abuses.

The Kano government requires that entrepreneurs pay corporate taxes, income taxes, and property taxes. Normally, taxes are paid to a government in exchange for vital goods or services. But when a government has not provided vital goods or services in the past, is not providing them in the present, and cannot be relied on to provide them in the future, are business owners morally justified in refusing to pay taxes to such a government?

One of the basic moral requirements for businesses is that they obey the laws and fundamental moral rules of society. This requirement is not absolute—some laws may be unjust. Moreover, there may be genuine questions about what the laws are, in particular in regions where the government is weak or contested. Official laws and constitutional principles may depart significantly from practice. For example, widespread practices such as bribery may officially be illegal, but nonetheless be widely tolerated and necessary to operate a business. How should entrepreneurs act under these circumstances?

One way of addressing questions about businesses' obligations is through the application of the social contract theory, according to which "all businesses are ethically obligated to enhance the welfare of society by satisfying consumer and employee interests without violating any of the general canons of justice."[3] Businesses owe the government or state respect for the general canons of justice, and this obligation is derived from a hypothetical contract in which businesses have (at least implicitly) consented to respect the general canons of justice in return for the goods and services (governance) which the government or state provides for the businesses and the general society.

Social contract theory in business ethics offers an explanation for the relationship between businesses and society and the obligations the former owe the latter. In view of the theory, *ceteris paribus*, entrepreneurs are supposed to pay taxes because they receive benefits from the state. But what about when the government has failed in its obligations to entrepreneurs? Does social contract theory then justify the refusal to pay taxes?

One response is that the entrepreneurs' obligations toward the government are contingent on the government upholding its part of the social contract. Even if this is true, it does not resolve what business owners should do. Should they close their businesses, continue to operate illicitly, or do the best they can to do their part despite a government that falls short of its own moral obligations? This position is complicated by the fact that businesses' actions do not only affect the government and its officials; businesses also have obligations to consumers and, arguably, to the wider society. Businesses may have an obligation to promote good government and governance, even at a cost to their owners.

Other issues arise because of the prohibition on the sale of alcohol. One question is whether it is unjust for the government to impose restrictions on alcohol. The right of the government to restrict or ban the use of intoxicants is widely accepted. The United States banned alcohol during prohibition in the 1920s and, like many countries, continues to ban the sale and use of many drugs. Are the prohibitions of alcohol under *Shari'a* unjust? This raises complex questions about what makes a law or a system of laws just. Furthermore, in many cases there are obligations to obey unjust laws and seek to change them through established political and legal challenges, especially if, like the prohibition of alcohol, they do not appear to jeopardize human rights or fundamental freedoms.

The social nature and economic condition of Nigerian society complicates matters. In Nigeria, two-thirds of the 180 million people live in poverty, with many people dependent on their relatives for economic survival. Without economic assistance from relatives (nuclear and extended family members) who are comparatively well off, many people are unable to afford basic necessities such as shelter, health care, education, water, and food.

This has two implications for many hospitality entrepreneurs. Firstly, many entrepreneurs must take out loans in order to start their businesses. Secondly, given the communitarian nature of the society, having a business—i.e., having a source of income—brings with it the burden of catering to members of the nuclear and extended family. If hospitality entrepreneurs do not sell alcohol (either smuggled into Kano or manufactured and sold with fake labels), then they will not be able to repay their loans and care for their dependent nuclear and extended family members.

NOTES

1   Lucy Fleming, "Secret Nigerian Drinking Dens in Kano," *BBC News* (March 21, 2015).
2   Ibid.
3   John Hasnas, "The Normative Theories of Business Ethics: A Guide for the Perplexed," *Business Ethics Quarterly* 8.1 (1998): 19–42, at 29.

DISCUSSION QUESTIONS

(1) Under what circumstances (if any) should entrepreneurs disobey laws because they have negative consequences on their businesses? Explain your answer and give examples.

(2) Is the Kano government's prohibition of alcohol just or unjust? If you think that this prohibition is unjust, what implications does this have for the obligations of businesses in the hospitality industry?

(3) How should businesses negotiate tensions when explicit laws and widespread social practice conflict?

(4) Is the social contract a useful way of thinking about the obligations of businesses to follow the law and contribute to society? Why or why not? What implications does it have for this particular case?

(5) Do the moral obligations of local entrepreneurs, especially in regions with political instability and frequent human rights violations, differ from entrepreneurs from other parts of the world? Why or why not?

FURTHER READINGS

Justin G. Longenecker et al., "Ethics in Small Business," *Journal of Small Business Management* 27.1 (1989): 2–31.

Vincent O. Nmehielle, "Sharia Law in the Northern States of Nigeria: To Implement or Not to Implement, the Constitutionality Is the Question," *Human Rights Quarterly* 26.3 (2004): 730–59.

O. Uche Ofili, "Challenges Facing Entrepreneurship in Nigeria," *International Journal of Business and Management* 9.12 (2014).

Christine K. Volkmann and Holger Berg, "Ethical Dilemmas in Entrepreneurial Decision Making" (2012), online.

35.

GOOGLE IN CHINA: CENSORSHIP REQUIREMENTS CHALLENGE THE INTERNET COMPANY

THERESA BAUER

BACKGROUND

GOOGLE INC. SEES ITSELF AS A GOOD CORPORATE CITIZEN. IT FOLLOWS the famous mission statement "Don't Be Evil," governs its business practices according to a code of conduct, and engages in philanthropy. Nevertheless, the company's compliance with censorship requirements in autocratic regimes such as China has attracted widespread criticism.

Since the Internet arrived in China in the 1990s, the response of the Chinese government has been twofold. Internet development has been supported as a chance to vitalize the economy. At the same time, the Chinese government has taken extensive measures to control online communication and suppress criticism, at least ostensibly to maintain political stability and social harmony. A number of laws have been developed to regulate the Internet, prohibiting the creation or dissemination of information that endangers national unification, damages the reputation of state organizations, instigates hatred or discrimination among nationalities, is sexually suggestive, or promotes gambling or violence.

Chinese authorities police the Internet by screening websites, email, and social media, stopping unwanted discussions, and arresting users who express negative opinions too freely.

In 2002, the "Golden Shield" project, also known as the "Great Firewall of China," was launched. This complex system automatically monitors the information flow within China and across borders through various techniques such as Internet address and domain name system tampering, IP address blocking, website blocking, and key-word filtering. Access to a number of websites (e.g., Human Rights Watch, Amnesty International) is completely blocked; in some cases users can access portions of websites while other parts (e.g., where there is mention of Tibet or Taiwan) are blocked.

Internet Service Providers are liable for all offensive content transmitted through their facilities. They are required to assist public security organizations in investigating breaches of the law and reporting illegal activities. Foreign companies wishing to obtain a Chinese operating license must sign the "Public Pledge on Self Discipline for the Chinese Internet Industry" (or "The Pledge"), which commits the companies to censoring content on their websites and in search engine results, and to turning over the names of users who post objectionable content.

Even in light of these extensive regulations, Western Internet companies have a great interest in the Chinese market and its large and growing number of users. Google decided to launch its Chinese-language search engine Google.cn in January 2006. Until then, Google.com could be accessed through Chinese local Internet providers, but the website was slow and unreliable inside China and results were automatically censored by the Great Firewall (though the wall only half-worked in Google's case, sometimes letting banned search results slip through). The new website Google.cn could operate more quickly and reliably. Yet, Google had to sign "The Pledge," committing itself to removing content banned under Chinese law. For example, when searching for "Tiananmen Square," Google.cn did not deliver any photos of the crackdown on student protesters in 1989 (as a search on the conventional version does), but merely presented photos of the square itself.[1] As a small measure of defiance, Google decided to display a pop-up warning to inform users when access had been restricted on certain search terms.

Google's decision to comply with Chinese Internet censorship laws stirred debate in the US and met with criticism from human rights organizations. In February 2006, company representatives, together with other US Internet companies operating in China, were called into Congressional hearings and had to defend their business practices in China.

Google changed its approach in 2010: in January, the company reported that hackers (allegedly on behalf of the Chinese government) had attempted to penetrate the Gmail accounts of human rights activists, and announced they would stop censoring results on Google.cn.[2] In March, Google began automatically redirecting Chinese users to unfiltered servers in Hong Kong, which is a special administrative region of China that is not subject to Chinese Internet censorship laws. After a warning by the Chinese government that the company's operating license would not be renewed if this practice continued, Google stopped the automatic rerouting in June 2010, but installed a landing page on Google.cn with a link to the Hong Kong website. However, observers noted that Chinese authorities allowed only a tiny fraction of traffic to reach Google's servers in Hong Kong.[3]

In 2013, Google stopped notifying users when a search term was censored after Chinese authorities had found new ways to hamper the search engine. In 2014, Google began encrypting searches, thus making it difficult for Chinese authorities to determine who was searching for illegal topics. Then in May 2014 all Google services were blocked, including Google.hk and Google.com as well as products such as Gmail, Calendar, and Translate.[4]

ANALYSIS

ON WHAT GROUNDS COULD GOOGLE'S DECISION TO LAUNCH Google.cn and to follow Chinese censorship requirements be justified? Should Google have resisted Chinese requirements because of human rights concerns? Defenders of Google's presence in China have given economic, legal, and moral justifications.

Google's decision to operate Google.cn could be justified on *economic* grounds. Most business ethicists see at least part of companies' obligations as being toward shareholders, which include pursuing opportunities for profit when legal and in conformity with widely accepted ethical norms.[5] In 2006, Google faced growing competition in China, as other Western companies such as Yahoo! Inc. were also present in the market and had chosen to follow censorship requirements. Most notably, Yahoo had surrendered emails and other information to the Chinese government in 2004, leading to the imprisonment of the prodemocracy journalist Shi Tao. Also, Chinese search engines had been developed and were gaining market share. Particularly, the Beijing-based Baidu arose as a strong competitor. In 2005, Google.com's new Chinese-character service had a search market share of 27 per cent, whereas Baidu was quickly gaining users and had already amassed nearly half of the Chinese search engine market.[6] Until the launch of Google.cn, Google could offer only a slow version of its search engine in China and had to be prepared for complete blockades of its website Google.com with the consequence of further losing market share. Indeed, the search market share of Google.cn had fallen to a mere 1.7 per cent by October 2013. Though there were economic grounds for pursuing opportunities in China, they were not straightforward. One consideration was the economic effects of the blow to the company's reputation. Resisting Chinese censorship requirements might even make sense in the light of diminishing market share in the country, as such a practice can help avoid reputation loss in Western countries and hence be important for business success.

In addition to *economic* considerations, *legal* considerations about the regulatory framework must be assessed. As Chinese law required Google to filter its content, Google.cn could not have been started without agreeing to assist in the censorship. This does not, however, settle matters. The fact that Google is an American company raises questions of jurisdiction: when operating abroad, which laws and legal norms should it respect? How should a company act when confronted with a violation of the right to freedom of expression? Google also presented *moral* arguments to defend the start of Google.cn. In the congressional hearing in February 2006, Google's Vice President Elliot Schrage underlined the company's commitment to considering the moral implications of all business decisions. Schrage pointed out that the launch of Google.cn had been a difficult decision, but was justified, as Google.cn would "make a meaningful—though imperfect—contribution to the overall expansion of access to information in China."[7] Schrage also stressed the higher degree of transparency compared to competitors due to the notification when links had been removed from search results. From Schrage's point of view, this disclosure "allows users to hold their legal systems accountable."[8]

Google was attempting to justify its presence in China by arguing that this produced more overall benefits than the alternatives. One challenge to this type of argument is that it is difficult to assess whether any benefits achieved by launching Google.cn actually outweighed the negative effects of censorship.[9] On the one hand, Google contributed to increased access to information by delivering high-quality search results. Even if politically sensitive websites had to be censored, Google "could still improve Chinese citizens' ability to learn about AIDS, environmental problems, avian flu, world markets."[10] Besides, the censorship required by the Chinese government included leeway for interpretation: Google—like the other signatories of "The Pledge"—had to follow the official guidelines on unwanted content, but these rules were often vague and Internet companies made different censoring choices. Hence, Google could attempt to censor less than its competitors. On the other hand, as US Representative Christopher Smith noted in 2006, "When Google sends you to a Chinese propaganda source on a sensitive subject, it's got the imprimatur of Google. And that influences the next generation—they think, maybe we can live with this dictatorship."[11]

Google's moral arguments face the criticism that they are incompatible with the universal concern for human rights, in particular the right to freedom of expression. Human rights are global, "inalienable rights of all members of the human family."[12] The right to freedom of expression includes the right to seek, receive, and impart information and ideas; it is a negative right that protects the individual from abuses and interference (in the form of blocking access to information) by governments and private actors.

Human rights are moral rights, but have gained a legal basis through international covenants such as the Universal Declaration of Human Rights (UNUDHR) adopted by the United Nations General Assembly in 1948. The right to freedom of expression is guaranteed by Article 19 of the UNUDHR as well as by Article 19 of the International Covenant on Civil and Political Rights (ICCPR), a multilateral treaty adopted by the United Nations General Assembly in 1966.

The moral responsibility of companies to respect human rights has been increasingly recognized. The work by the United Nations (UN) Special Representative John Ruggie contributed to this development with the introduction of the UN "Protect, Respect and Remedy" Framework[13] and "Guiding Principles on Business and Human Rights."[14] According to Ruggie, companies must respect human rights and may not infringe on the rights of others as the baseline expectation. They should seek to prevent or mitigate adverse human rights impacts that are directly linked to their operations, products, or services. Companies must also avoid becoming complicit in human rights violations, whereas complicity means any "indirect ways in which companies can have an adverse effect on rights through their relationships."[15]

The exact implications and limits of the concept of complicity are debated. Various categories of complicity have been identified: the idea of "direct complicity" is widely accepted, i.e., cases where the company knowingly "participates through assistance in the commission of human rights abuses"; "beneficial complicity" means that a company benefits from human rights abuses without assisting or causing them; the most debated category is "silent complicity," which refers to the failure to address human rights abuses with the appropriate authorities.[16]

Google's operations in China meant cooperating with the Chinese government in blocking websites. Google.cn restricted Chinese users in their access to websites to which they have a right of access. This kind of complicity has been called "obedient complicity" in which a company "follows laws or regulations of a government to act in ways that support its activities that intentionally and significantly violate people's human rights."[17]

Overall, does this mean Google should not have launched Google.cn due to human rights concerns? Although the right to freedom of expression has been violated, determining what Google should have done in 2006 (and what it should do today) is not straightforward. One may argue that this is a case where "moral compromise" is defensible, as the situation in 2006 was highly complex and the exact consequences of the decision to launch Google.cn uncertain.[18] Besides, Google's management has not opted for the easy way out, but has been monitoring the situation in China constantly and has taken current assessments as the basis to decide what actions are required and acceptable with respect to censorship requirements. Correspondingly, it revised its decision to follow censorship requirements in 2010.

Censorship and filtering requirements continue to challenge Google and other Internet companies—not only in China, but in many countries around the world. This issue is complex, as it involves economic and legal issues, but also necessitates distinguishing just from unjust laws and balancing freedom of expression and local cultural norms. One important step for Internet companies to clarify human rights obligations has been the start of the Global Network Initiative (GNI), co-founded by Google in 2008. The initiative commits participants to a set of principles, including respecting and protecting the freedom of expression of their users "by seeking to avoid or minimize the impact of government restrictions on freedom of expression" and by removing content or otherwise limiting access to information and ideas "in a manner inconsistent with internationally recognized laws and standards."[19]

NOTES

1   Silla Brush, Danielle Knight, and Bay Fang, "Learning to Live with Big Brother," *U.S. News & World Report* 140.7 (February 27, 2006): 29–d31.

2   David Drummond, "A New Approach to China," Official Google Blog (January 12, 2010).

3   Keith Bradsher and Paul Mozursept, "China Clamps Down on Web, Pinching Companies like Google," *New York Times* (September 21, 2014).
    Dan Levin, "China Escalating Attack on Google," *New York Times* (June 2, 2014).

4   Ibid.

5   Economic responsibility can be conceptualized as one part of overall corporate responsibilities along with legal, ethical, and philanthropic responsibilities. See A.B. Carroll, "A Three-Dimensional Conceptual Model of Corporate Social Performance," *Academy of Management Review* 4 (1979): 497–505.

6   Clive Thompson. "Google's China Problem (and China's Google Problem)," *New York Times* (April 23, 2006).

7   Elliot Schrage, "Testimony of Google Inc. before the Subcommittee on Africa, Global Human Rights, and International Operations Committee on International Relations," United States House of Representatives (February 15, 2006), online.

8   Ibid.

9   See Gary Dann and Neil Haddow, "Just Doing Business or Doing Just Business: Google, Microsoft, Yahoo! and the Business of Censoring China's Internet," *Journal of Business Ethics* 79.3 (2008): 227.

10 Clive Thompson, "Google's China Problem (and China's Google Problem)," *New York Times* (April 23, 2006).

11 Ibid.

12 UN General Assembly, "Universal Declaration of Human Rights" (1948), online.

13   United Nations, "Protect, Respect and Remedy: A Framework for Business
     and Human Rights Report of the Special Representative of the Secretary-
     General on the Issue of Human Rights and Transnational Corporations
     and Other Business Enterprises, John Ruggie. Human Rights Council,
     Eighth Session, a/Hrc/8/5" (2008), online.
14   United Nations, "Report of the Special Representative of the Secretary-
     General on the Issue of Human Rights and Transnational Corporations
     and Other Business Enterprises, Guiding Principles on Business and
     Human Rights: Implementing the United Nations 'Protect, Respect
     and Remedy' Framework, Human Rights Council Seventeenth Session,
     a/Hrc/17/31" (2011), online.
15   United Nations, "Protect, Respect and Remedy: A Framework for Business
     and Human Rights. Report of the Special Representative of the Secretary-
     General on the Issue of Human Rights and Transnational Corporations
     and Other Business Enterprises, John Ruggie. Human Rights Council,
     Eighth Session, a/Hrc/8/5" (2008), online.
16   Andrew Clapham and Scott Jerbi, "Categories of Corporate Complicity
     in Human Rights Abuses," *Hastings International and Comparative Law
     Review* 24 (2001): 339–49.
17   George Brenkert, "Google, Human Rights, and Moral Compromise,"
     Journal of Business Ethics 85.4 (2009): 459.
18   Ibid.
19   Global Network Initiative, "The GN Principles," https://
     globalnetworkinitiative.org/principles/index.php.

DISCUSSION QUESTIONS

(1)   Google argued in 2006 that filtering Internet content is less harmful than
      not making its search engine available to the Chinese market. Do you
      agree? If this is true, does it justify Google doing business in China?
(2)   Is Google complicit in human rights abuses in China?
(3)   Some have dismissed the human rights approaches as a mere Western
      idea. Should the critics of the launch of Google.cn be castigated for their
      "ethical imperialism"?
(4)   Do governments of democratic countries have the responsibility to ensure
      proper conduct of internationally active companies abroad, i.e., should
      the US government prevent Google from working with autocratic regimes
      such as China?

FURTHER READINGS

George Brenkert, "Google, Human Rights, and Moral Compromise," *Journal of Business Ethics* 85.4 (2009): 453–78.

Gary Dann and Neil Haddow, "Just Doing Business or Doing Just Business: Google, Microsoft, Yahoo! and the Business of Censoring China's Internet," *Journal of Business Ethics* 79.3 (2008): 219–34.

Lyombe Eko, Anup Kumar, and Yao Qingjiang, "Google This: The Great Firewall of China, the IT Wheel of India, Google Inc., and Internet Regulation," *Journal of Internet Law* 15.3 (2011): 3–14.

J. Brooke Hamilton, Stephen B. Knouse, and Vanessa Hill, "Google in China: A Manager-Friendly Heuristic Model for Resolving Cross-Cultural Ethical Conflicts," *Journal of Business Ethics* 86.2 (2009): 143–57.

Clive Thompson, "Google's China Problem (and China's Google Problem)," *New York Times* (April 23, 2006).

36.

BUYING INFLUENCE IN CHINA: THE CASE OF AVON PRODUCTS INCORPORATED

PETER JONKER

BACKGROUND

AVON PRODUCTS INCORPORATED IS A MANUFACTURER OF COS-
metics and beauty-related products. The company was founded in 1886
and is headquartered and listed in New York. With annual revenues of
nearly US$9 billion and over 30,000 employees,[1] Avon is one of the larg-
est players in the market. Avon relies on a network of six million sales
representatives to sell their products directly to customers.

In 2014, Avon and the US Department of Justice settled a corruption
case related to Avon's operations in China with a Deferred Prosecution
Arrangement (DPA).[2] The case involved violations of the US Foreign
Corrupt Practices Act between 2004 and 2008 and resulted in a settlement of US$135 million, an agreement to have an external monitor for
18 months, and an obligation to report on the progress in its compliance
efforts in the 18 months afterwards.

Until the law was changed in 2006, it was not possible for (foreign) companies to sell products in China via a direct selling approach.

To ensure that it would be among the first companies to obtain a license to sell in China—a growing market of one billion consumers—Avon tried to influence Chinese government officials, offering them between 2004 and 2008 exclusive personal luxury items by Gucci or Louis Vuitton, dinners, entertainment, luxurious trips, and even cash. According to the DPA with the US Department of Justice, these payments amounted to around US$8 million to buy influence, obtain licenses, avoid fines, and avoid negative publicity.

Avon's revenues have been under pressure in recent years. Especially in China, sales targets were not achieved. Over the fiscal year 2014, the company reported a decline in its global sales of 18 per cent. In China, sales dropped over 40 per cent.[3]

ANALYSIS

THERE ARE SEVERAL DEFINITIONS OF BRIBERY IN USE AND THERE is an ongoing debate on their scope. For example, the United States distinguishes between facilitation payments and bribes when it comes to enforcement of its Foreign Corrupt Practices Act. Facilitation payments are small payments to speed up administrative processes that one has a right to receive (e.g., paying a customs official a few dollars to process a shipment). Bribes are payments to induce officials to do things they would not otherwise necessarily do. Most international treaties and several countries do consider facilitation payments to be bribes.

We follow Transparency International, an internationally recognized NGO promoting the fight against corruption, in defining bribery as follows:

> The offering, promising, giving, accepting or soliciting of an advantage as an inducement for an action which is illegal, unethical or a breach of trust. Inducements can take the form of gifts, loans, fees, rewards or other advantages (taxes, services, donations, favors etc.).

THIS IS A BROAD DEFINITION, BUT THE CORE IS THAT THE "ADVANTAGE" offered leads to an action which is illegal, unethical or a breach of trust.

Many companies have defined gift policies these days, restricting routine external gifts to a maximum "nominal value." If the value of a gift surpasses a threshold of, say, US$50, one should ask for internal approval or report it in a "gift register." Although this is an easy-to-understand rule, focusing on the value of the gift diverts attention from the real point: the intention behind the gift. If you are giving a gift to induce someone to do something illegal, it is a bribe.

Ethical questions surrounding bribery become especially complex in international business. In many countries, bringing gifts is a generally accepted business custom, which underscores the value of the relationship. In many Asian countries it is regarded as disrespectful not to accept a gift. In the Middle East a gift is sometimes used to express how wealthy the giver is. People conducting business internationally need to navigate these customs while respecting legal and ethical obligations not to allow gifts to provide an unfair advantage.

According to the Statement of Facts in Avon's DPA with the US Department of Justice, Avon representatives offered Chinese officials gifts, entertainment, and even cash "in order to obtain and retain direct selling licenses, avoid fines or negative media reports, obtain favorable judicial treatment and obtain government approval to sell nutritional supplements and healthcare apparel products, via direct selling, that did not meet or had yet to meet government standards."

The intention behind the gifts and entertainment was clearly to buy influence and make sure the government officials would rule in favor of Avon's petition for a license. A US$8 million "investment" to secure potential revenues of hundreds of millions could be viewed as making smart business sense. Executives and employees of Avon were very well aware of the sensitivity of their actions, as they deliberately changed the description of these expenses in their books and records, misleading or falsely describing them as "employee travel," "samples," or "public relations business entertainment." In addition, they also used a consulting company to send false invoices. Avon transferred money to this company, which then made payments into personal accounts of government officials. In 2005, the internal audit department of Avon made management aware of irregularities in China. But this did not lead to fundamental changes. After a whistleblower's report in 2008, Avon's Group management started a full-blown internal investigation and decided to voluntarily disclose its findings to the SEC.

Though Avon's wrongdoing in this case appears fairly straightforward, we need to inquire into the business environment that led them to bribe officials. Bribery is bad because it allows companies to receive contracts and licenses because of their ability to influence officials, not because of their ability to deliver goods and services more efficiently than their competition. The problem is that this does not explain why individual companies operating in an environment where corruption is widespread should refrain from bribery. Where governments are not committed to enforcing anti-corruption laws and bribery is widespread, companies that refuse to engage in corrupt practices may not be able to compete.

There are also complex questions remaining about the ethics of bribery and corruption from companies operating in multiple jurisdictions. As mentioned above, Avon was charged under the United States' Foreign Corrupt Practices Act, which governs companies that have a "footprint" (e.g., a listing, subsidiary, or history of transactions in US dollars) in the US. Avon is a US company with a listing on the New York stock exchange, so there is little confusion in this case. The legal and ethical ramifications are less clear for companies that have a more tangential connection to the United States. For example, the US's "extra-territorial" reach may be more problematic in cases where the US chooses to charge foreign companies that only have subsidiaries in the US. Questions of legitimate political authority are particularly pressing in international matters where the parties affected do not have democratic representation. We can question the ethics of the US using its economic power to enforce regulations abroad, especially since these regulations do not command universal recognition: i.e., countries and cultures disagree about what constitutes bribery and when it is problematic.

In recent years, other countries have adopted laws governing corruption abroad. Until recently, the US was the only country having vigorously enforced anti-corruption laws. Canada, the UK, and Brazil have all recently adopted laws with an extra-territorial reach. This raises practical and moral questions. In its anti-corruption law, Brazil, for instance, names penalties up to 20 per cent of the company's annual revenue in corruption cases. Will they also go after Avon, for corruption in China, because Avon has a subsidiary in Brazil as well? And what is the role of China, the country where the corruption took place? Will they also take action against Avon? Who has a right to go after a company? In the case of Avon, would it be the US (as the company is listed on the NYSE), or China (as the crime happened there) or the UK (as Avon might have a "footprint" in the UK)? Could a company be fined more than once for the same scheme? Or, if the US collects a fine, should part of it be transferred to China, to support the Chinese government's efforts to tackle corruption?

A final question concerns the morality of punishment. Was the US\$135 million fine appropriate? When answering this question, it is important to reflect on all of the potential costs of the Deferred Prosecution Arrangement. One cost is the appointment of a Monitor, an independent external expert to monitor and report to the US authorities on the progress Avon makes in its anti-corruption and compliance efforts. Where appropriate the Monitor decides to appoint additional external resources (for instance auditors) to verify the process. Avon must pay for the costs of those external consultants and invest internal management time to deal with compliance topics and improve processes and procedures, and also to report on progress and deal with authorities, legal experts, and media.

Furthermore, the fine may impact the company's reputation and/or its share price and potentially lead to lower revenues. Other companies with corruption issues have faced blacklisting, with governments deciding not to buy products from them for a certain period of time. In China, Avon was also confronted with falling revenues and has had to adjust its sales targets in recent years.

When assessing the fine imposed, we should ask about the function and proportionality of punishment. Is the purpose of the fine and accompanying actions to deter Avon and other companies from violating the Foreign Corrupt Practice Act? Is the punishment proportional? Is the fine comparable to what other companies have received for similar violations? Is a fine even the most appropriate punishment given that companies may come to see it as a cost of doing business, and merely take it into account in their overall plans? Are there any extenuating factors that deserve consideration? When pondering this question, is it relevant to take into account that Avon had already spent US\$344 million on the investigation prior to the settlement?

NOTES

1 Avon, *Annual Report* 2014, online.
2 *US Department of Justice v. Avon Products Inc.*, December 2014, online.
3 Avon, *Annual Report* 2014, online, at 40.

DISCUSSION QUESTIONS

(1) In a well-known article, A.W. Cragg argues that "we have no right to impose moral values that define corruption for us on cultures where what we call immoral is thought to be commonplace and widely accepted." In your view, should all countries, like the US, UK, Brazil, and Canada, start to implement and enforce laws against overseas bribery?

(2) Avon settled with the US authorities for US$135 million for improper payments of around $8 million. Do you think this is a fair and proportional penalty? Please explain your considerations.

(3) There are different considerations to identify if a gift is "appropriate." What would be practical rules of thumb a company could use to determine if a gift is "appropriate" or "lavish"?

FURTHER READINGS

Christopher Baughn, Nancy L. Bodie, Mark A. Buchanan, and Michael B. Bixby, "Bribery in International Business Transactions," *Journal of Business Ethics* 92.1 (2010): 15–32.

Margot Cleveland, Christopher M. Favo, Thomas J. Frecka, and Charles L. Owens, "Trends in the International Fight against Bribery and Corruption," *Journal of Business Ethics* 90.S2 (2009): 199–244.

A.W. Cragg, "Business, Globalization, and the Logic and Ethics of Comparison," *International Journal* 53.4 (1998): 643–60. https://www.jstor.org/stable/40203720?seq=1#page_scan_tab_contents.

Transparency International, https://www.transparency.org/.

US Department of Justice, "*United States v. Avon Products Inc.*, Deferred Prosecution Agreement," online.